XSLT Quickly

XSLT Quickly

Bob DuCharme

MANNING

Greenwich
(74° w. long.)

For online information and ordering of this and other Manning books, go to www.manning.com. The publisher offers discounts on this book when ordered in quantity. For more information, please contact:

Special Sales Department
Manning Publications Co.
32 Lafayette Place   Fax: (203) 661-9018
Greenwich, CT 06830   email: orders@manning.com

♾ Recognizing the importance of preserving what has been written, it is Manning's policy to have the books we publish printed on acid-free paper, and we exert our best efforts to that end.

Library of Congress Cataloging-in-Publication Data
DuCharme, Bob
   XSLT Quickly/Bob DuCharme.
         p.   cm.
   Includes bibliographical references and index.
   ISBN 1-930110-11-1
      1. XSLT (Computer language program) I. Title

QA76.X58 D83   2001
005.7'2—dc21   2001030931
                                                CIP

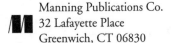
Manning Publications Co.   Copyeditor: Adrianne Harun
32 Lafayette Place   Typesetter: Syd Brown
Greenwich, CT 06830   Cover designer: Leslie Haimes

Printed in the United States of America
1 2 3 4 5 6 7 8 9 10 – VHG – 05 04 03 02 01

contents

Part 3   Appendices   257

preface

Perhaps the most astonishing thing about XML's rapid growth is how this meta-language came to be used for so much more than its inventors had imagined. What started off as a subset of SGML designed for easier delivery to web browsers has become the standard way to ship data between processors, computers, or businesses that need to share data but don't have identical setups for their respective information processing systems.

Much of the original excitement about XML assumed that DTDs (and eventually, schemas) would pop up to serve the data description needs of everyone who wanted to share data. As it turned out, they each had different, specific needs, and joint efforts to develop DTDs that satisfied multiple parties involved a huge amount of work—often *too* much work.

Then the Extensible Stylesheet Language Transformations (XSLT) came along. XSLT made it easy to specify the conversion of data that conforms to one schema, into data that conforms to another. Free software that allows you to run these conversions began appearing everywhere. Because XSLT is a W3C standard, like XML itself, developers could be confident that no one company would start changing its syntax solely to meet their marketing needs.

At the time, I had spent several years working with languages and tools that converted SGML documents into other formats, so I had a pretty good idea of the basic tasks that should be easy to perform when making such conversions.

The first time I saw an XSLT script, I thought it looked a little strange—it didn't look like a program, but like an odd XML document. Then I started playing with it. Even as a beginner, I discovered that each time I set a goal, I usually got an XSLT script to achieve my goal the first or second time I ran the script.

XSLT was clearly a language that could make users of XML very productive. As more XSLT processors appeared, I saw that XSLT was going to become popular quickly, and although no XSLT books were available at the time, I knew that there would eventually be plenty of them.

As someone familiar with the tasks that XSLT was trying to achieve, even before I was familiar with XSLT itself, I thought I had the right perspective to put together a truly task-oriented explanation of how to get work done with XSLT, rather than just listing all the features of its syntax and how to use each one. The result, I hope, is something that will enable developers with a broad range of skill sets to productively use XSLT quickly.

acknowledgments

I was fortunate to have extensive help in the tech reviewing of this book from a sharp-eyed cast of XSLT folk: first and foremost, Mario Jeckle and Dave Pawson, who in addition to reading the text, ran all the examples and reported back to me on the success or problems of doing so. Other patient reviewers, many of whom saw the manuscript more than once as I progressed through it, also made many excellent suggestions: David Marston of the Xalan team, Laurie Mann, Aidan Killian, Juergen Baier, Phil Gooch, David Halsted, Jean-Francois Halleux, Darrin Bishop, Matthew Bentley, Karri Mikola, Dan Vint, Jim Gabriel, Bill Humphries, Olivier Gerardin, and Evan Lenz. Mike J. Brown and Michael Dyck also made very helpful suggestions. Of the good people at Manning, I'd like to start with review editor, Ted Kennedy, who assembled and coordinated the stellar cast mentioned so far, and Marjan Bace, publisher, as well as Syd Brown, Mary Piergies, and Adrianne Harun.

Lastly, I owe the most thanks and love to my wife Jennifer and my daughters, Madeline (sitting on the piano bench behind me reading a Nancy Drew book as I write this) and Alice (currently enjoying her bath enough to demand more time from Jennifer before getting out), for putting up with my constant attempts to squeeze in some time on one computer or the other to write this book.

about this book

This book is for people who need to learn XSLT quickly. While it isn't meant to be a complete reference of everything you might want to do in XSLT, it will show you the twenty percent of XSLT that you'll probably use eighty percent of the time. It also includes a user's guide for looking up simple solutions to the most common problems you will encounter when doing more advanced XSLT development.

The two parts of the book address the two parts of this goal.

Part 1 is a step-by-step tutorial that will bring you up to speed with basic concepts and document manipulation techniques necessary for the most common XSLT tasks. More importantly, part 1 will give you the background to understand part 2.

Part 2 is a task-oriented user's guide to various issues you may need to tackle in XSLT. Instead of being organized by XSLT features (for example, attribute value templates, namespace aliasing, and the document () function), part 2 is organized by the goals of your tasks (for example, converting elements to attributes, writing stylesheets to create other stylesheets, and reading in multiple documents at once). This format will make it easier for readers who don't already know XSLT to find solutions to their stylesheet development problems.

Unlike part 1, part 2 is not meant to be read from start to finish. It's a place to find complete answers to specific problems. If a section seems repetitive in places, it's only to ensure that each section can stand on its own. For example, certain techniques basic to both deleting elements and moving elements are explained in both sections.

When you do know a particular XSLT concept or specialized element type but are not sure how to use it, the book's glossary and index will help you find the explanation you need. For example, looking up the document () function in the index will point you to the section in part 2 on reading multiple documents at the same time.

WHAT YOU SHOULD ALREADY KNOW

This book assumes that if you're interested in transforming XML documents, you're already familiar with the basics of XML: elements, attributes, well-formedness, and entity references. Readers who want to know how XSLT handles more complex XML topics such as CDATA, namespaces, and unparsed entities will find these covered in part 2, chapter 4, "Advanced XML markup," on page 84.

HTML is simpler than XML, and because XSLT is so popular for converting XML to HTML, this book assumes a basic familiarity with HTML: the p element used for paragraphs, the img element used for images, b for bolding, i for italicizing, the h1, h2, and h3 elements used for different levels of headers, and the a element used for linking.

SAMPLE CODE

For more updated information on the book's material, as well as a downloadable zip file with all the sample code and input, see http://www.manning.com/ducharme or http://www.snee.com/XSLTQuickly.

Each stylesheet (or stylesheet excerpt) in the book begins with an XML comment listing its filename in the zip file. If the book shows you input created for and output created by that stylesheet, the comment tells you their filenames as well. For example, the following comment at the beginning of a stylesheet means that the stylesheet has the name xq1023.xsl in the zip file and that it converts the zip file's xq1022.xml file into xq1024.xml:

```
<!-- xq1023.xsl: converts xq1022.xml into xq1024.xml -->
```

Instead of showing the xsl:stylesheet start- and end-tags around each example, the book often shows only the template rules (the xsl:template elements) that demonstrate the topic at hand. The zip file's version of the example will be a complete, working stylesheet so that you can try the example. In these stylesheet files, I used processing instructions to show the beginning and end of the part of the stylesheet that I wanted to appear in the book. When you see an example like this in the book,

```
<!-- xq1023.xsl: converts xq1022.xml into xq1024.xml -->

<xsl:template match="wine">
  <xsl:value-of select="price"/>
</xsl:template>
```

the xq1023.xsl disk file will look more like this:

```
<xsl:stylesheet xmlns:xsl="http://www.w3.org/1999/XSL/Transform"
    version="1.0">
  <xsl:output method="xml" omit-xml-declaration="yes" indent="no"/>
  <?startSampleFile ?>

  <!-- xq1023.xsl: converts xq1022.xml into xq1024.xml -->

  <xsl:template match="wine">
 <xsl:value-of select="price"/>
  </xsl:template>
  <?endSampleFile ?>
</xsl:stylesheet>
```

TIP   The sample output shown in the book's examples sometimes has more carriage returns and other spacing between elements than you'll actually see when you apply the corresponding stylesheet to the included sample document. I added these to make the sample output more readable in the book, and only did so where it wouldn't make any difference to an application (particularly an XML application) reading one of these files.

Many of the book's samples refer to the DocBook, a DTD maintained by the Organization for the Advancement of Structured Information (OASIS) that has been popular for technical documentation since before XML was invented. (It began its career as an SGML DTD.) The XML version of DocBook lets you create simple and complex documents, and stylesheets are available to convert them to HTML and Acrobat files. I use it in examples for two reasons: First, it's the DTD I'm using to write this book. Secondly, and more importantly, you don't even need to know the DTD to understand the structure of a simple DocBook document like the following, because the element names make the structure clear enough:

```
<!DOCTYPE chapter PUBLIC "-//OASIS//DTD DocBook XML V4.0beta1//EN"
  "docbook.dtd">

<chapter><title>My Chapter</title>

  <para>This paragraph introduces the chapter's sections.</para>

  <sect1><title>Section 1 of "My Chapter"</title>
    <para>Here is the first section's first paragraph.</para>
    <para>Here is the first section's second paragraph.</para>
  </sect1>

  <sect1><title>Section 2 of "My Chapter"</title>
    <para>Here is the first section's first paragraph.</para>

    <sect2><title>Section 2.2</title>
      <para>This section has a subsection.</para>
    </sect2>

  </sect1>

</chapter>
```

(See http://www.docbook.org for more on DocBook and links to the DTD itself and its stylesheets.)

Finally, sample documents showing portions of a poem use excerpts from John Milton's "Paradise Lost," with spelling rendered in the modern style.

CONVENTIONS USED IN THIS BOOK

The following typographical conventions are used throughout the book:

Code examples and fragments are set in a `Courier` fixed-width font. Parts of the code examples referenced by the accompanying descriptions may be set in **boldface** to draw attention to them, but this has no bearing on how they work. Downloaded versions of the same samples will not have markup to indicate the bolding.

XML element and attribute names are also set in a `Courier` fixed-width font.

Author Online

Purchase of *XSLT Quickly* includes free access to a private web forum run by Manning Publications where you can make comments about the book, ask technical questions, and receive help from the authors and from other users. To access the forum and subscribe to it, point your web browser to http://www.manning.com/ducharme. This page provides information on how to get on the forum once you are registered, what kind of help is available, and the rules of conduct on the forum.

Manning's commitment to readers is to provide a venue where a meaningful dialog between individual readers and between readers and the authors can take place. It is not a commitment to any specific amount of participation on the part of the author, whose contribution to the AO remains voluntary (and unpaid). We suggest you try asking the authors some challenging questions, lest his interest stray!

The Author Online forum and the archives of previous discussions will be accessible from the publisher's web site as long as the book is in print.

about the cover illustration

The figure on the cover of *XSLT Quickly* is a "Soldado Japon de Cavalleria" or Japanese Cavalryman. While the details of his military rank and assignment are lost in historical fog, there is no doubt that we are facing a man of courage and prowess. The illustration is taken from a Spanish compendium of regional dress customs first published in Madrid in 1799. The book's title page informs us:

> *Coleccion general de los Trages que usan actualmente todas las Nacionas del Mundo desubierto, dibujados y grabados con la mayor exactitud por R.M.V.A.R. Obra muy util y en special para los que tienen la del viajero universal*

Which we loosely translate as:

> *General Collection of Costumes currently used in the Nations of the Known World, designed and printed with great exactitude by R.M.V.A.R. This work is very useful especially for those who hold themselves to be universal travelers*

Although nothing is known of the designers, engravers, and artists who colored this illustration by hand, the "exactitude" of their execution is evident in this drawing. The "Soldado Japon de Cavalleria" is just one of a colorful variety of figures in this collection which reminds us vividly of how distant and isolated from each other the world's towns and regions were just 200 years ago. Dress codes have changed since then and the diversity by region, so rich at the time, has faded away. It is now often hard to tell the inhabitant of one continent from another. Perhaps we have traded a cultural and visual diversity for a more varied personal life—certainly a more varied and interesting world of technology.

At a time when it can be hard to tell one computer book from another, Manning celebrates the inventiveness and initiative of the computer business with book covers based on the rich diversity of regional life of two centuries ago—brought back to life by the pictures from this collection.

P A R T **1**

Getting started with XSLT

This tutorial will acquaint you with the XSLT techniques necessary to perform basic transformation operations as you convert one document into another: reordering, renaming and deleting elements, renaming and deleting attributes, converting attributes into elements and elements into attributes, and selecting elements for processing based on their attribute values.

There's much more to XSLT than these operations, as the rest of this book illustrates, but these operations will take you far in tasks such as:

- converting your company's XML data to conform to an industry standard
- converting XML data that conforms to an industry standard schema or DTD, into a form that works with your company's systems
- converting your company's XML into a form that a client or supplier can understand as part of an XML-based electronic transaction
- converting a client or supplier's XML so that it works with your company's systems as part of an electronic transaction

All of these tasks usually involve taking a subset of some data, rearranging the order of the pieces, and renaming them. Once you can do these operations, you're ready to take part in the assembly of some of the most important parts of an ecommerce system.

C H A P T E R   1

A brief tutorial

1.1   WHAT IS XSLT (AND XSL, AND XPATH)?

Extensible Stylesheet Language Transformations (XSLT) is a language that lets you convert XML documents into other XML documents, into HTML documents, or into almost anything you like. When you specify a series of XSLT instructions for converting a class of XML documents, you do so by creating a "stylesheet," an XML document that uses specialized XML elements and attributes that describe the changes you want made. The definition of these specialized elements and attributes comes from the World Wide Web Consortium (W3C), the same standards body responsible for XML and HTML.

Why is XSLT necessary? XML's early users were excited about their new ability to share information, but they gradually realized that sharing this information often assumed that both sharing parties used the same schema or DTD—a lot to assume. Assembling a schema that both parties could agree on was a lot of trouble, especially if they didn't need to exchange information often. XSLT solves this problem by providing an easy, W3C-sanctioned way to convert XML documents that conform to one schema into documents that conform to others, making information much easier to pass back and forth between different systems.

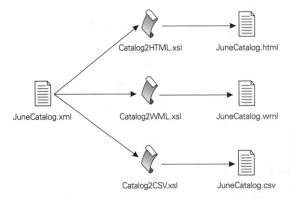

Figure 1.1
XSLT stylesheets can automate the conversion of the same input into multiple output formats.

XSLT was originally part of the Extensible Stylesheet Language (XSL). In fact, XSLT is still technically a part of XSL. The XSL specification describes XSL as a language with two parts: a language for transforming XML documents and an XML vocabulary for describing how to format document content. This vocabulary is a collection of specialized elements called "formatting objects," which specify page layout and other presentation-related details about the text marked up with these elements' tags: font family, font size, margins, line spacing, and other settings.

Because a powerful formatting language should let you rearrange your input document in addition to assigning these presentation details, the original XSL specification included specialized elements that let the stylesheet delete, rename, and reorder the input document's components. As they worked on this collection of elements, the W3C XSL Working Group saw that it could be useful for much more than converting documents into formatting object files—that it could convert XML documents into almost *anything* else. They called this transformation language XSLT and split it out into its own separate specification, although the XSL specification still said that everything in the XSLT specification was considered to be part of the XSL specification as well.

One great feature of XSLT is its ability, while processing any part of a document, to grab information from any other part of that document. The mini-language developed as part of XSLT for specifying the path through the document tree from one part to another is called "XPath." XPath lets you say things like "get the `revisionDate` attribute value of the element before the current element's `chapter` ancestor element." This ability proved so valuable that the W3C also broke XPath (see figure 1.2) out into its own specification so that other W3C specifications could incorporate this language. For example, an XLink link can use an XPath expression as part of an XPointer expression that identifies one end of a link.

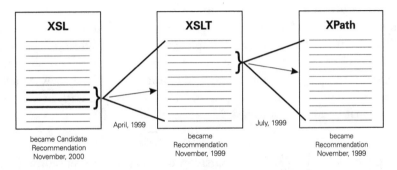

Figure 1.2   The W3C released the first Working Draft of XSL in August 1998, split XSLT out into its own Working Draft in April of 1999, then split XPath out from XSLT into its own working Draft in July 1999.

1.1.1   XSLT and alternatives

Other ways exist for transforming XML documents. These options fall into two categories:

- XML-related libraries added to general purpose programming languages such as Java, Perl, Visual Basic, Python, and C++
- languages such as Omnimark and Balise designed specifically for manipulating XML (and, typically, SGML) documents

So why use XSLT? For one thing, it's a standard. This doesn't necessarily make XSLT a good language, but it does mean that multiple vendors worked on it together, each contributed to its design, and each has committed to supporting it in their products. XSLT wasn't invented by some guy who started a company to sell it and then added and dropped features and platform support over the years as it fit the needs of the company's bigger customers. XSLT's features and platform support reflect a broad range of interests, and the wide availability of open source implementations make it easy for most programmers to put together their own customized XSLT processors with any features they may want to add.

Being a W3C standard also means that XSLT fits in with other W3C standards and that future W3C standards will also fit in with it. The phrase "standards-driven" is nearing tiresome buzzword status these days as more products take advantage of XML; unfortunately, many ignore important related W3C standards. For example, one XML transformation product has various specialized element types whose names you're not allowed to use for your own element types. If this product declared and used a namespace for their specialized element types they wouldn't need to impose such arbitrary constraints on your application development—for example, if they declared a URI and a prefix for this set of element and attribute names, and then used that prefix in the document with those names to prevent an XML parser from confusing them with other elements and attributes that may have the same name.

Another advantage of XSLT over other specialized XML transformation languages is that a series of XSLT document transformation instructions are themselves stored as an XML document. This gives XSLT implementers a big head start because they can use one of the many available XML parsers to parse their input. It also means that developers learning XSLT syntax don't need to learn a completely new syntax to write out their instructions for the XSLT processor. They must just learn new elements and attributes that perform various tasks.

1.1.2 Documents, trees, and transformations

Speaking technically, an XSLT transformation describes how to transform a source tree into a result tree. Informally, we talk about how XSLT lets you transform documents into other documents, but it's really about turning one tree in memory into another one. Why?

Most XSLT processors read a document into the source tree, perform the transformations expressed by the XSLT stylesheet to create a result tree, and write out the result tree as a file, with the net result of converting an input XML document into an output document. Nothing in the XSLT specification requires these processors to read and write disk files; by leaving files and input/output issues out of it, the spec offers more flexibility in how XSLT is used. Instead of an XML file sitting on your hard disk, the input may come from a Document Object Model (DOM) tree in memory or from any process capable of creating a source tree—even another XSLT transformation whose result tree is the source tree for this new transformation. (The DOM is a W3C standard for representing and manipulating a document as a tree in memory.) How would you tell a processor to treat the result tree of one transformation as the source tree of another? See the documentation for your XSLT processor. As I said, the XSLT spec deliberately avoids input and output issues, so that's up to the people who designed each processor.

Similarly, the processor doesn't have to write out the result tree as a disk file, but can store it as a DOM tree, pass it to a new XSLT stylesheet that treats that result tree as the source tree of a new transformation to perform, or pass it along for use by another program via some means that hasn't been invented yet. Figure 1.3 shows these relationships when using XSLT to create an HTML file from a poem document type.

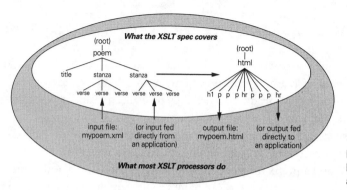

Figure 1.3
Document trees, XSLT, and XSLT processors

Dealing with an input tree instead of an input document also gives you an important advantage that XML developers get from DOM trees: at any given point in your processing, the whole document is available to you. If your program sees a word in the document's first paragraph that's defined in the glossary at the end, it can go to the glossary to pull out the term's definition. Using an event-driven model such as the Simple API for XML (SAX) to process a document instead of a tree-based model like XSLT uses, your program would process each XML element as it read the element in. While doing this, if you want to check some information near the end of your document when reading an element in the beginning, you need to create and keep track of data structures in memory, which makes your processing more complicated.

TIP When a discussion of XSLT issues talks about a source tree and a result tree, you can think of these trees as temporary representations of your input and output documents.

Not all nodes of a document tree are element nodes. A diagram of the tree that would represent this document

```
<?xml-stylesheet href="article.xsl" type="text/xsl"?>
<article>
  <!-- here is a comment -->
  <title author="bd">Sample Document</title>
  <para>My 1st paragraph.</para>
  <para>My 2nd paragraph.</para>
</article>
```

shows that there are nodes for elements, attributes, processing instructions, comments, and the text within elements. (There are also nodes for namespaces, but this document has no namespace nodes.)

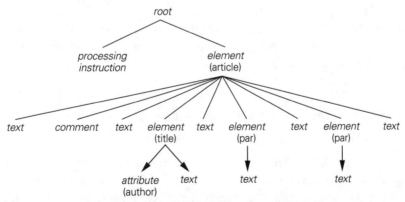

Figure 1.4   A document tree with several different node types

It's easy to match up the parts of the tree with the parts of the corresponding document, except that it might appear that the document has too many "text" nodes. The tree diagram shows text between the comment and the `title` element, and text between the two `para` elements; where is this text in the document? You can't see this text, but it's there: it's the carriage returns that separate those components of the document. If the two `para` elements had been written as one line, like this,

```
<para>My 1st paragraph.</para><para>My 2nd paragraph.</para>
```

no text node would exist between those two elements, and you wouldn't see a text node between them in the tree diagram. (See section 6.11, "Whitespace: preserving and controlling," page 229 for more on this.)

You also might wonder why, if `article` is the root element of the document, it's not the root node of the tree. According to XSLT's view of the data (its "data model"), the root element is a child of a predefined root node of the tree (shown as a slash in the diagram) because it may have siblings. In the example above, the processing instruction is not inside the `article` element, but before it. It is therefore not a child of the `article` element, but its sibling. Representing both the processing instruction and the `article` element as the children of the tree's root node makes this possible.

1.2   A SIMPLE XSLT STYLESHEET

An XSLT transformation is specified by a well-formed XML document called a stylesheet. The key elements in a stylesheet are the specialized elements from the XSLT namespace. (A namespace is a unique name for a given set of element and attribute names. Their use is usually declared in an XML document's document element with a short nickname that the document uses as a prefix for names from that namespace.) When an XSLT processor reads one of these stylesheets, it recognizes these specialized elements and executes their instructions.

XSLT stylesheets usually assign "xsl" as the prefix for the XSLT namespace (ironically, XSL stylesheets usually use the prefix "fo" to identify their "formatting objects"), and XSLT discussions usually refer to these element types using the "xsl" prefix. This way, when something refers to the `xsl:text` or `xsl:message` elements you can assume that they mean the text and message element types from the XSLT namespace and not from somewhere else.

An XSLT stylesheet doesn't have to use "xsl" as the namespace prefix. For example, if the stylesheet below began with the namespace declaration

```
xmlns:harpo="http://www.w3.org/1999/XSL/Transform"
```

the stylesheet's XSLT elements would need names like `harpo:text` and `harpo:message` for an XSLT processor to recognize them and perform their instructions.

The following stylesheet demonstrates many common features of an XSLT stylesheet. It's a well-formed XML document with a root element of `xsl:stylesheet`. (You can also use name `xsl:transform` for your stylesheet's root element, which means the same thing to the XSLT processor.):

```
<!-- xq15.xsl: converts xq16.xml into xq17.xml -->
```

```
<xsl:stylesheet xmlns:xsl="http://www.w3.org/1999/XSL/Transform"
 version="1.0">

  <xsl:template match="year">
    <vintage>
      <xsl:apply-templates/>
    </vintage>
  </xsl:template>

  <xsl:template match="price">
  </xsl:template>

  <!-- Copy all the other elements and attributes, and text nodes -->
  <xsl:template match="*|@*|text()">
    <xsl:copy>
      <xsl:apply-templates select="*|@*|text()"/>
    </xsl:copy>
  </xsl:template>

</xsl:stylesheet>
```

1.2.1 Template rules

An XSLT stylesheet has a collection of template rules. Each template rule has a pattern that identifies the source tree nodes to which the pattern applies and a template that is added to the result tree when the XSLT processor applies that template rule to a matched node.

In a stylesheet document, the template rules that comprise a stylesheet are represented as `xsl:template` elements; the stylesheet above has three. The value of each `xsl:template` element's `match` attribute is the pattern that gets matched against source tree nodes. The element's content—that is, everything between its start- and end-tag—is the template that gets added to the result tree for each source tree node that corresponds to the match pattern. An `xsl:template` element essentially tells the XSLT processor, "as you go through the source tree, when you find a node of that tree whose name matches the value of my `match` attribute, add my contents to the result tree."

For example, the first template rule in the preceding stylesheet tells the XSLT processor what to do when it sees a `year` element node as the child of another node in the source tree. (The "year" attribute value is actually an abbreviation of "child::year.") The template rule has one element as its template to add to the result tree: a `vintage` element. This element contains an `xsl:apply-templates` element that tells the processor to apply any relevant templates to the children of the matched element node (in this case, `year`). The ultimate result of this template is the contents of the input `year` element surrounded by `vintage` tags—in effect, renaming the source tree's `year` element to a `vintage` element for the result tree. Figure 1.5 shows where the pattern and template are in one example of a template rule.

Figure 1.5   The two parts of a template rule

[Pattern → template)

The specialized elements in a template from the XSLT namespace are sometimes called "instructions," because they are instructions to the XSLT processor to add something to the result tree. What does this make the elements in the template that don't use the "xsl" namespace prefix, such as the vintage element? The stylesheet is a legal, well-formed XML document, and the vintage element is an element in that stylesheet. Because this element is not from the XSLT namespace, the XSLT processor will pass it along just as it is to the result tree. In XSLT, this is known as a "literal result element."

Like all template rules, the second xsl:template rule in the stylesheet on page 9 tells the XSLT processor "if you find a source tree node whose name matches the value of my match attribute, add my contents to the result tree." The string "price" is the pattern to match, but what are the template's contents? There are no contents; it's an empty element. So, when the XSLT processor sees a price element in the source tree, the processor will add nothing to the result tree—in effect, deleting the price element.

Because the stylesheet is an XML document, the template rule would have the same effect if it were written as a single-tag empty element, like this:

```
<xsl:template match="price"/>
```

XSLT has other ways to delete elements when copying a source tree to a result tree, but a template rule with no template is the simplest.

Unlike the first two template rules, the third one is not aimed at one specific element type. It has a more complex match pattern that uses some XPath abbreviations to make it a bit cryptic but powerful. The pattern matches any element, attribute, or text node, and the xsl:copy and xsl:apply-templates elements copy any element, attribute, or text node children of the selected nodes to the result tree. Actually, the pattern doesn't match *any* element—an XSLT processor uses the most specific template it can find to process each node of the source tree, so it will process any year and price elements using the stylesheet's templates designed to match those specific tree nodes. Because the processor will look for the most specific template it can find, it doesn't matter whether the applicable template is at the beginning of the stylesheet or at the end—the order of the templates in a stylesheet means nothing to an XSLT processor.

> **TIP**   If more than one xsl:template template rule is tied for being most appropriate for a particular source tree node, the XSLT processor may output an error message or it may just apply the last one to the node and continue.

The values of all of the xsl:template elements' match attributes are considered "patterns." Patterns are like XPath expressions that limit you to using the child and attribute axes, which still gives you a lot of power. (see chapter 2, "XPath," on page 23, for more on axes and the abbreviations used in XPath expressions and patterns.) The "year" and "price" strings are match patterns just as much as "*|@*|text()" is, even though they don't take advantage of any abbreviations or function calls.

That's the whole stylesheet. It copies a source tree to a result tree, deleting the price elements and renaming year elements to vintage elements. For example, the stylesheet turns this wine element

```
<wine grape="chardonnay">
  <product>Carneros</product>
  <year>1997</year>
  <price>10.99</price>
</wine>
```

into this:

```
<?xml version="1.0" encoding="utf-8"?>
<wine grape="chardonnay">
  <product>Carneros</product>
  <vintage>1997</vintage>

</wine>
```

Although the price element was deleted, the carriage returns before and after it were not, which is why the output has a blank line where the price element had been in the input. This won't make a difference to any XML parser.

This is not an oversimplified example. Developers often use XSLT to copy a document with a few small changes such as the renaming of elements or the deletion of information that shouldn't be available at the document's final destination.

1.2.2 Running an XSLT processor

The XSLT specification intentionally avoids saying "here is how you apply stylesheet A to input document B in order to create output document C." This leaves plenty of flexibility for the developers who create XSLT processors. The input, output, and stylesheet filenames might be entered in a dialog box; or they might be entered at a command line; or they might be read from a file.

Many XSLT processors are designed to give a range of options when identifying the inputs and outputs. Some are programming libraries which you can invoke from a command line or call from within a program. For example, an XSLT processor supplied as a Java class library often includes instructions for using it from a Windows or Linux command line, but its real power comes from your ability to call it from your own Java code. This way, you can write a Java program that gets the input, stylesheet, and output filenames either from a dialog box that you design yourself, from a file sitting on a disk, or from another XML file that your application uses to control your production processes. Your program can then hand this information to the XSLT processor.

In fact, the input, stylesheet, and output don't even have to be files. Your program may create them in memory or read them from and write them to a process communicating with another computer. The possibilities are endless, because the input and output details are separate from the transformation.

One example of a Java library that you can use from the command line or as part of a larger Java application is Xalan (pronounced "Zalan"). This XSLT processor was written at IBM and donated to the Apache XML project (http://xml.apache.org). To run release 2.0 of this particular XSLT processor from the command line with an input file of winelist.xml, a stylesheet of winesale.xsl, and an output file of winesale.xml, enter the following as one line (to fit on this page, the example below is split into two lines):

```
java org.apache.xalan.xslt.Process -in winelist.xml
  -xsl winesale.xsl -out winesale.xml
```

(This assumes that the appropriate Java libraries and system paths have been set up; directions come with each Java processor.) For examples of how to run other XSLT processors, see appendix A, "XSLT quick reference" on page 259.

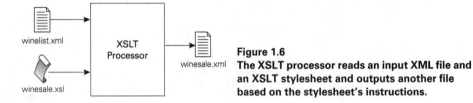

Figure 1.6
The XSLT processor reads an input XML file and an XSLT stylesheet and outputs another file based on the stylesheet's instructions.

1.2.3   An empty stylesheet

What would an XSLT processor do with a stylesheet that contained no template rules? In other words, what effect would an empty stylesheet, such as the following, have on an input document?

```
<!-- xq21.xsl: converts xq22.xml into xq23.xml -->

<xsl:stylesheet xmlns:xsl="http://www.w3.org/1999/XSL/Transform"
    version="1.0"/>
```

XSLT has several built-in default templates that tell the XSLT processor to output the text content (or, in XML terms, the PCDATA) of the elements, leaving out the attributes and markup. For example, the processor would turn this

```
<winelist date="20010626">

<wine grape="chardonnay">
  <product>Carneros</product>
  <year>1997</year>
  <price>10.99</price>
</wine>
</winelist>
```

into this:

```
<?xml version="1.0" encoding="UTF-8"?>

  Carneros
  1997
  10.99
```

An XSLT processor's default behavior adds an XML declaration as well. This can be overridden with the optional `xsl:output` element if you want to create HTML, plain text, or other non-XML output.

The built-in templates also tell the XSLT processor to apply any relevant templates to the children of the elements being processed. (Otherwise, when the `wine-list` element in the above example gets processed, no reason would exist for the XSLT processor to do anything with the `wine` element.) If the stylesheet has no template for one of the children, the most appropriate template for that child element may be the same built-in template that the processor applied to the child's parent. The XSLT processor will do the same thing to the child: add any character data nodes to the result tree and apply the most appropriate templates to any grandchildren elements.

1.3 MORE ELEMENT AND ATTRIBUTE MANIPULATION

In our first stylesheet, we saw that an `xsl:apply-templates` element with no attributes tells the XSLT processor to apply any relevant templates to all the matched node's children. By using this element type's `select` attribute, you can be pickier about exactly which children of a node should be processed and in what order.

For example, this stylesheet

```
<!-- xq25.xsl: converts xq26.xml into xq27.xml -->
<xsl:template match="wine">
  <wine>
    <price><xsl:apply-templates select="price"/></price>
    <product><xsl:apply-templates select="product"/></product>
  </wine>
</xsl:template>
```

will turn this XML element

```
<wine grape="chardonnay">
  <product>Carneros</product>
  <year>1997</year>
  <price>10.99</price>
</wine>
```

into this:

```
<wine>
  <price>10.99</price>
  <product>Carneros</product>
</wine>
```

The stylesheet performs two important operations on this element:

- It moves the `price` element before the `product` element.
- It deletes the `year` element.

The first technique that we saw for deleting an element—using an empty template for that element type—is often simpler than adding `xsl:apply-templates` elements for each of an element's children (except the ones you want to delete). If you're reordering the children anyway, as with the preceding example, omitting an xsl:apply-templates element for the elements in question can be an easier way to delete them.

1.3.1 Manipulating attributes

We've seen how to delete and rename elements. How do you delete and rename attributes? For example, how would you delete the following wine element's price attribute and rename its year attribute to vintage?

```
<wine price="10.99" year="1997">Carneros</wine>
```

We want the result to look like this:

```
<wine vintage="1997">Carneros</wine>
```

(Because an XML declaration is optional, it won't make any difference if that shows up as well.) The first template rule in the following stylesheet makes both of these changes:

```
<!-- xq30.xsl: converts xq28.xml into xq29.xml -->

<xsl:stylesheet xmlns:xsl="http://www.w3.org/1999/XSL/Transform"
     version="1.0">

<xsl:template match="wine">
<wine vintage="{@year}"> <!-- price attribute omitted -->
    <xsl:apply-templates/>
  </wine>
</xsl:template>

<!-- Copy all the other source tree nodes. -->
<xsl:template match="@*|node()">
  <xsl:copy>
    <xsl:apply-templates
         select="@*|node()"/>
  </xsl:copy>
</xsl:template>

</xsl:stylesheet>
```

Deleting the price attribute was easy: the template just left the attribute out of the wine start-tag in the template. To rename the year attribute to vintage, the year start-tag includes the attribute specification vintage="{@year}". The part between the quotation marks says "put the value of the source tree wine element's year attribute here." The @ character is shorthand for the XPath notation that means "get the value of the attribute with this name," and the curly braces tell the XSLT processor that the expression they contain is an attribute value template—not a literal string to appear in the result tree exactly as shown, but an expression to be evaluated and replaced with the result of the evaluation. If this attribute specification had said vintage="{2+2}", the XSLT processor would have added vintage="4" to the result tree. In the example, the processor understands the meaning of @ and plugs in the appropriate attribute value between the quotation marks on the result tree.

1.3.2   Attribute value templates

You can do a lot with attribute value templates. For example, these templates make converting elements to attributes simple. The @ character makes it easy to insert an attribute value where that value will be used as element content in the result. To demonstrate this, let's convert the grape attribute in the following to a product subelement of the wine element. While we're at it, we'll convert the year subelement to a vintage attribute.

```
<wine grape="Chardonnay">
  <product>Carneros</product>
  <year>1997</year>
  <price>10.99</price>
</wine>
```

The result should look like this:

```
<wine vintage="1997">
  <product>Carneros</product>
  <category>Chardonnay</category>
  <price>10.99</price>
</wine>
```

The following template converts the grape attribute into a category subelement by using the @ character, and the message uses the xsl:value-of element to put each grape attribute value between a pair of category start- and end-tags. (As with attribute value templates, an XSLT processor takes what the xsl:value-of element hands it in its select attribute, evaluates it, and adds the result to the appropriate place on the result tree.)

```
<!-- xq33.xsl: converts xq31.xml into xq32.xml. -->
<xsl:template match="wine">
  <wine vintage="{year}">
    <product><xsl:apply-templates select="product"/></product>
    <category><xsl:value-of select="@grape"/></category>
    <price><xsl:apply-templates select="price"/></price>
  </wine>
</xsl:template>
```

To convert an element to an attribute, the same template uses an attribute value template—the curly braces around "year"—to put the source tree wine element's year subelement after vintage= in the result tree's wine element.

Another great trick is selective processing of elements based on an attribute value. Because an XSLT processor applies the most specific template it can find in the stylesheet for each source tree node, it will apply the first template in the following stylesheet for each wine element that has a value of "Cabernet" in its grape attribute, and the second for all the other wine elements. (The [@grape='Cabernet'] part that specifies this is a special part of a match pattern or XPath expression called a "predicate.") The first template copies the element, while the second doesn't. The output will therefore only have wines with "Cabernet" as their grape value.

```
<!-- xq34.xsl -->

<xsl:stylesheet xmlns:xsl="http://www.w3.org/1999/XSL/Transform"
    version="1.0">

<xsl:template match="wine[@grape='Cabernet']">
  <xsl:copy><xsl:apply-templates/></xsl:copy>
</xsl:template>

<xsl:template match="wine"/>

<xsl:template match="@*|node()|processing-instruction()|comment()">
  <xsl:copy>
    <xsl:apply-templates
        select="@*|node()|processing-instruction()|comment()"/>
  </xsl:copy>
</xsl:template>

</xsl:stylesheet>
```

How useful is this? Think about the importance of a database system's ability to extract subsets of data based on certain criteria. The creation of such customized reports can be the main reason for developing a database in the first place. The ability to generate customized publications and reports from your XML documents can give you similar advantages in a system that uses those documents, because the more you can re-use the document components in different permutations, the more value the documents have.

For related information, see

- chapter 2, "XPath," on page 23 for more on the use of expressions in square brackets ("predicates") to filter out a subset of the nodes that you want
- section 3.5, "Converting elements to attributes for the result tree," page 55
- section 3.8, "Deleting elements from the result tree," page 63
- section 3.14, "Converting attributes to elements," page 79

1.4   *SUMMING UP THE TUTORIAL*

So far, this brief tour has only given you a taste of XSL's capabilities—yet we've already covered the features that will let you do four-fifths of your XSLT work! We've shown you how to:

- delete elements
- rename elements
- reorder elements
- delete attributes
- rename attributes
- convert elements to attributes
- convert attributes to elements
- process elements based on an attribute's value

These are the most basic changes that you'll want to make when converting XML documents that conform to one schema or DTD into documents that conform to another. If data is shared between two organizations that designed their data structures independently, those organizations probably have many types of information in common—after all, that's why they're sharing it. Yet, it's also likely that they assigned different names to similar information, or ordered their information differently, or stored extra information that the other organization doesn't need (or hasn't paid for!). XSLT makes most of these conversions painless and quick.

Before moving on, let's review what the XSLT processor is doing now that you've seen it in action a few times. Imagine that an XSLT processor has just started processing the children of the chapter element in the following document,

```
<book><title>Paradise Lost</title>
  <chapter><title>The Whiteness of the Whale</title>
    <para>He lights, if it were Land that ever burned</para>
    <para>With solid, as the Lake with liquid fire</para>
  </chapter>
<chapter><title>The Castaway</title>
    <para>Nine times the Space that measures Day and Night</para>
    <para>To mortal men, he with his horrid crew</para>
  </chapter>
</book>
```

and it's using a stylesheet with the following two template rules to process it:

```
<!-- xq37.xsl -->

  <xsl:template match="title">
    Title: <xsl:apply-templates/>
  </xsl:template>

  <xsl:template match="chapter/title">
    Chapter title: <xsl:apply-templates/>
  </xsl:template>
```

(The match pattern "chapter/title" in the second template element shows that this template rule is for the title elements that are children of chapter elements. The first is for all the other title elements.) The diagram in figure 1.7 shows the steps that take place. The chapter title's content is the only text node shown in the source tree; the rest are omitted to simplify the diagram.

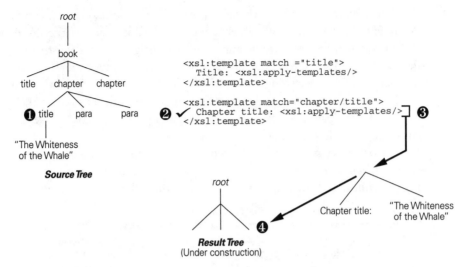

Figure 1.7 How the XSLT processor handles an element node

1 It finds the first child of the `chapter` element, a `title` element node.

2 It checks the stylesheet for a matching template rule. It finds two, and picks the most specific one it can find.

3 Once it's found the best template rule for the node, it gets the template rule's template to add to the result tree.

4 It adds the template, which consists of a text node ("Chapter title:") and the result of processing the template's `xsl:apply-templates` element to the title element's lone text node child: the string "The Whiteness of the Whale."

Of course, XSLT can do much more than what we've seen so far. If you'd like more background on key XSLT techniques before you dive into stylesheet development, the following sections of part 2, "XSLT user's guide: How do I work with...," on page 21 of this book are good candidates for "Advanced Beginner" topics:

- chapter 2, "XPath," on page 23
- chapter 3, "Elements and attributes," on page 47
- section 3.6, "Copying elements to the result tree," page 57
- section 5.1, "Control statements," page 110
- section 6.1, "HTML and XSLT," page 187
- section 6.5, "Non-XML output," page 202
- section 6.6, "Numbering, automatic," page 205
- section 6.9, "Valid XML output: including DOCTYPE declarations," page 225

If your stylesheet absolutely depends on these potentially unavailable elements, the xsl:message element can do more than just output a message about the problem: it can abort the processing of the source document with its terminate attribute. (See section 5.4.1, "Runtime messages, aborting processor execution," page 134, for more on the use of xsl:message.)

XSLT user's guide: How do I work with...

Part 2 explores advanced aspects of XSLT in more detail. It doesn't attempt to be exhaustive, because this isn't a reference book but a user's guide. As a user's guide this part of the book presents background and examples for different areas of XSLT so that you can put them to work in your stylesheets as quickly as possible.

The chapters here cover the following areas:

- *XPath*   You can do a lot with simple XPath expressions, and chapter 2 outlines the full range of possibilities for putting together axis specifiers, node tests, and predicates into an XPath expression of one or more location steps, you can grab almost anything you want from anywhere on the source document tree, regardless of the node you're processing.

- *Elements and attributes*   Part 1 illustrated simple ways to manipulate elements and attributes; chapter 3, "Elements and attributes," on page 47, demonstrates a broader range of techniques for inserting, deleting, moving, and reordering elements, as well as ways to count, combine, and duplicate them. This chapter also describes how to find empty elements in the source tree and how to create them in the result tree, as well as how to deal with sibling elements, and to select elements based on their name, content, children, and parents.

  Chapter 3 also covers the adding of new attributes to the result tree, converting them to elements, getting their values and names, testing for their existence and values within a particular element, and defining and reusing groups of attributes in different result document element types.

- *Advanced XML markup* XML is more than elements and attributes. Sophisticated documents can take advantage of entities (especially to incorporate images and other non-XML data), namespaces, processing instructions, comments, and namespaces. Chapter 4, "Advanced XML markup," on page 84, offers ways to find these in your source documents as well as techniques for creating and controlling them in your result documents.

- *Programming issues* Developers coming to XSLT with a programming background want to know how to perform certain operations offered by most other programming languages: "if" statements, case (or in XSLT, "choose") statements, loops, setting and using variables, passing values to functions and programs (or in XSLT's case, to named templates and stylesheets), special functions for string and number manipulation, the adding of new functions to use in stylesheets, and the use of other developers' extension functions and elements. Chapter 5, "Programming issues," on page 110, covers these topics as well as techniques that make it easier to create and manage larger, more complex stylesheets. In addition to explaining how to combine stylesheets, this chapter covers the use of named templates, which let you apply templates explicitly instead of waiting for the XSLT processor to do so for you. It also reviews several debugging techniques and provides a guide to using the W3C's official XSLT specification.

- *Specialized input and output* XSLT can be used to read all kinds of XML input and to create all kinds of XML and non-XML output, but certain formats are particularly popular and present their own set of advantages and disadvantages. Chapter 6, "Specialized input & output," on page 187, introduces techniques for dealing with HTML as both input and output, using Web browsers, stripping XML markup for plain text output, creating valid XML documents, and creating formatting object files that conform to the XSL specification. It also covers sorting and automatic numbering, handling of white space, creating IDs and links, and splitting of output into multiple files.

C H A P T E R   2

XPath

XPath is a specialized language for addressing parts of an XML document. XPath started off as part of the XSLT spec, but when the XSL Working Group realized how useful it could be to other W3C specifications—for example, an XLink link can use an XPath expression as part of an XPointer expression to identify one resource in a link—they split XPath out into its own specification.

Like the core of the SQL language used to manipulate relational databases, XPath is important because it gives you a flexible way to identify the information you want to pull out from a larger collection. When you create a custom version of an XML document collection, the global replacements and deletions that you might perform with a word processor are useful, but XPath's ability to point at any branch of a document tree makes it possible for XSLT to move beyond deletions and global replacements and really create new documents out of old ones.

WARNING   You may see values that look like XPath expressions in match patterns—that is, as the value of a `match` attribute that identifies which nodes an `xsl:template` element's template rule should process. The syntax used for match patterns defines a language that is actually a subset of the XPath language; they're like XPath expressions that only allow the use of the `child` and `attribute` axes.

2.1 LOCATION PATHS, AXES, NODE TESTS, AND PREDICATES

The syntax of XPath expressions can be confusing because the fully spelled-out versions have a lot of rarely used syntax. This syntax is rarely used, not because stylesheets don't take advantage of it, but because the most useful forms have compact abbreviations to use instead. You've probably seen the "at" sign (@), the slash (/), and the two periods (. .) used in XSLT stylesheets. Once you know what these symbols are abbreviating, you'll more easily see how these pieces fit together, and you can then create your own powerful XPath expressions.

An XPath expression consists of a location path, which is a series of one or more location steps separated by slashes. The following template rule uses an XPath expression with a two-step match pattern to say "when any `year` node is found with a `wine` parent, output its contents surrounded by `vintage` tags":

```
<!-- xq41.xsl -->

<xsl:template match="wine/year">
  <vintage><xsl:apply-templates/></vintage>
</xsl:template>
```

Each location step can have up to three parts:

1 An axis specifier
2 A node test
3 A predicate

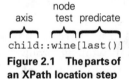

Figure 2.1 The parts of an XPath location step

Only the node test is required in each step, which is why each of the two location path steps in the example above (`wine` and `year`) are just simple node names. When an axis is specified, two colons separate it from the node test, and a predicate is enclosed by square braces after the node test.

> **TIP** When discussing the mechanics of XPath, the term "context node" comes up a lot. In general, this refers to the source tree node with which the XSLT processor is currently dealing as it traverses that tree. (Inside of an `xsl:for-each` loop, the context node is the one currently being processed by the loop.)

2.2 AXES

A location step's axis describes the selected nodes' relationship to the context node in terms of their location on the tree. For example, in the location step, the `child` axis part tells an XSLT processor to look at the child nodes of the context node, and the `wine` node test part tells it the name of the child nodes in which it's interested. Besides `child`, other available "tree relationships" are `descendant`, `parent`, `ancestor`, `following-sibling`, `preceding-sibling`, `following`, `preceding`, `attribute`, `namespace`, `self`, `descendant-or-self`, and `ancestor-or-self`.

TIP Despite the singular form of most axis specifier names, such as `ancestor` and `preceding-sibling`, only `self` and `parent` always refer to a single node. The others might be more aptly named "children," "ancestors," "preceding-siblings," and so forth, so that's how you should think of them: as ways of accessing those particular *sets* of nodes. As we'll see later, the node test and predicate parts of a location step let you select a subset of the group of nodes to which a particular axis specifier points.

2.2.1 The child, parent, and attribute axes

Figure 2.2 shows the `parent`, `attribute`, and `child` nodes of the `excerpt` element in this sample document:

```
<!-- xq638.xml -->
<poem>
  <excerpt source="book 1">
    <verse>He lights, if it were Land
           that ever burned</verse>
    <verse>With solid, as the Lake
           with liquid fire</verse>
  </excerpt>
</poem>
```

The next example shows how to access the `parent`, `child`, and `attribute` nodes. Let's say that when processing the `prices` element, you want to look up the grape attribute value of the `prices` element's parent element.

```
<wine grape="Cabernet Sauvignon">
    <winery>Los Vascos</winery>
    <year>1998</year>
    <prices>
       <list>13.99</list>
       <discounted>11.99</discounted>
       <case>143.50</case>
    </prices>
</wine>
```

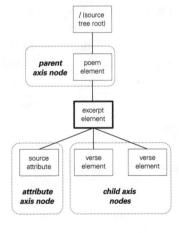

Figure 2.2
This poem's excerpt element has one node in its parent axis, one in its attribute axis, and two in its child axis.

The following template tells the XSLT processor, "As you traverse the source tree, when you find a `prices` element node, use `xsl:value-of` to add a certain value to the result tree. To get that value, first go to the parent node named `wine` and then go to its attribute node named `grape`."

```
<!-- xq45.xsl: converts xq44.xml into xq46.xml -->

<xsl:template match="prices">
  parent element's grape:
  <xsl:value-of select="parent::wine/attribute::grape"/>
</xsl:template>
```

Each of the two steps in the `select` attribute's location path have both an axis specifier (`parent` and `attribute`) and a node test (`wine` and `grape`).

This template rule creates the following result from the `wine` XML document above:

```
    Los Vascos
    1998

  parent element's grape:
  Cabernet Sauvignon
```

The `parent` and `attribute` axes look pretty handy. Why do you see them so rarely when you look at XSLT stylesheets? Because they're so handy that XSLT offers abbreviations for them. The "at" sign (@) abbreviates `attribute::`, and two periods (`..`) abbreviate `parent::node()`. (The `node()` node test points to the current node.) Knowing this, you can write the preceding template rule like this with the same effect:

```
<xsl:template match="prices">
  parent element's grape:
  <xsl:value-of select="../@grape"/>
</xsl:template>
```

The most abbreviated abbreviation is the one for the child axis: if no axis at all is specified in an XPath location step, an XSLT processor assumes that `child` is the axis. For example, take a look at the following template, which (among other things) plugs in the value of the `wine` element's `year` child as the value of the `vintage` attribute in the result tree version. (The curly braces tell the XSLT processor to evaluate the string "child::year" as an expression—that is, to figure out what it's supposed to represent instead of putting that actual string as the value of the `vintage` elements.)

```
<!-- xq48.xsl -->

<xsl:template match="wine">
  <wine vintage="{child::year}">
    <xsl:apply-templates select="product"/>
    <category><xsl:value-of select="@grape"/></category>
    <xsl:apply-templates select="price"/>
  </wine>
</xsl:template>
```

Written like this (with the `child` axis specification removed) it will have the same effect and be more compact:

```
<!-- xq49.xsl -->

<xsl:template match="wine">
  <wine vintage="{year}">
    <xsl:apply-templates select="product"/>
    <category><xsl:value-of select="@grape"/></category>
    <xsl:apply-templates select="price"/>
  </wine>
</xsl:template>
```

2.2.2   ancestor and ancestor-or-self

Figure 2.3 shows the `ancestor` and `ancestor-or-self` nodes of the first `verse` element in the poem example from the following document:

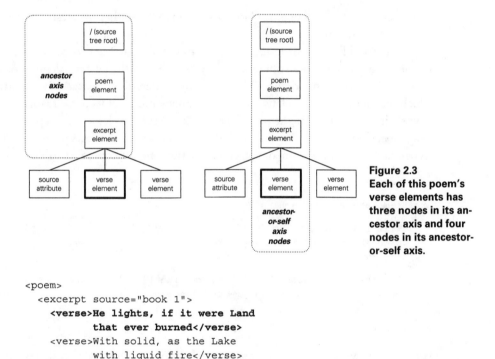

Figure 2.3
Each of this poem's verse elements has three nodes in its ancestor axis and four nodes in its ancestor-or-self axis.

```
<poem>
  <excerpt source="book 1">
    <verse>He lights, if it were Land
          that ever burned</verse>
    <verse>With solid, as the Lake
          with liquid fire</verse>
  </excerpt>
</poem>
```

The `ancestor` axis is great when you want to apply special treatment to elements that exist somewhere inside another element but you're not sure how many levels down. In the next example, let's say you want to format your `para` elements differently when they're in an `appendix` element. These `para` elements may be children of an `appendix` element, or children of `section` elements inside an `appendix` element, or children of `subsect` or `warning` elements inside a `section` element.

The "para" template rule in the following example uses the ancestor axis to add one set of markup to the result tree if the para source node element has an appendix element as an ancestor and another if it has a chapter element as an ancestor.

```
<!-- xq51.xsl -->

<xsl:template match="para">

  <xsl:if test="ancestor::appendix">
    <p><font face="arial"><xsl:apply-templates/></font></p>
  </xsl:if>

  <xsl:if test="ancestor::chapter">
    <p><font face="times"><xsl:apply-templates/></font></p>
  </xsl:if>

</xsl:template>
```

(See section 5.4, "Debugging," on page 133 for another interesting use of the ancestor attribute.)

Why would you want to use the ancestor-or-self axis? Suppose you want to check the value of an attribute that may be either in the current element or one of its ancestors. For example, the XML specification describes the xml:lang attribute, which indicates the spoken language of an element and all of its descendants that don't have their own xml:lang attribute. To check whether an element has a particular language specified for it, you could check that element, then check its parent, then check its parent's parent, and so on, or you could use the ancestor-or-self axis like this:

```
<!-- xq52.xsl: converts xq53.xml into xq54.xml -->

<xsl:template match="warning">

  <xsl:if test="ancestor-or-self::*[@xml:lang][1]/@xml:lang='en'">
    <p><b>Warning! </b><xsl:apply-templates/></p>
  </xsl:if>

  <xsl:if test="ancestor-or-self::*[@xml:lang][1]/@xml:lang='de'">
    <p><b>Achtung! </b><xsl:apply-templates/></p>
  </xsl:if>

</xsl:template>
```

Each of the two xsl:if elements has a two-step location path in its test attribute value. If the first step said ancestor-or-self::warning, this would tell the XSLT processor to check the current node and its ancestors and select any of those nodes named warning. Instead, it uses the asterisk to select the ancestor-or-self nodes with *any* name and a double predicate to select, of those nodes in that axis that have an xml:lang attribute, the first one. The location path's second step checks whether the node selected by the first step has a value of "en" or "de" for its attribute value. When the current node or its closest ancestor with an xml:lang attribute has a value of "en" for that attribute, the first xsl:if instruction adds the

English string "Warning!" to the result tree. If that `xml:lang` attribute has a value of "de", the second `xsl:if` statement adds the German "Achtung!"

With the following document in the source tree,

```
<chapter>
  <section xml:lang="de">
    <warning>Make a backup first.</warning>
  </section>
</chapter>
```

the template above adds the string "Achtung!" at the start of the result tree's version of the `warning` element whether the `xml:lang` attribute was part of the warning, `section`, or `chapter` start-tags:

```
<p><b>Achtung! </b>Make a backup first.</p>
```

2.2.3 preceding-sibling and following-sibling

The term "sibling" refers to another node with the same parent as the context node. The `preceding-sibling` axis refers to all the siblings before the context node, and `following-sibling` refers to all the siblings after it. Figure 2.4 shows the `preceding-sibling` and `following-sibling` nodes of this poem document's third excerpt child element:

```
<!-- xq640.xml -->
<poem>
  <excerpt>
    <verse>Then with expanded wings he steers his flight</verse>
    <verse>Aloft, incumbent on the dusky Air</verse>
  </excerpt>
  <excerpt>
    <verse>I therefore, I alone first undertook</verse>
    <verse>To wing the desolate Abyss, and spy</verse>
  </excerpt>
  <excerpt>
    <verse>This new created World, whereof in Hell</verse>
    <verse>Fame is not silent, here in hope to find</verse>
  </excerpt>
  <excerpt>
    <verse>Better abode, and my afflicted Powers</verse>
    <verse>To settle here on Earth or in mid-air</verse>
  </excerpt>
  <excerpt>
    <verse>Spirit of happy sort: his gestures fierce</verse>
    <verse>He marked and mad demeanor, then alone</verse>
  </excerpt>
</poem>
```

The template in this next example copies chapter elements from the source tree to the result tree and uses these two axis specifiers to add messages about the preceding and following chapters at the beginning of each chapter.

```
<!-- xq56.xsl: converts xq57.xml into xq58.xml -->

<xsl:template match="chapter">
  <chapter>
  Previous chapter:
  (<xsl:value-of select="preceding-sibling::chapter[1]/title"/>)
  Next chapter:
  (<xsl:value-of select="following-sibling::chapter/title"/>)
  <xsl:text>
  </xsl:text>
  <xsl:apply-templates/>
  </chapter>
</xsl:template>
```

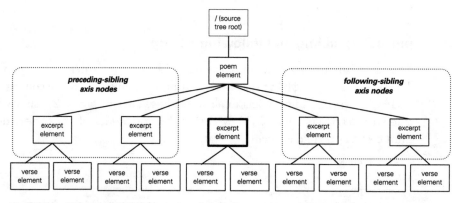

Figure 2.4   This poem's third excerpt element has two nodes in its preceding-sibling axis and two in its following-sibling axis.

Understanding how this is done will be easier if we first see the effect this has. This template turns the following input

```
<story>

  <chapter><title>Chapter 1</title>
    <para>A Dungeon horrible, on all sides round</para>
  </chapter>

  <chapter><title>Chapter 2</title>
    <para>More unexpert, I boast not: them let those</para>
    <para>Contrive who need, or when they need, not now.</para>
    <sect><title>Chapter 2, Section 1</title>
      <para>For while they sit contriving, shall the rest,</para>
      <para>Millions that stand in Arms, and longing wait</para>
    </sect>
  </chapter>

  <chapter><title>Chapter 3</title>
    <para>So thick a drop serene hath quenched their Orbs</para>
  </chapter>

</story>
```

into this:

```
<chapter>
Previous chapter:
()
Next chapter:
(Chapter 2)

Chapter 1
  A Dungeon horrible, on all sides round
</chapter>

<chapter>
Previous chapter:
(Chapter 1)
Next chapter:
(Chapter 3)

Chapter 2
  More unexpert, I boast not: them let those

  Contrive who need, or when they need, not now.
  Chapter 2, Section 1
    For while they sit contriving, shall the rest,

    Millions that stand in Arms, and longing wait

</chapter>

<chapter>
Previous chapter:
(Chapter 2)
Next chapter:
()

Chapter 3
  So thick a drop serene hath quenched their Orbs
</chapter>
```

Each of the two xsl:value-of elements in the template rule has a two-step XPath expression as its select attribute. For the second of these elements, the two steps are following-sibling::chapter and title, telling the XSLT processor "go to the sibling node named chapter that is after the context node (which is also named chapter, as we see from the xsl:template element's match attribute) and grab the value of its title child element." Although following-sibling can refer to multiple nodes, the xsl:value-of element only adds a text version of the first one to the result tree. For the first chapter in the source document, the second chapter is that first node; for the second chapter, the third chapter is; and for the third chapter, no such node exists, so nothing appears in the parentheses after the final "Next chapter" in the result document.

The first `xsl:value-of` element in the example template resembles the second with this exception: we don't want `xsl:value-of` to get a text version of the first node in the set of nodes to which that `preceding-sibling::chapter` points. Chapter 3 has two preceding siblings, but the first of those is not the preceding chapter. To tell the XSLT processor to grab the preceding sibling just before the context node, the location step includes the predicate `[1]`, telling the XSLT processor "get the first one as you count along these nodes." This may seem confusing, because we're adding the number "1" to show that we don't want the first node, but we don't want the first one in document order; we want the first one counting backwards—the one preceding the context node. The XSLT processor counts backwards through a node set when you add a number predicate to an XPath expression using the `preceding-sibling`, `preceding`, `ancestor`, or `ancestor-or-self` axes. Just as your parent is your first ancestor and your grandparent is your second ancestor, your first preceding sibling is the one just before you, and your second preceding sibling is the one before that. The XSLT processor counts forward, in document order, for any other axis.

In the example, the two steps of the `preceding-sibling::chapter[1]/title` XPath expression say "go to the first preceding sibling named `chapter`, then get its `title` element's contents." The first chapter has no preceding `chapter` sibling, so nothing shows up in the parentheses after the first "Previous chapter" text in the result.

2.2.4 preceding and following

The `preceding` and `following` axis specifiers let you address nodes that aren't necessarily siblings. The `preceding` axis contains *all* the nodes that end before the context node begins, and the `following` axis contains all the nodes that begin after the context node ends. Figure 2.5 shows how the poem element's third `excerpt` element in the following document has six nodes in its `preceding` axis and six in its `following` axis:

```
<!-- xq641.xml -->
<poem>
  <excerpt>
    <verse>Then with expanded wings he steers his flight</verse>
    <verse>Aloft, incumbent on the dusky Air</verse>
  </excerpt>
  <excerpt>
    <verse>I therefore, I alone first undertook</verse>
    <verse>To wing the desolate Abyss, and spy</verse>
  </excerpt>
  <emphasis><excerpt>
    <verse>This new created World, whereof in Hell</verse>
    <verse>Fame is not silent, here in hope to find</verse>
  </excerpt></emphasis>
  <excerpt>
    <verse>Better abode, and my afflicted Powers</verse>
```

```
      <verse>To settle here on Earth or in mid-air</verse>
    </excerpt>
    <excerpt>
      <verse>Spirit of happy sort: his gestures fierce</verse>
      <verse>He marked and mad demeanor, then alone</verse>
    </excerpt>
  </poem>
```

In the next example, we'll use these axes in a template rule for the sample document's
`test` elements. We want this template to add messages naming the titles of the preceding and following chapters.

In the following document, what if we want the "Previous chapter" and "Next
chapter" messages that we saw in section 2.2.3, "preceding-sibling and following-sibling," page 29, to show up where the `test` elements are?

```
<story>

  <chapter><title>Chapter 1</title>
    <para>A Dungeon horrible, on all sides round</para>
  </chapter>

  <chapter><title>Chapter 2</title>
    <para>More unexpert, I boast not: them let those</para>
    <test/>
    <para>Contrive who need, or when they need, not now.</para>
    <sect><title>Chapter 2, Section 1</title>
      <para>For while they sit contriving, shall the rest,</para>
      <test/>
      <para>Millions that stand in Arms, and longing wait</para>
    </sect>
  </chapter>

  <chapter><title>Chapter 3</title>
    <para>So thick a drop serene hath quenched their Orbs</para>
  </chapter>

</story>
```

The first `test` element needs to point at the nodes preceding and following its grandparent, because it's in a `para` element inside a `chapter` element. The second `test`
element must point at the nodes preceding and following its great-grandparent,
because it's in a `para` element in a `sect` element in a `chapter` element.

Despite the two `test` element's different levels of depth in the source tree, the
`preceding` and `following` axes let a stylesheet use the same template rule:

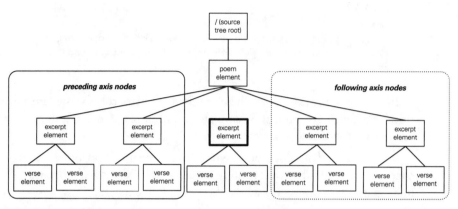

Figure 2.5 This poem's third excerpt element has six nodes in its preceding axis and six in its following axis.

```
<!-- xq61.xsl: converts xq60.xml into xq62.xml -->

  <xsl:template match="test">

    Previous chapter:
    (<xsl:value-of select="preceding::chapter[1]/title"/>)
    Next chapter:
    (<xsl:value-of select="following::chapter/title"/>)
    <xsl:apply-templates/>

  </xsl:template>
```

The first `xsl:value-of` element's XPath expression tells the XSLT processor "go to the first node named "chapter" that finished before the context node (for this template, the `test` element) started, and get its `title` element's contents." As with the `preceding-sibling` example earlier, this XPath expression needs the [1] predicate to show that of all the `chapter` elements preceding the context node, the XSLT processor should grab the first one. Because the counting is done from the end of the node list when using the `preceding` axis, that means the first one counting backwards.

The second `xsl:value-of` element's XPath expression tells the XSLT processor to get the contents of the `title` element in the first `chapter` element that begins after the context node ends. When a stylesheet with this template is run with the sample document above, the output for both `test` elements in chapter 2 is the same:

```
<story>

  <chapter><title>Chapter 1</title>
    <para>A Dungeon horrible, on all sides round</para>
  </chapter>

  <chapter><title>Chapter 2</title>
    <para>More unexpert, I boast not: them let those</para>

    Previous chapter:
```

```
(Chapter 1)
Next chapter:
(Chapter 3)

<para>Contrive who need, or when they need, not now.</para>
<sect><title>Chapter 2, Section 1</title>
  <para>For while they sit contriving, shall the rest,</para>

Previous chapter:
(Chapter 1)
Next chapter:
(Chapter 3)

  <para>Millions that stand in Arms, and longing wait</para>
</sect>
</chapter>

<chapter><title>Chapter 3</title>
  <para>So thick a drop serene hath quenched their Orbs</para>
</chapter>

</story>
```

2.2.5   descendant and descendant-or-self

The descendant axis refers to the context node's children, the children's children, and any other descendants of the context node at any level. Figure 2.6 shows how the poem element in the following document has four descendant nodes and five descendant-or-self nodes in the following document:

```
<!-- xq642.xml -->
<poem>
  <excerpt source="book 1">
    <verse>He lights, if it were Land
           that ever burned</verse>
    <verse>With solid, as the Lake
           with liquid fire</verse>
  </excerpt>
</poem>
```

In this next example, let's say that when we transform the following document we want to list all of a chapter's pictures at the beginning of the result tree's chapter element. Of its three figure elements, the first is a child of the chapter element; the second is a grandchild (being in the sect1 child); and the third is a great-grandchild:

```
<chapter>
  <para>Then with expanded wings he steers his flight</para>
  <figure><title>"Incumbent on the Dusky Air"</title>
  <graphic fileref="pic1.jpg"/></figure>
  <para>Aloft, incumbent on the dusky Air</para>
  <sect1>
   <para>That felt unusual weight, till on dry Land</para>
   <figure><title>"He Lights"</title>
   <graphic fileref="pic2.jpg"/></figure>
```

```
<para>He lights, if it were Land that ever burned</para>
<sect2>
 <para>With solid, as the Lake with liquid fire</para>
 <figure><title>"The Lake with Liquid Fire"</title>
 <graphic fileref="pic3.jpg"/></figure>
</sect2>
</sect1>
</chapter>
```

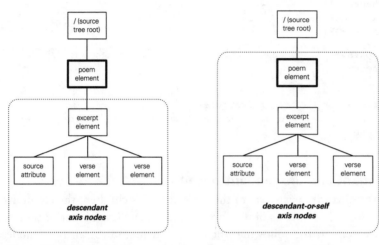

Figure 2.6   This poem element has four descendant nodes and five descentant-or-self nodes.

After the `chapter` start-tag in the result tree document, we want to see the string "Pictures:" as a header. After that, we want the titles of all the chapter's `figure` elements, like this:

```
<chapter>
Pictures:
"Incumbent on the Dusky Air"
"He Lights"
"The Lake with Liquid Fire"
  <para>Then with expanded wings he steers his flight</para>
  <figure><title>"Incumbent on the Dusky Air"</title>
  <graphic fileref="pic1.jpg"/></figure>
  <para>Aloft, incumbent on the dusky Air</para>
  <sect1>
    <para>That felt unusual weight, till on dry Land</para>
    <figure><title>"He Lights"</title>
    <graphic fileref="pic2.jpg"/></figure>
    <para>He lights, if it were Land that ever burned</para>
    <sect2>
       <para>With solid, as the Lake with liquid fire</para>
       <figure><title>"The Lake with Liquid Fire"</title>
```

```
      <graphic fileref="pic3.jpg"/></figure>
    </sect2>
  </sect1>
</chapter>
```

The following template rule uses the `descendant` axis specifier to find these figure titles even though they are at three different levels in the source tree document. The template first adds the string "Pictures:" to the result tree after the `chapter` start-tag.

In our earlier examples of using axis specifiers, we saw that `xsl:value-of` returns a text node of only the first node to which the axis points. In this case, we want all the nodes in that axis, so the template uses an `xsl:for-each` instruction to iterate across the node set. The `xsl:for-each` element's `select` attribute names the node set to iterate over, and an `xsl:value-of` instruction adds the contents of each `figure` element's `title` to the result tree. (See "Iteration across nodes with xsl:for-each," on page 118 for more on this instruction.) The `xsl:text` element (with only a carriage return as its contents) adds this character after each title that the `xsl:value-of` element instruction adds to the result tree:

```
<!-- xq66.xsl: converts xq64.xml into xq65.xml -->

<xsl:template match="chapter">
  <chapter>
  Pictures:
  <xsl:for-each select="descendant::figure">
  <xsl:value-of select="title"/>
  <xsl:text>
  </xsl:text>
  </xsl:for-each>
  <xsl:apply-templates/>
  </chapter>
</xsl:template>
```

As you may guess from the name `descendant-or-self`, this axis checks a context node's descendants and the context node itself. For example, imagine that you want to list all the people who worked on the following chapter by listing the values of any `author` attributes in the entire work:

```
<chapter author="jm">
  <para>Then with expanded wings he steers his flight</para>
  <para author="ar">Aloft, incumbent on the dusky Air</para>
  <sect1 author="bd">
    <para>That felt unusual weight, till on dry Land</para>
    <para>He lights, if it were Land that ever burned</para>
    <sect2 author="jm">
      <para>With solid, as the Lake with liquid fire</para>
    </sect2>
  </sect1>
</chapter>
```

The chapter template rule that makes this possible uses an asterisk node test with a descendant-or-self axis specifier in an xsl:for-each instruction to go through all the elements, regardless of their names, that qualify as descendant-or-self nodes.

```
<!-- xq68.xsl: converts xq67.xml into xq69.xml -->

<xsl:stylesheet xmlns:xsl="http://www.w3.org/1999/XSL/Transform"
    version="1.0">

<xsl:template match="chapter">
  <chapter>
Authors
<xsl:for-each select="descendant-or-self::*/@author">
<xsl:value-of select="."/><xsl:text>
</xsl:text>
    </xsl:for-each>
    <xsl:apply-templates/>
  </chapter>
</xsl:template>

</xsl:stylesheet>
```

The descendant-or-self part is the first step of the location path in the xsl:for-each element's select attribute. The second step (@author) checks for an author attribute of each of these descendant-or-self nodes. (Remember, @author is an abbreviation of attribute::author, which would have the same effect.) Inside the xsl:for-each instruction, the xsl:value-of element grabs a string version of each selected node and adds it to the result tree; the xsl:text element after that adds a carriage return.

The output shows *every* author value in document order:

```
<?xml version="1.0" encoding="utf-8"?>
<chapter>
Authors
jm
ar
bd
jm

  Then with expanded wings he steers his flight
  Aloft, incumbent on the dusky Air

    That felt unusual weight, till on dry Land
    He lights, if it were Land that ever burned

      With solid, as the Lake with liquid fire

</chapter>
```

(For information on removing duplicates, see section 3.9, "Duplicate elements, deleting," on page 64.) An abbreviation for this axis exists as well, or rather, an abbreviation exists for a common XPath fragment that uses this axis: "//" means the same as

"/descendant-or-self::node()/." Note the slashes beginning and ending the fragment represented by this abbreviation; it's almost as though you can just leave out the "descendant-or-self::node()" part when you want to write "/descendant-or-self::node()/" to leave you with "//".

It's a nice shortcut to refer to any descendant of a given element with a particular name. For example, while chapter/title means "any title child of a chapter element," chapter//title means "any title descendant of a chapter element." An XPath expression that begins with these two slashes refers to any descendant of the document's root described by the part after the "//". This is an easy way to refer to any node in a document that meets a certain condition; for example, //title refers to any title element anywhere in the document.

This "//" abbreviation doesn't have to be used with elements. The XPath expression chapter//@author refers to any author attribute in a chapter or one of its descendants, and //comment() refers to all the comments in a document.

The // abbreviation has one interesting advantage over the XPath fragment that it represents: In addition to using it in XPath expressions, you can use it in match patterns (that is, in the value of an xsl:template instruction's match attribute). Match pattern syntax is a subset of XPath expression syntax; there are various features of XPath syntax that aren't allowed in a match pattern. The descendant-or-self axis is one, but you are free to use the // abbreviation in both XPath expressions and match patterns.

2.2.6   self

The self node refers to the context node itself. We've already used an abbreviation of it several times in the last few examples: the single period (.) is an abbreviation of self::node(), which says "give me the context node, whatever its type is." (The node() node test is true for any node. The XPath expression needs it there because the node test is a required part of an XPath expression or match pattern.) Where you see <xsl:value-of select="."/> in the last few examples, the stylesheets would work exactly the same if the select attribute had the value self::node(). Figure 2.7 shows how the excerpt element in the following document has only one node at its self axis:

```
<!-- xq643.xml -->
<poem>
  <excerpt source="book 1">
    <verse>He lights, if it were Land
            that ever burned</verse>
    <verse>With solid, as the Lake
            with liquid fire</verse>
  </excerpt>
</poem>
```

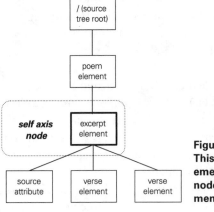

Figure 2.7
**This poem's excerpt el-
ement has one self
node: the excerpt ele-
ment node.**

2.2.7   namespace

The last axis is `namespace`. This axis consists of the default `xml` namespace and any additional ones that are in scope for the context node.

Figure 2.8 shows how the `excerpt` element in the following document has three namespace nodes: the default "xml" one, and "foo" one declared by its parent element, and the "bar" one declared in its own start-tag:

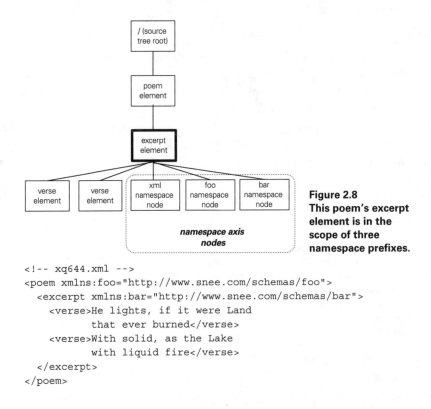

Figure 2.8
**This poem's excerpt
element is in the
scope of three
namespace prefixes.**

```
<!-- xq644.xml -->
<poem xmlns:foo="http://www.snee.com/schemas/foo">
  <excerpt xmlns:bar="http://www.snee.com/schemas/bar">
    <verse>He lights, if it were Land
            that ever burned</verse>
    <verse>With solid, as the Lake
            with liquid fire</verse>
  </excerpt>
</poem>
```

In the next example, the template rule lists the prefixes for a `test` element's namespace nodes:

```
<!-- xq72.xsl: converts xq73.xml into xq74.xml -->

<xsl:template match="test">
  <xsl:for-each select="namespace::*">
    <xsl:value-of select="name()"/><xsl:text> </xsl:text>
  </xsl:for-each>
</xsl:template>
```

For a document like this with three namespaces declared,

```
<test xmlns:snee="http://www.snee.com/dtds/test"
      xmlns:glikk="http://www.glikk.com/dtds/test"
      xmlns:flunn="http://www.flunn.com/dtds/test">
this is a test.
</test>
```

the stylesheet lists the prefixes for the default `xml` namespace as well as the three declared namespaces with a space after each:

```
xml flunn glikk snee
```

WARNING   Despite the requirements of the XPath specification, not all XSLT processors assume the existence of a default "xml" namespace node, so you may not see it listed if you run the above example.

For related information, see section 4.3, "Namespaces," on page 91.

2.3   NODE TESTS

In an XPath expression's location step, a node test is a way of saying "of the nodes that the axis specifier refers to, I'm interested in the one (or ones) with this name." An asterisk (*) node test means "I'm interested in all of them"; a node test of `price` means "I want the ones named 'price'."

How does an XSLT processor know whether a node test of `price` refers to a `price` element, a `price` attribute, or a `price` namespace? Each axis has a principal node type, or a specific node type to which it refers. They're easy to remember: the `attribute` axis refers to attributes; the `namespace` axis refers to namespaces; the rest all refer to elements. The XPath expression `ancestor::price` selects all the `price` elements that are ancestors of the context node, and the XPath expression `attribute::price` refers to a `price` attribute of the context node. (In the latter case, the abbreviation `@price` is more likely to be used.)

A node test is the only part of an XPath location step that must be included, because predicates are optional, and when no axis specifier is included, the XSLT processor assumes a default axis of `child`. Knowing this, you can see why the value of the `select` attribute in the following template rule's `xsl:value-of` element is a complete XPath expression: it's a location path with only one step that omits the axis specifier (so we can assume the default of "child::") and doesn't need a predicate. This node test of price is a complete XPath expression, telling the XSLT processor to add the value of the wine element's price child to the result tree when the XSLT processor finds a wine element in the source tree.

```
<!-- xq76.xsl -->

<xsl:template match="wine">
  <xsl:value-of select="price"/>
</xsl:template>
```

The XPath expression in the select attribute of the next template rule's xsl:value-of element has a two-step location path. Both steps are merely node tests. Because both steps take the default axis value of child, they tell the XSLT processor, "go to the context node's price child, then go to the price element's retail child, and add a text node with the retail child's contents to the result tree."

```
<!-- xq77.xsl -->

<xsl:template match="wine">
  <xsl:value-of select="prices/retail"/>
</xsl:template>
```

The node() node test is true for any node regardless of its type. This is broader than a node test of *, which refers to all the sibling nodes of the axis specifier's principal node type. For example, let's look at the child nodes of the book element in the following document:

```
<book author="jm">
  <chapter>Daughter of God and Man, accomplished Eve</chapter>
  <!-- here is a comment -->
  <?xml-stylesheet href="ss.css" type="text/css" ?>
</book>
```

The book element has three children: a chapter element, a comment, and a processing instruction. When processing this document, the XPath expression in the select attribute of the following template's xsl:for-each element only selects the book element node's chapter child element, because the XPath expression's axis is the default child axis. The child axis has a principal node type of element, so the XPath expression only looks for element children of the book element.

```
<!-- xq79.xsl -->

<xsl:template match="book">
  <xsl:for-each select="*">
    <xsl:value-of select="."/>
  </xsl:for-each>
</xsl:template>
```

The following template (whose only difference from the previous one is its use of the node() node test in the xsl:for-each element's select attribute instead of *) selects *all* the children of the book element node: the chapter element, the comment, and the processing instruction. Again, the lack of an axis specifier in this XPath expression means that child is the relevant axis, and the child axis's principal node type is still "element", but the node() node test doesn't care; it wants all the context node's children regardless of their type.

```
<!-- xq80.xsl -->

<xsl:template match="book">
  <xsl:for-each select="node()">
    <xsl:value-of select="."/>
  </xsl:for-each>
</xsl:template>
```

2.4   PREDICATES

The third part of a location step is the optional part known as the predicate. This is an expression in square brackets that lets you be more specific about which node you really want from the set selected by the axis specifier and node test. Any nodes for which the predicate expression is true are selected, and any others are left out.

For example, the one-step XPath expression in the select attribute of the following template rule's xsl:for-each element does not use a predicate. It tells the processor that when it finds a winelist element node in the source tree, it should go through all of its wine children and add a text node with the value of each one's winery subelement to the result tree:

```
<!-- xq82.xsl -->

<xsl:template match="winelist">
  <xsl:for-each select="child::wine">
    <xsl:value-of select="winery"/>
  </xsl:for-each>
</xsl:template>
```

The next template is the same, except that the XPath expression in the xsl:for-each element's select attribute has a predicate. The Boolean expression @grape='Cabernet' tells the XSLT processor, "of the nodes that the axis specifier and node test child::wine point to, I only want the ones that have a grape attribute value of 'Cabernet' specified."

```
<!-- xq83.xsl -->

<xsl:template match="winelist">
  <xsl:for-each select="child::wine[@grape='Cabernet']">
    <xsl:value-of select="winery"/>
  </xsl:for-each>
</xsl:template>
```

The expression @grape='Cabernet' is obviously Boolean: for a given node it's either true or false. Other handy predicates may not look like Boolean expressions, but the XSLT processor will treat them as true for each node that they apply to, and false for the others. For example, the predicate in the XPath expression `child::wine[@grape]` selects any `wine` child that has a `grape` attribute specified at all. The expression `child::wine[year]` returns a true value only for `wine` elements that have a `year` subelement.

When a predicate has a number, it returns a true value for a node that has that number's position in the node set. For example, `child::wine[4]` is true for the fourth wine child.

XSLT offers many built-in functions useful in predicates. (Technically, some are actually XPath functions. The rest are XSLT's additions to the available repertoire.) In fact, the use of a number such as 4 as a predicate expression is really an abbreviation of the predicate expression `position() = 4`, which definitely has a more Boolean look to it—either a node's position in the node list equals 4 or it doesn't. Other functions that you can use in predicates include

- `last()` returns the number of nodes in the node list, making it easy to get a list's last node when you don't know how long the node list is. For example, if you have five `wine` nodes, `child:wine[last()]` gives you the fifth one.

- `text()` is true for any node that has text content. For example, if some `year` elements have text content and others are empty, `child::year[text()]` is only true for the ones with text content. (Technically, `text()` is a node test and not a function.)

- `not()` takes a Boolean expression as an argument and returns the opposite value of that expression. For example, `child::year[not(text())]` selects all the `year` elements that have no text. You can do this with an attribute name to get all the elements that *don't* have that attribute value set; for example, `child::wine[not(@grape)]` gives you all the wine nodes that don't have a `grape` attribute.

Why would you select the nodes that don't have text or a particular attribute set? Maybe you need to know which ones are missing text or a value for a certain attribute. For example, let's say you're going to publish your wine price list but first need to check which wines have no `discounted` value specified yet. Of your 200 entries, here are three:

```
<winelist>
  <wine grape="Chardonnay">
   <winery>Benziger</winery>
   <product>Carneros</product>
   <year>1997</year>
   <prices>
    <list>10.99</list>
    <discounted>9.50</discounted>
   </prices>
  </wine>

  <wine grape="Cabernet">
```

```
  <winery>Duckpond</winery>
  <product>Merit Selection</product>
  <year>1996</year>
  <prices>
    <list>13.99</list>
    <discounted></discounted>
  </prices>
</wine>

<wine grape="Chardonnay">
  <winery>Lindeman's</winery>
  <product>Bin 65</product>
  <year>1998</year>
  <prices>
    <list>6.99</list>
    <discounted>5.99</discounted>
  </prices>
</wine>
</winelist>
```

The template uses an xsl:for-each element to look at the discounted value of each of the winelist element's wine children.

```
<!-- xq85.xsl: converts xq84.xml into xq86.txt -->

<xsl:template match="winelist">
Wines needing their "discount" value set:
  <xsl:for-each select="wine/prices/discounted[not(text())]">
    <xsl:value-of select="../../year"/><xsl:text> </xsl:text>
    <xsl:value-of select="../../winery"/><xsl:text> </xsl:text>
    <xsl:value-of select="../../product"/>
  </xsl:for-each>
</xsl:template>
```

For each wine element whose prices child has a discounted child containing no text, the XSLT processor adds the year, winery, and product values, separated by spaces, to the result tree. Here is the result for the preceding document:

```
Wines needing their "discount" value set:
  1996 Duckpond Merit Selection
```

The paths used in the three xsl:value-of elements' select attributes need further explanation. Each has two slashes, meaning that each is a three-step location path. The first and second step of each are two periods, which is an abbreviation of the axis specifier and node test parent::node(). So, the XPath expression ../../year in the first xsl:value-of element's select attribute tells the XSLT processor, "follow a path to the context node's parent, then to the parent's parent (the grandparent), and then to the grandparent's year child." (In effect, the year "uncle" node.) How did it know where to start following this path? In most situations, the context node is the one named in the xsl:template element's match attribute, but inside an xsl:for-each loop, the context node is the node that the loop is currently counting off as it goes through the nodes—in this case, a `discounted` element. Why is the loop counting off discounted elements? Because, as complicated as the XPath expression `wine/prices/discounted[not(text())]` may look, the type of the nodes that the XPath expression is ultimately talking about is always the type of the nodes named by the node test in the XPath expression's last location path step. Here, the last step is `discounted[not (text())]`, and its node test is discounted.

> **WARNING** While predicates may mention certain kinds of elements or other nodes, they don't affect the *type* of node being selected; they specify a condition to apply to the nodes selected by the axis specifier and node test. For example, "wine[year]" (or "child::wine[child::year]", which means the same thing) selects not `year` elements, but `wine` elements that happen to have a `year` child.

Fancy XPath expressions can be intimidating, but they're not too bad if you remember a few things:

- Look at the slashes first. These show how the expression breaks down into steps.
- The last step has some of the most important information: the type of node that the expression is ultimately addressing, and, in the predicate, any conditions for filtering out a subset of them.
- "@" abbreviates `attribute::`, ".." abbreviates `parent::node()`, and "//" abbreviates "`/descendant-or-self::node()/`".

The more you learn about how the parts can be assembled to create XPath expressions, the more options you'll have to put together your own powerful XPath expressions.

CHAPTER 3

Elements and attributes

3.1 ADDING NEW ELEMENTS TO THE RESULT TREE

An XSLT processor's main job is to look through a stylesheet for specialized elements from the XSLT namespace and execute the instructions specified by each of those elements on the source tree where the input document resides in memory. When the processor finds elements from outside of the XSLT namespace (or any namespace declared as an XSLT extension, which is how XSLT processors let you incorporate their nonstandard instructions into a stylesheet) in any of a stylesheet's templates, it passes them along to the result tree untouched. We call these "literal result elements."

This makes it easy to add new elements to your output documents: simply add elements from outside of the XSLT namespace inside of the appropriate templates.

The stylesheet below demonstrates this. When the stylesheet's first template rule sees a poem element, it adds its contents to the result tree using `xsl:apply-templates` and surrounds those contents with ode tags, effectively renaming the element from poem to ode. After that ode start-tag, and before the `xsl:apply-template` element that shows where to put the poem element's contents, the template rule adds two new `child` elements of this ode element to the result tree: an `author` element and a `year` element. The `author` element has a hard-coded value of "John Milton," which remains the same for all `author` elements output by this template rule. The `year` element uses the `xsl:value-of` element to output the value of the poem element's year attribute:

```
<!-- xq89.xsl: converts xq90.xml into xq91.xml -->

<xsl:stylesheet xmlns:xsl="http://www.w3.org/1999/XSL/Transform"
     version="1.0">

  <xsl:template match="poem">
    <ode>
    <author>John Milton</author>
    <year><xsl:value-of select="@year"/></year>
    <xsl:apply-templates/>
    </ode>
  </xsl:template>

  <xsl:template match="verse">
    <verse><xsl:apply-templates/></verse>
  </xsl:template>

</xsl:stylesheet>
```

The result is the conversion of a document like this one

```
<poem year="1667" type="epic">
<verse>Nine times the Space that measures Day and Night</verse>
<verse>To mortal men, he with his horrid crew</verse>
</poem>
```

to this:

```
<?xml version="1.0" encoding="utf-8"?>
<ode><author>John Milton</author><year>1667</year>
<verse>Nine times the Space that measures Day and Night</verse>
<verse>To mortal men, he with his horrid crew</verse>
</ode>
```

The `xsl:xsl:element` element offers another way to create new elements for your result tree. The following stylesheet does the same thing as the last one, but it uses `xsl:element` elements instead of literal result elements. Their name attributes name the elements being created, and the XSLT processor adds start- and end-tags for those elements to the result tree:

```
<!-- xq92.xsl: converts xq90.xml into xq91.xml -->

<xsl:stylesheet xmlns:xsl="http://www.w3.org/1999/XSL/Transform"
     version="1.0">

  <xsl:template match="poem">
   <xsl:element name="ode">
      <xsl:element name="author">John Milton</xsl:element>
      <xsl:element name="year"><xsl:value-of select="@year"/>
      </xsl:element>
      <xsl:apply-templates/>
   </xsl:element>
  </xsl:template>

  <xsl:template match="verse">
    <verse><xsl:apply-templates/></verse>
  </xsl:template>

</xsl:stylesheet>
```

This name attribute is the key to the advantage of `xsl:element` elements over literal result elements. It offers greater flexibility, letting you create element names dynamically by concatenating strings, calling functions, and retrieving element content and attribute values from elsewhere in the document. For instance, the template in the next example resembles the first one in the stylesheets above except that, instead of converting the source tree's poem element into an ode element using an ode literal result element or an `xsl:element` element with a hard-coded name value, the template uses an `xsl:element` element to create an element that gets its name from the poem element's type attribute value:

```
<!-- xq93.xsl: converts xq90.xml into xq94.xml -->

<xsl:template match="poem">
   <xsl:element name="{@type}">
     <author>John Milton</author>
     <year><xsl:value-of select="@year"/></year>
     <xsl:apply-templates/>
   </xsl:element>
</xsl:template>

  <xsl:template match="verse">
    <verse><xsl:apply-templates/></verse>
  </xsl:template>
```

When applied to the earlier poem document which had a type attribute value of "epic" in its poem element, the template creates the following epic element:

```
<epic><author>John Milton</author><year>1667</year>
<verse>Nine times the Space that measures Day and Night</verse>
```

```
<verse>To mortal men, he with his horrid crew</verse>
</epic>
```

Using this same technique for specifying element names, a template can add an element to a result tree without even knowing its element type name in advance.

While literal result elements are less powerful than `xsl:element` elements, their simplicity and ease of use often makes them more convenient. Considering the tasks performed by the templates above, literal result elements make more sense to add the examples' `author` and `year` elements to the result tree.

3.2 CHANGING ELEMENT NAMES FOR THE RESULT TREE

While `xsl:copy` copies an element node or other nodes, `xsl:apply-templates` processes only the children of the current node. For an element, this means processing everything between the tags, but nothing in the tags themselves.

When you use `xsl:apply-templates` to copy the content of an element to the result tree without the element's tags, you can surround that content with anything you want, as long as it doesn't prevent the document represented by that result tree from being well-formed. For example, the template rule below takes any `article` elements in the source tree and copies their contents to the result tree. The template wraps this content in a `body` element and wraps that `body` element with an `html` element.

```
<!-- xq96.xsl -->

<xsl:template match="article">
  <html><body>
    <xsl:apply-templates/>
  </body></html>
</xsl:template>
```

3.3 PARENT, GRANDPARENT, SIBLING, UNCLE, AND OTHER RELATIVE ELEMENTS: GETTING THEIR CONTENT AND ATTRIBUTES

Chapter 2, "XPath," on page 23, describes how XPath expressions work—the pieces used to construct them, how they fit together, and the abbreviations that you can substitute for some of the pieces. This section provides a quick reference for some handy XPath expressions.

In the following example, the `list` element is a child of the `prices` element, which is a child of the `wine` element:

```
<wine grape="Chardonnay">
  <winery>Lindeman's</winery>
  <product>Bin 65</product>
  <year>1998</year>
  <desc>Youthful, with a cascade of spicy fig.</desc>
  <prices>
```

```
        <list>6.99</list>
        <discounted>5.99</discounted>
        <case>71.50</case>
      </prices>
    </wine>
```

The following template rule tells the XSLT processor to add information about the list element and its relatives to the result tree. Much of the template is comprised of text nodes such as "~~~~ Start of list element's template ~~~~" to show where the template's output begins and "1. List price (current node): {" to label the results of the xsl:apply-templates element. The curly braces around the xsl:apply-templates and the xsl:value-of elements make it easier to see where the results of these elements begin and end:

```
<!-- xq99.xsl: converts xq98.xml into xq100.xml -->

<xsl:template match="list">
~~~~ Start of list element's template  ~~~~
1. List price (current node): {<xsl:apply-templates/>}
2. Parent element (prices) contents: {<xsl:value-of select=".."/>}
3. Grandparent element contents: {<xsl:value-of select="../.."/>}
4. Attribute of grandparent: {<xsl:value-of select="../../@grape"/>}
5. Sibling node {<xsl:value-of select="../discounted"/>}
6. "Uncle" node {<xsl:value-of select="../../product"/>}
7.  Parent node's name: {<xsl:value-of select="name(..)"/>}
8.  Grandparent node's name: {<xsl:value-of select="name(../..)"/>}
~~~~ End of list element's template   ~~~~
</xsl:template>
```

Before we examine the template in detail, let's look at the result created using the wine element above as input:

```
~~~~ Start of list element's template   ~~~~
1. List price (current node): {6.99}
2. Parent element (prices) contents: {
        6.99
        5.99
        71.50
      }
3. Grandparent element contents: {
      Lindeman's
      Bin 65
      1998
      Youthful, with a cascade of spicy fig.

        6.99
        5.99
        71.50

    }
4. Attribute of grandparent: {Chardonnay}
5. Sibling node {5.99}
```

```
6.  "Uncle" node {Bin 65}
7.   Parent node's name: {prices}
8.   Grandparent node's name: {wine}
~~~~ End of list element's template  ~~~~
```

1   The line labeled "1. List price" has an xsl:apply-templates element that tells the XSLT processor to apply any relevant templates to the node's children. The list node named by the xsl:template element's match attribute has only one child: a text node, and the default processing for a text node is to add its contents to the result tree. The text string "6.99," which makes up the list element's character data, gets added to the result between the template line's curly braces.

2   The line labeled "2. Parent element" has ".." as the xsl:value-of element's select attribute value. This abbreviation tells the XSLT processor to output the contents of the list element node's parent prices. With no template rule for prices or its other children in the stylesheet, the built-in rules output the character data content between that line's curly braces: the contents of the three children of the prices element, complete with their carriage returns. As this shows, relying on built-in template rules to output the contents of an element enclosing element children leads to less control over the appearance of the children's contents.

3   The third line outputs the content of the grandparent wine element using the ".." abbreviation twice to say "the parent of the parent." The slash separates these two location path steps. As with line 2, the contents of this element are output using built-in template rules, resulting in a flat dump of the source tree text (including its carriage returns) to the result tree.

4   The fourth line, "4. Attribute of grandparent", uses the same XPath expression as the xsl:value-of element's select attribute in line 3, with an addition: one more location path step to say "after going to the parent of the parent of the context node (../..), get the value of its grape attribute." The attribute value "Chardonnay" shows up between line 4's curly braces in the result.

5   Line 5 gets the value of a sibling by first looking to the list node's parent and then looking at its child named discounted. The discounted element's content of "5.99" shows up between line 5's curly braces in the result.

6   Line 6 looks at an "uncle" node by looking at a child of the grandparent much the same way that line 3 looked at an attribute of the grandparent: by adding a new location step (product, to look at the child element with that name) to the "../.." expression that looks at the parent of the context node's parent.

7   Line 7 uses the name() function to get the name of the node's parent. The template passes the ".." expression for "parent" to the function.

8 Line 8 resembles 7 except that it passes the "parent of parent" XPath expression (../..) to the name() function. The element type name wine shows up between the curly braces in the result.

The pieces of these expressions mix and match well. For example, if the context node's desc "uncle" node has a color attribute, and you want this attribute's value when processing the context node, the xsl:value-of element's select attribute can use the expression ../../desc/@color.

3.4   PREVIOUS, NEXT, FIRST, THIRD, LAST SIBLINGS

The previous section showed how to access nodes siblings of the context nodes as well as nodes at different levels of the source tree from the context node, such as the parent and grandparent. Sometimes, when you want a sibling node, specifying its name isn't good enough, because other siblings may have the same name. Maybe you want a particular node because of its order among the siblings.

You can use the preceding-sibling and following-sibling axes to refer to sibling elements, or you use a two-step location path to refer to the child of the parent node that has a particular name. The latter method sounds more cumbersome, but using the abbreviation of the parent axis (..) often makes it the more convenient form to use. The next template rule uses both methods to access the siblings of the third item element in the following document:

```
<list>
<item flavor="mint">First node.</item>
<item flavor="chocolate">Second node.</item>
<item flavor="vanilla">Third node.</item>
<item flavor="strawberry">Fourth node.</item>
</list>
```

If the following template rule's match pattern only said "item," the template rule would apply to all item elements, but this one includes a predicate of "3". This way, when the XSLT processor finds item children of a node that it's processing, it will only apply this template rule to the third item child. (Remember, when no axis is specified in a template rule's match pattern, a default of "child::" is assumed, so the template is looking for item elements that are the child of another node currently being processed.) The template also includes text nodes (for example, "~~~~ Start of item element's template ~~~~" and "1. This node: {") to show the beginning, the end and the numbered individual steps of the template's actions in the result. The curly braces show exactly where the xsl:apply-templates element and xsl:value-of elements results begin and end in the result.

```
<!-- xq103.xsl: converts xq102.xml into xq104.txt -->

<xsl:template match="item[3]">
~~~~ Start of item element's template ~~~~
1. This node: {<xsl:apply-templates/>}
```

```
2. First node: {<xsl:value-of select="../item[1]"/>}
3. Last node: {<xsl:value-of select="../item[last()]"/>}
4. Preceding node:
   {<xsl:value-of select="preceding-sibling::item[1]"/>}
5. Next node: {<xsl:value-of select="following-sibling::item[1]"/>}
6. flavor attribute value of first node:
   {<xsl:value-of select="../item[1]/@flavor"/>}
~~~~ End of item element's template ~~~~
</xsl:template>
```

Applying this template creates a result that places the contents of each referenced node between curly braces:

```
~~~~ Start of item element's template ~~~~
1. This node: {Third node.}
2. First node: {First node.}
3. Last node: {Fourth node.}
4. Preceding node:
   {Second node.}
5. Next node: {Fourth node.}
6. flavor attribute value of first node:
   {mint}
~~~~ End of item element's template ~~~~
```

1 Line 1 ("This node:") adds the contents of the current item element to the result tree to show the XSLT processor's location in the source tree document during the execution of this template rule.

2 Line 2 has a two-step location path. The first step (..) tells the XSLT processor to look at the node's parent, and the second step tells it to look at the first item child of that parent. Without the second step's predicate in square brackets, the expression ../item would refer to *all* of the parent node's item children, but because xsl:value-of only returns a string version of the first one, the [1] predicate in this case is not completely necessary. It's still worth including because it makes the stylesheet's intent clearer.

Any number could go in that predicate, although a number for which no item exists—for example, a predicate of [8] when there are four nodes in the list—tells the XSLT processor to look for something that isn't there, so it won't get anything. The match pattern in the xsl:template element's start-tag is a good example of selecting a node by its number; it uses [3] to indicate that this template should be applied to the third item child of the node currently being processed.

3 Line 3 uses the last() function in its predicate. The XSLT processor replaces this with the number of nodes in the node set selected by the axis and node test (in this case, by the default child axis and the item node test). This gives the same result as putting the actual number (in this case, 4) between those square brackets. When you put this node test of "item" and predicate of [last()]

together, you're asking for the last of the parent node's item elements. When the context node and all of its siblings are item elements, this is the simplest way to get the last sibling, especially if you don't know how many siblings exist.

4 Line 4 (which is actually split over two lines to fit on this book's page) uses the preceding-sibling axis to access the node before the context node. Without the [1] predicate, it would take the first node in the preceding-sibling node set in document order, but with the explicit inclusion of the number "1," the XSLT processor counts from the end of the node set instead of from the beginning. It only counts from the end with axes for which this makes sense; for the preceding-sibling axis, the first sibling node that precedes the context node is the one just before it. XSLT processors also count backwards like this for the ancestor axis (for example, ancestor[1] refers to the parent node and ancestor[2] refers to the grandparent node), the ancestor-or-self axis, and the preceding axis.

5 Line 5 looks like line 4 except that it uses the following-sibling axis specifier to look at the siblings after the context node. The predicate of [1] is not necessary, because when the XSLT instruction xsl:value-of is pointed at a node list, it returns a string value of the first one it can find in document order, but including the predicate here makes it easier to see the exact intent of the XPath expression.

6 Line 6 (which is also split over two lines) shows how easily you can get an attribute value from one of these siblings. Its XPath expression repeats the one from line 2 and adds one more step to the location path, @flavor, to get the flavor attribute value of that first item sibling. You could add this location step to any of the XPath expressions in this example to get the corresponding item element's flavor attribute value.

3.5 CONVERTING ELEMENTS TO ATTRIBUTES FOR THE RESULT TREE

While the xsl:value-of element is a great way to pick out a value on the input tree and insert it someplace in the result tree—especially when converting attributes to elements—you can't use this element just anywhere. For example, you can't use it to assign an attribute value to an element on the result tree. The following template shows a misguided attempt at doing just that, which puts the xsl:value-of element inside the start-tag of a wine literal result element. This very ill-formed template will make any XML parser choke, and, if the XML parser doesn't like the template, it's never going to get to the XSLT processor:

```
<!-- xq106.xsl: won't work -->
<xsl:template match="wine">
<wine brand="<xsl:value-of select='winery'>"> <!-- WRONG! -->
</xsl:template>
```

This next template, on the other hand, does take the content of two input elements and makes them attribute values in the output document:

```
<!-- xq107.xsl: converts xq108.xml into xq109.xml -->
<xsl:template match="wine">
<wine varietal="{@grape}" brand="{winery}" year="{../year}"/>
</xsl:template>

<xsl:template match="year"/>
```

For example, this template turns the `winery` element content "Los Vascos" in the input

```
<vintage>
  <year>1998</year>
  <wine grape="Cabernet Sauvignon">
    <winery>Los Vascos</winery>
  </wine>
</vintage>
```

into the `brand` attribute's value in the output:

```
<wine varietal="Cabernet Sauvignon" brand="Los Vascos" year="1998"/>
```

Although the first template grabs the value of the `year` element, and puts it in the result tree `wine` element's start-tag, XSLT's built-in template rules will still add the `year` element value just before that `wine` element in the result tree. To prevent this, the second template above tells the XSLT processor "when you find a `year` element node, add nothing to the result tree."

Why isn't this necessary for the `winery` element? The first template also grabs its value and adds that value as an attribute value of the result tree's `wine` element, but that template has no `xsl:apply-templates` element, which would tell the XSLT processor to apply any relevant templates to the `wine` element's children. So, even the built-in templates won't be applied to the `winery` element. (This didn't affect the `year` element because that element isn't a child of the `wine` element.)

Using the same technique, the `year` element's content "1998" becomes the value of a `year` attribute in the result.

The template does this using attribute value templates. An attribute value template is an expression between curly braces ({ }) that you can use for the dynamic generation of certain attribute values in an XSLT stylesheet. When an XSLT processor finds an attribute value template, it evaluates the expression and replaces the attribute value template with the result of the evaluation.

The preceding template uses three attribute value templates:

- One attribute value template inserts the value of the `wine` element's `grape` attribute as the value of the result tree's `varietal` attribute.

- Another uses the content of the `wine` element's `winery` child element as the value for the `brand` attribute.

- And one inserts the value of the `wine` element's `year` sibling element as the value of the `year` output attributes.

The attribute value template for the `brand` attribute value shows how simple the conversion of an element to an attribute can be if the element to convert is a child of the element named in the match pattern. In this case, the `year` element is a child of the `wine` element named by the `xsl:template` element's `match` attribute. The `year` attribute's attribute value template shows that you have a broad range of options if you want to use the value of an element that isn't a child of the match pattern element as your result tree attribute value—and remember, you have the full power of XPath available to identify the text that you want to plug in there.

For related information, see

- section 3.3, "Parent, grandparent, sibling, uncle, and other relative elements: getting their content and attributes," page 50 for background on the use of the @ and `../` notation.

- section 3.13, "Adding new attributes," page 77 for more on ways to add new attributes to your output elements.

3.6 COPYING ELEMENTS TO THE RESULT TREE

A template can copy an element from the source tree to the result tree by putting its contents either between literal result element tags or in an `xsl:element` instruction that gives the result element the same name it had in the source tree. If the source element has attributes, a template rule can copy them with explicitly named `xsl:attribute` elements, or it can add them directly to the literal result element.

For example, to copy the `prices` element in this document,

```
<wine grape="Cabernet">
  <winery>Duckpond</winery>
  <product>Merit Selection</product>
  <year>1996</year>
  <prices date="12/1/01">
    <list>13.99</list>
    <discounted>11.00</discounted>
  </prices>
</wine>
```

the following template uses a literal result element and adds its `date` attribute value with an attribute value template:

```
<!-- xq112.xsl -->

<xsl:template match="prices">
  <prices date="{@date}">
    <xsl:apply-templates/>
  </prices>
</xsl:template>
```

XSLT offers better ways to copy elements. For example, you shouldn't have to write out the copied element's name in the literal result element or xsl:element instruction. Once you tell the XSLT processor to copy certain elements and attributes to the result tree, it should be able to copy their names as well as contents.

The simplest way to copy a node is with the xsl:copy element, which copies the node named in the template rule's match attribute. It doesn't copy any of the node's children. If you're copying an element, this means it won't copy any of its child elements, character data, or attributes. For example, the following template rule

```
<!-- xq113.xsl: converts xq111.xml into xq114.xml -->

<xsl:template match="prices">
  <xsl:copy/>
</xsl:template>
```

turns the prices element above into this:

```
<prices/>
```

This prices element has the element type name, but with no attributes or content, it doesn't even need an end-tag, so it comes out as a single empty element.

With an xsl:apply-templates instruction inside that xsl:copy instruction to process the element's content, like this,

```
<!-- xq115.xsl: converts xq111.xml into xq116.xsl -->

<xsl:template match="prices">
  <xsl:copy>
    <xsl:apply-templates/>
  </xsl:copy>
</xsl:template>
```

the result has the prices start- and end-tags with only the descendant elements' character data, because the list and discounted elements' handling are left to XSLT's built-in templates:

```
<prices>
  13.99
  11.00
</prices>
```

Neither the xsl:copy element nor XSLT's built-in templates copy the prices element's attribute. You can include attributes yourself in the xsl:copy element, as in the following, which copies the prices element's date attribute and inserts a new, hard-coded vendor attribute:

```
<!-- xq117.xsl: converts xq111.xml into xq118.xsl -->

<xsl:template match="prices">
  <xsl:copy>

    <xsl:attribute name="date">
      <xsl:value-of select="@date"/>
```

```
    </xsl:attribute>

    <xsl:attribute name="vendor">
        <xsl:text>Snee Wines</xsl:text>
    </xsl:attribute>
    <xsl:apply-templates/>
  </xsl:copy>
</xsl:template>
```

This template creates the following result from the same source document:

```
<prices date="12/1/01" vendor="Snee Wines">
    13.99
    11.00
</prices>
```

If you really want to copy the element node and its attribute and children elements, the xsl:copy-of element makes this easy. For example, the following template

```
<!-- xq119.xsl: converts xq111.xml into xq120.xml -->

<xsl:template match="wine">
  <xsl:copy-of select="."/>
</xsl:template>
```

makes an exact copy of the wine element shown earlier:

```
<wine grape="Cabernet">
  <winery>Duckpond</winery>
  <product>Merit Selection</product>
  <year>1996</year>
  <prices date="12/1/01">
    <list>13.99</list>
    <discounted>11.00</discounted>
  </prices>
</wine>
```

The xsl:copy-of instruction has a required select attribute to tell this instruction what to copy. In the example above, the single period (an abbreviation of the XPath expression self::node()) tells it to copy the context node. Because it's an xsl:copy-of instruction and not an xsl:copy one, it copies all the node's children as well. (The xsl:copy instruction has no attributes to tell it what to copy; the xsl:copy instruction can only copy the context node.) You can use any XPath expression you like as the select value. With a select attribute value of something other than ".", the xsl:copy-of element can grab almost any set of nodes in the source tree and group them together wherever you want in the result tree.

To really understand the power of xsl:copy-of, let's compare it to the xsl:value-of instruction. Both help you grab an arbitrary part of the source tree while the XSLT processor is processing another part of the tree. The xsl:value-of element doesn't add a copy of the grabbed node to the result tree, but a text node with a string representation of it. When `xsl:value-of` is told to convert a set of nodes to a string, it only gets the first one in that set, so it's only useful for getting one node's value at a time. The `xsl:copy-of` element, on the other hand, gets a whole node set and all of the nodes' children.

TIP   The `xsl:copy-of` element copies an element and all its element children, but `xsl:copy-of` does more than that: if it's copying an element node, it copies all of its *node* children (and descendants), whether they're element, attribute, comment, namespace, text, or processing instruction nodes.

Let's look at a stylesheet that demonstrates the difference between the `xsl:value-of` and `xsl:copy-of` instructions. The template in the following example has one of each, with the same XPath expression in both `select` attributes:

```
<!-- xq121.xsl: converts xq111.xml into xq122.xml -->

<xsl:template match="product">

  xsl:values-of:
  <xsl:value-of select="following-sibling::*"/>

  xsl:copy-of:
  <xsl:copy-of select="following-sibling::*"/>
</xsl:template>
```

The XPath expression `following-sibling::*` refers to all the sibling nodes, regardless of their name, following the current one. In the XML document above, `product` has two siblings after it: `year` and `prices`. The `prices` sibling has two element children. When `xsl:value-of` converts this set of nodes to a text node to add to the result tree, this instruction only gets the first one, and it gets the node's value—its character data, which is just the string "1996" in this case:

```
xsl:value-of:
1996

xsl:copy-of:
<year>1996</year><prices date="12/1/01">
  <list>13.99</list>
  <discounted>11.00</discounted>
</prices>
```

With the same XPath expression in its `select` attribute, the `xsl:copy-of` element adds a lot more to the result tree: the tags, attributes, and content of *all* the nodes to which the expression refers.

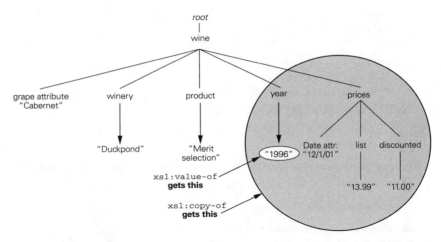

Figure 3.1 Getting the "`following-sibling::`" node set for a context node of "product":`xsl:value-of vs. xsl:copy-of`

Remember, `xsl:copy-of` is getting *copies* of the `year`, `prices`, and other elements retrieved by the `following-sibling::*` expression. If those nodes have their own template rules with instructions about processing them, the XSLT processor will still apply those templates to them. The `product` template rule's actions with its `xsl:copy-of` instruction have no effect on the actions of the element's own templates.

For more information on `xsl:value-of`, see section 3.11.2, "Moving text with xsl:value-of," page 71.

3.7   *COUNTING ELEMENTS AND OTHER NODES*

The `count()` function returns the number of nodes in the node set passed to it. In effect, it counts the number of nodes described by an XPath expression. To demonstrate, we'll count different groups of nodes in this document:

```
<employees>

  <employee hireDate="04/23/1999" officer="yes">
    <last>Hill</last>
    <first>Phil</first>
    <salary>100000</salary>
  </employee>

  <employee hireDate="09/01/1998" officer="no">
    <last>Herbert</last>
    <first>Johnny</first>
    <!-- Salary may need updating -->
    <salary>95000</salary>
  </employee>

  <employee hireDate="08/20/2000">
    <last>Hill</last>
```

```
    <first>Graham</first>
    <salary>89000</salary>
  </employee>

  <employee hireDate="10/16/2000">
    <last>Sterling</last>
    <first>Moss</first>
    <salary>97000</salary>
  </employee>

</employees>
```

The document element is an employees element, and the following template rule counts four sets of nodes within that document:

```
<!-- xq125.xsl: converts xq124.xml into xq126.txt -->

<xsl:template match="employees">
  A. Number of employees:
  <xsl:value-of select="count(employee)"/>
  B. Number of officers:
  <xsl:value-of select="count(employee[@officer='yes'])"/>
  C. Number of employees without 'officer' attribute set:
  <xsl:value-of select="count(employee[not(@officer)])"/>
  D. Number of comments in 'employees' element:
  <xsl:value-of select="count(//comment())"/>
</xsl:template>

<xsl:template match="employee"/>
```

Before we look at the ways in which this template uses the count() function, let's consider the result of counting each node set:

```
A. Number of employees:
4
B. Number of officers:
1
C. Number of employees without 'officer' attribute set:
2
D. Number of comments in 'employees' element:
1
```

The first use of the function, in part A, counts the number of employee child elements of the employees element. The answer is 4. By passing "employee" as an argument to the count() function, the template tells the XSLT processor to count all the child elements of the context node (employees) that have that name.

Part B adds a predicate to the employee node test passed as an XPath expression to the count() function: [@officer='yes']. This way, only employee elements with an officer attribute value of "yes" are counted. As the result shows, the answer is 1.

A predicate of [@officer] with a node test of employee would tell the count() function to count all the employee elements having the officer attribute set. Part C of the preceding stylesheet takes the opposite approach: a predicate that puts the `@officer` part inside of a `not()` function tells the `count()` function to count all the `employee` elements that don't have the `officer` attribute set. The answer is 2.

Finally, part D of the template illustrates that you don't have to count elements with the `count()` function; you can count any kind of node type you want. Part D counts comments, and because the expression begins with the XPath abbreviation `//` (meaning "`/descendant-or-self::node()/`") part D's expression counts all the comments in the document, and finds 1.

This is just a sample of what you can do with the `count()` function. Remember that if you can describe a subset of a document's nodes using an XPath expression, you can count the nodes in that subset, whether they are element nodes or any other kind of nodes.

3.8 DELETING ELEMENTS FROM THE RESULT TREE

A template rule essentially says "when you find a source node that corresponds to the value of my `match` attribute, add the template in my contents to the result tree." If the template rule has no contents, then nothing gets added to the result tree for that source node, essentially deleting it from the result tree copy of the source tree.

For example, this template rule says "when you find a `project` element, add nothing to the result tree":

```
<!-- xq128.xsl -->
<xsl:template match="project"></xsl:template>
```

(Of course, this `xsl:template` element could also be written as a single empty-element tag.)

The next template takes advantage of the flexibility allowed in the patterns allowed in the `template` element's `match` attribute. While a `match` value of "project" would delete *all* the `project` elements from the output, the following template rule only deletes `project` elements whose `status` attributes have the string "canceled" as their value:

```
<!-- xq129.xsl -->
<xsl:template match="project[@status='canceled']"/>
```

Another way to delete an element is to be selective about which of its parent's children get processed. With no `select` attribute specified, an `xsl:apply-templates` element processes all the children of the tree node being processed. When an `xsl:apply-templates` element does include a `select` attribute, you can be pickier about which children to process. For example, the following template will process all of a `customer` element's children:

```
<!-- xq130.xsl -->
  <xsl:template match="customer">
```

```
   <client>
     <xsl:apply-templates/>
   </client>
 </xsl:template>
```

And this template will only output the lastName and phone children of the customer elements, omitting any others:

```
<!-- xq131.xsl -->

<xsl:template match="customer">
  <client>
    <xsl:apply-templates select="lastName"/>
    <xsl:apply-templates select="phone"/>
  </client>
</xsl:template>
```

3.9   *DUPLICATE ELEMENTS, DELETING*

When we copy a source tree to a result tree, the basic idea of deleting duplicate elements as we make a copy of a source tree document sounds simple: Don't copy an element from the source tree to the result tree if an identical one has already been
copied. But what do we mean by "identical"? According to the XPath specification,
two node sets are considered equal if their string values are equal. The string values
are the concatenation of any text node descendants of the elements. Text nodes store
character data contents of elements—the part between start- and end-tags that aren't
child elements—so two nodes with different attributes or with different values in the
same attribute are still considered equal, because attributes aren't taken into account
in the XPath version of element equality. So, if you only want to compare element
content when determining which elements are duplicates, an equal sign will do, but if
you want to consider attribute values, you have to explicitly say so.

Let's look at an example. While no two line elements in the following document are exactly the same—each, for instance, has at least a different lid ("line ID")
attribute value—we'll examine several ways to avoid copying certain elements to the
result tree because they have content or an attribute value in common with others.

```
<sample>
    <line lid="u1">hello</line>
    <line color="red" lid="u2">hello</line>
    <line color="blue" lid="u3">hello</line>
    <line lid="u4">hello there</line>
    <line color="blue" lid="u5">hello there</line>
    <line color="blue" lid="u6">hello</line>
</sample>
```

The first stylesheet has a template rule for line elements that copies only one element to the result tree if it's not equal to any of the line elements in the preceding axis—that is, not equal to any line element that finished before the one being

processed began. (See section 2.2.4, "preceding and following," page 32, for more on this axis.) The other template copies all the other nodes verbatim:

```
<!-- xq495.xsl: converts xq494.xml into xq496.xml -->
<xsl:stylesheet xmlns:xsl="http://www.w3.org/1999/XSL/Transform"
    version="1.0">
  <xsl:output method="xml" omit-xml-declaration="yes"/>

  <xsl:template match="line">
    <xsl:if test="not(. = preceding::line)">
    <xsl:copy>
    <xsl:apply-templates select="@*|node()"/>
  </xsl:copy>
    </xsl:if>
  </xsl:template>

  <xsl:template match="@*|node()">
   <xsl:copy>
    <xsl:apply-templates select="@*|node()"/>
   </xsl:copy>
  </xsl:template>

</xsl:stylesheet>
```

As I mentioned above, the XPath spec considers elements equal if the string values that represent their contents are equal. The contents are the parts between the tags, so attribute values aren't considered in this kind of equality test. Once one line element with the contents "hello" is added to the result tree, no more may be added, regardless of their attribute values, and likewise for the "hello there" elements:

```
<sample>
<line lid="u1">hello</line>

<line lid="u4">hello there</line>

</sample>
```

This variation on the line template rule above has a different condition in the test attribute of its xsl:if instruction. It won't add a line element to the result tree if any preceding line element had the same value in its color attribute as that in the context node line element.

```
<!-- xq497.xsl: converts xq494.xml into xq498.xml -->

  <xsl:template match="line">
    <xsl:if test="not(@color = preceding::line/@color)">
      <xsl:copy>
        <xsl:apply-templates select="@*|node()"/>
      </xsl:copy>
    </xsl:if>
  </xsl:template>
```

Once the XSLT processor adds one line element with a color attribute value of "blue", it won't add any more, even when the line element has different content, such as the "u5" one with "hello there" as its content:

```
<sample>
<line lid="u1">hello</line>
<line lid="u2" color="red">hello</line>
<line lid="u3" color="blue">hello</line>
<line lid="u4">hello there</line>

</sample>
```

The next version of the same template rule won't copy any `line` element with the same content and the same `color` attribute value as any earlier `line` element. This version is more complicated than the earlier examples. First, this template rule sets two local variables with the contents and `color` attribute value of the context node to use in the comparison. Then, the comparison in the predicate (that is, in the square brackets) has a Boolean and to connect the two conditions. It's checking for preceding nodes that meet both conditions. The `not()` function wrapped around the whole XPath expression tells the XSLT processor to only process `list` elements that don't meet both of these conditions:

```
<!-- xq499.xsl: converts xq494.xml into xq500.xml -->

  <xsl:template match="line">
    <xsl:variable name="contents" select="."/>
    <xsl:variable name="colorVal" select="@color"/>
    <xsl:if test =
      "not(preceding::line[(. = $contents) and
           (@color = $colorVal)])">
      <xsl:copy>
        <xsl:apply-templates select="@*|node()"/>
      </xsl:copy>
    </xsl:if>
  </xsl:template>
```

The result of running the source document with this version of the template has all the `line` elements except the "u6" one, which is the only one with contents and a `color` attribute that match the contents and `color` attribute of an earlier `line` element ("u3"):

```
<sample>
    <line lid="u1">hello</line>
    <line lid="u2" color="red">hello</line>
    <line lid="u3" color="blue">hello</line>
    <line lid="u4">hello there</line>
    <line lid="u5" color="blue">hello there</line>

</sample>
```

To compare the `lid` attribute value along with the contents and `color` attribute value of the `line` elements you would declare another local variable and add another condition inside the square brackets. Remember, though, that the more complicated a comparison condition you have, the more work the XSLT processor must do, and the slower the stylesheet will run.

If you know that all potential duplicate elements are siblings, as they are in this chapter's examples, you can speed things up by using the preceding-sibling axis instead of the preceding axis so that the XSLT processor won't try to check as many nodes for equality. (See section 2.2.3, "preceding-sibling and following-sibling," page 29, for more on this axis.) This chapter's examples use the preceding axis because it does a more complete check that would cover a wider variety of cases.

3.10   EMPTY ELEMENTS: CREATING, CHECKING FOR

To an XML parser, the elements <sample/> and <sample></sample> are the same: they're both empty sample elements. When your stylesheet adds an element to the result tree, if it creates no content for that element, it has created an empty element, whether that element type was declared as being empty in a DTD or not. To demonstrate, let's look at a template rule that copies the following element and adds empty sample elements to the copy:

```
<test>Dagon his Name, Sea Monster</test>
```

The stylesheet adds seven empty sample elements after the result tree's test start-tag. The fourth, fifth, and sixth resemble the first three except that each of these empty elements includes an attribute specification:

```
<!-- xq135.xsl: converts xq134.xml into xq476.xml -->

<xsl:template match="test">
  <test>
    1. <sample/>
    2. <sample></sample>
    3. <xsl:element name="sample"/>

    4. <sample color="green"/>
    5. <sample color="green"></sample>
    6. <xsl:element name="sample">
         <xsl:attribute name="color">green</xsl:attribute>
       </xsl:element>

    7. <sample> </sample>

    <xsl:apply-templates/>
  </test>
</xsl:template>
```

Whether elements are shown in the stylesheet as a single-tag empty element, a start- and end-tag pair with nothing between them, or as xsl:element instruction with no content specified, they all show up in the result tree as empty elements:

```
<test>
    1. <sample/>
    2. <sample/>
    3. <sample/>

    4. <sample color="green"/>
```

```
5. <sample color="green"/>
6. <sample color="green"/>


7. <sample/>Dagon his Name, Sea Monster</test>
```

The seventh `sample` is a special case. If space characters (tabs, carriage returns, or spacebar spaces) and no others occur between two tags, an XML parser does not treat those characters as character data, which is why that seventh `sample` element is considered empty. This does look a little confusing in the stylesheet, so it's a good idea to avoid it when possible.

How about checking for empty elements so that your stylesheet can perform certain actions if they're empty and others if they're not? The following `test` document has seven sample elements, and the first four are empty.

```
<test>
  <sample eid="A"/>
  <sample eid="B"></sample>
  <sample eid="C">  </sample>
  <sample eid="D">
</sample>
  <sample eid="E">some text</sample>
  <sample eid="F"><color>blue</color></sample>
  <sample eid="G"><color>red</color>more text</sample>
</test>
```

How can a template rule know which ones are empty? When the node set "`.`" (an abbreviation of "`self::node()`") is passed to the `normalize-string()` function, the function converts this node set to a string (because it only acts on strings) and then does its real job: it converts any multispace sequences to a single space and removes all leading and trailing spaces. (See section 5.7.1, "Extracting and comparing strings," page 153 for more on this function.) If there's anything left, this means that the `sample` element was not empty, and that makes the Boolean value of the `xsl:when` element's `test` attribute true.

The following template checks this Boolean value before adding a message about the `sample` element to the result tree (see section 3.8, "Deleting elements from the result tree," page 63, for more on these):

```
<!-- xq137.xsl: converts xq136.xml into xq138.txt -->

<xsl:template match="sample">
  <xsl:choose>
    <xsl:when test="normalize-space(.)">
      Sample element <xsl:value-of select="@eid"/> isn't empty.
    </xsl:when>
    <xsl:otherwise>
      Sample element <xsl:value-of select="@eid"/> is empty.
    </xsl:otherwise>
  </xsl:choose>
</xsl:template>
```

When the `test` value is true, the stylesheet adds a message to the result tree about that sample element not being empty. When run with the XML document above, the stylesheet adds that message for `sample` elements E, F, and G:

```
Sample element A is empty.

Sample element B is empty.

Sample element C is empty.

Sample element D is empty.

Sample element E isn't empty.

Sample element F isn't empty.

Sample element G isn't empty.
```

When nothing is left after `normalize-space()` deletes any unnecessary space, the `xsl:choose` instruction's `xsl:otherwise` element adds a message to the result tree about that `sample` element being empty. The `xsl:otherwise` element adds that message for `sample` elements A, B, C, and D.

Some stylesheets use simpler syntax to check for empty elements, but it's safer to use the `normalize-space()` function to catch odd cases as well as more typical empty elements.

3.11 MOVING AND COMBINING ELEMENTS FOR THE RESULT TREE

Two ways exist to move an element from one position in the source tree to a different position in the result tree: reordering an element's children with `xsl:apply-templates`, and moving text with `xsl:value of`.

3.11.1 Reordering an element's children with xsl:apply-templates

The first way to move an element is the easiest: change the order of the parent element's children by selectively applying `xsl:apply-templates` elements for each sibling in the order you want them to appear on the source tree. A single `xsl:apply-templates` element with no attributes will process the element's children in order. In contrast, a series of `xsl:apply-templates` elements, each using the `select` attribute to specify a particular child, lets you process the children in any order you wish.

For example, this template rule

```
<!-- xq141.xsl -->

  <xsl:template match="customer">
    <client>
      <xsl:apply-templates/>
    </client>
  </xsl:template>
```

will process all of this `customer` element's child elements in order:

```
<customer>
  <last>Hill</last>
  <first>Phil</first>
  <phone>212-555-1212</phone>
  <address>166 Main St.</address>
  <city>New York</city>
  <state>NY</state>
  <zip>10001</zip>
</customer>
```

The following template rule, however, outputs them in a different order: the order specified by the `select` values in the template's `xsl:apply-templates` elements. (You don't have to list all child elements; section 3.8, "Deleting elements from the result tree," page 63, shows how the inclusion of `xsl:apply-templates` for only certain child elements is an effective way to delete elements from your output.)

```
<!-- xq143.xsl: converts xq144.xml into xq145.xml -->

<xsl:template match="customer">
  <customer>
    <xsl:apply-templates select="phone"/>
    <xsl:apply-templates select="firstName"/>
    <xsl:apply-templates select="lastName"/>
  </customer>
</xsl:template>
```

This template will turn this customer element

```
<customer>
  <lastName>Hill</lastName>
  <firstName>Phil</firstName>
  <phone>212-555-1212</phone>
</customer>
```

into this:

```
<customer>
  <phone>212-555-1212</phone>
  <firstName>Phil</firstName>
  <lastName>Hill</lastName>
</customer>
```

TIP   Along with the template for the element whose children are being reordered, the children elements themselves need a template rule or rules to pass along their tags as well as their contents. Many stylesheets address this need by including a template rule such as the following for all the nodes that have no more specific rules in that stylesheet. This template rule just copies them to the result tree:

```
<!-- xq146.xsl -->

<xsl:template match="@*|node()">
  <xsl:copy>
```

```
        <xsl:apply-templates select="@*|node()"/>
    </xsl:copy>
</xsl:template>
```

XSLT's default templates aren't enough to copy, because while they copy element content, they don't copy tags or attributes. (See section 6.8, "Stripping all markup from a document," page 224.)

3.11.2 Moving text with xsl:value-of

For more complex reordering, you'll need the xsl:value-of element. This adds the text specified by its select attribute to the point in the result tree being defined by the template. Because the select attribute can have an XPath expression value, you can grab an element from anywhere in the source tree. As long as you remember to delete the source node so that it doesn't show up in its original position in the output, you've moved that element from one place in the input to another in the output.

For example, the first template below converts a grape element to a product element. Before the grape element's content, the template inserts the value of the grape element's brand sibling. (The xsl:text element between them ensures that a space gets inserted there.) The second template prevents the brand element from being copied to the result tree:

```
<!-- xq148.xsl: converts xq149.xml into xq150.xml -->

<xsl:template match="grape">
  <product>
    <xsl:value-of select="../brand"/><xsl:text> </xsl:text>
    <xsl:apply-templates/>
  </product>
</xsl:template>

<xsl:template match="brand"/>
```

Working together, these two templates will convert this

```
<wine>
  <grape>Cabernet Sauvignon</grape>
  <brand>Los Vascos</brand>
</wine>
```

to this:

```
<product>Los Vascos Cabernet Sauvignon</product>
```

For related information, see:

- section 3.8, "Deleting elements from the result tree," page 63 for more on deleting elements from their default position in the result tree and eventual output
- section 6.11, "Whitespace: preserving and controlling," page 229

3.12 SELECTING ELEMENTS BASED ON: ELEMENT NAME, CONTENT, CHILDREN, PARENTS

A template rule can select elements for processing based on their element type name, their children, or their parents by using the appropriate match expression in the select attribute of the xsl:template element that specifies the template rule. Match expressions are a subset of XPath expressions. (Section 2.3, "Node tests," page 41, and section 2.4, "Predicates," page 43 go into more detail on these two building blocks of XPath and match expression syntax.)

This chapter summarizes the form of the node tests as well as the predicates that may be necessary to select elements based on their name, children, or parents. It also describes a predicate that lets you select elements based on their contents.

Selecting elements based on their element type name is a basic task in XSLT. The first template in the following, for example, selects all figure elements and adds their contents (which, considering the actions of the rest of the stylesheet, means the character data in each figure element's title element) to the result tree with square brackets around it:

```
<!-- xq153.xsl: converts xq477.xml into xq154.txt -->
<xsl:stylesheet xmlns:xsl="http://www.w3.org/1999/XSL/Transform"
    version="1.0">
  <xsl:output method="text"/>

  <xsl:strip-space elements="*"/>

  <xsl:template match="figure">
    [<xsl:apply-templates/>]
  </xsl:template>

  <xsl:template match="para | chapter/title |
                       sect1/title | sect2/title "/>

</xsl:stylesheet>
```

(The second template suppresses a few elements to keep the result from being too cluttered; the xsl:strip-space element removes extraneous whitespace from the output. See section 6.11.1, "xsl:strip-space and xsl:preserve-space," page 230, for more.) When applied to this document,

```
<chapter><title>The Chapter</title>
 <sect1><title>First Section</title>
   <figure><title>First picture in book</title>
     <graphic fileref="pic1.jpg"/></figure>
 </sect1>
 <sect1><title>Second Section</title>
  <sect2>
   <title>Second Section, First Subsection</title>
   <figure><title>Second picture in book</title>
     <graphic fileref="pic2.jpg"/></figure>
  </sect2>
```

```
   <sect2>
    <title>Second Section, Second Subsection</title>
        <para>This one has no figure.</para>
   </sect2>
   <sect2>
    <title>Second Section, Third Subsection</title>
    <figure><title>Fourth picture in book</title>
       <graphic fileref="pic3.jpg"/></figure>
   </sect2>
  </sect1>
 </chapter>
```

the result shows square brackets around the text content of each figure element—the figure's `title` followed by a carriage return.

```
[First picture in book]

[Second picture in book]

[Fourth picture in book]
```

To select an element based on its parent, your match pattern should have at least two location steps: one identifying the parent and one identifying the appropriate child element. For example, the first template in the following stylesheet will be applied only to `title` elements that are children of `sect1` elements. Those elements will be added to the result tree with square brackets around their contents:

```
<!-- xq155.xsl: converts xq477.xml into xq156.txt -->
<xsl:stylesheet xmlns:xsl="http://www.w3.org/1999/XSL/Transform"
    version="1.0">
  <xsl:output method="text"/>

  <xsl:template match="sect1/title">
   [<xsl:apply-templates/>]
  </xsl:template>

  <xsl:template match="para"/> <!-- reduce output clutter -->

</xsl:stylesheet>
```

Although the source document had many `title` elements, only the ones that are children of `sect1` elements have square brackets around them in the result tree:

```
The Chapter

   [First Section]

    First picture in book

   [Second Section]

    Second Section, First Subsection
    Second picture in book

    Second Section, Second Subsection

    Second Section, Third Subsection
    Fourth picture in book
```

To select elements based on their children, the node test of the match condition's final location step (or only location step, if there's just one) should name the element in which you're interested, and the predicate can then name the child element that must be present in that element to qualify that element for processing by this template rule.

For example, the following stylesheet's single template rule is looking for sect2 elements. As the predicate in square brackets shows, this template rule only wants sect2 elements that have a figure element in them. When it finds them, it outputs their contents surrounded by square brackets:

```
<!-- xq157.xsl: converts xq477.xml into xq158.txt -->
<xsl:stylesheet xmlns:xsl="http://www.w3.org/1999/XSL/Transform"
    version="1.0">
  <xsl:output method="text"/>

  <xsl:strip-space elements="*"/>

  <xsl:template match="sect2[figure]">
   <xsl:value-of select="title"/>
   [<xsl:apply-templates/>]
  </xsl:template>

</xsl:stylesheet>
```

The square brackets in the result show the contents of the sect2 elements that were processed by this template rule. There are no square brackets around the sect2 element with the paragraph that says "This one has no figure", because it didn't qualify for processing by this template. Instead, the XSLT default template rules built into all XSLT processors passed this sect2 element's text content along to the result tree:

```
The Chapter

  First Section

    First picture in book

  Second Section
   Second Section, First Subsection
   [
    Second Section, First Subsection
    Second picture in book

   ]

    Second Section, Second Subsection
       This one has no figure.

   Second Section, Third Subsection
   [
    Second Section, Third Subsection
    Fourth picture in book

   ]
```

Using the XPath `contains()` function in the predicate of a match condition lets a template rule select an element based on its content. For example, in the following document let's say we're only interested in the `para` elements that have the text string "the" in them:

```
<story>

  <chapter><title>Chapter 1</title>
    <para>A Dungeon horrible, on all sides round</para>
  </chapter>

  <chapter><title>Chapter 2</title>
    <para>More unexpert, I boast not: them let those</para>
    <para>Contrive who need, or when they need, not now.</para>
    <sect><title>Chapter 2, Section 1</title>
      <para>For while they sit contriving, shall the rest,</para>
      <para>Millions that stand in Arms, and longing wait</para>
    </sect>
  </chapter>

  <chapter><title>Chapter 3</title>
    <para>So thick a drop serene hath quenched their Orbs</para>
  </chapter>

</story>
```

The first of the following two templates for `para` elements has a predicate that tells the XSLT processor to apply this template rule only to `para` elements with the string "the" in their contents. The second template rule processes all the other `para` elements:

```
<!-- xq160.xsl: converts xq159.xml into xq161.txt -->
<xsl:stylesheet xmlns:xsl="http://www.w3.org/1999/XSL/Transform"
      version="1.0">

  <xsl:output method="text"/>

  <xsl:template match="para[contains(,'the')]">
    *** This para has "the" in it: ***
    <xsl:apply-templates/>
  </xsl:template>

  <xsl:template match="para">
    *** This para element not processed by other template: ***
    <xsl:apply-templates/>
  </xsl:template>

  <xsl:template match="title"/> <!-- reduce output clutter -->
</xsl:stylesheet>
```

Each template rule adds two things to the result tree: a message identifying the template that was called, and the `para` element's contents.

```
    *** This para element not processed by other template: ***
    A Dungeon horrible, on all sides round
```

```
*** This para has "the" in it: ***
More unexpert, I boast not: them let those

*** This para has "the" in it: ***
Contrive who need, or when they need, not now.

*** This para has "the" in it: ***
For while they sit contriving, shall the rest,

*** This para element not processed by other template: ***
Millions that stand in Arms, and longing wait

*** This para has "the" in it: ***
So thick a drop serene hath quenched their Orbs
```

Only one of the para elements that triggered the first template rule had the word "the" in it, but several others contained words that had the string "the"—for example, "them," "they," and "their."

This works even when the string is in a child or other descendant element. For example, this next stylesheet is identical to the last one, except that the first template is looking for chapter elements, not para elements, with "the" in them:

```
<!-- xq162.xsl: converts xq159.xml into xq163.txt -->
<xsl:stylesheet xmlns:xsl="http://www.w3.org/1999/XSL/Transform"
    version="1.0">

  <xsl:output method="text"/>

  <xsl:template match="chapter[contains(,'the')]">
    *** This chapter has "the" in it: ***
    <xsl:apply-templates/>
  </xsl:template>

  <xsl:template match="chapter">
    *** This chapter element not processed by other template: ***
    <xsl:apply-templates/>
  </xsl:template>

  <xsl:template match="title"/>
</xsl:stylesheet>
```

The result shows that the first chapter doesn't have "the" in it, and the other two do:

```
*** This chapter element not processed by other template: ***

A Dungeon horrible, on all sides round

*** This chapter has "the" in it: ***

More unexpert, I boast not: them let those
Contrive who need, or when they need, not now.

  For while they sit contriving, shall the rest,
  Millions that stand in Arms, and longing wait

*** This chapter has "the" in it: ***

So thick a drop serene hath quenched their Orbs
```

XSLT offers many functions for use in predicates. The contains() function is particularly valuable because, while typical match condition tricks (like the ones we saw earlier in this chapter) base their logic on a document's structure, the contains() function lets you base processing logic on a document's contents.

3.13   ADDING NEW ATTRIBUTES

Adding an attribute to a result tree can be as simple as putting the attribute in the start-tag of a literal result element. For example, the line start-tag in the following template has four attributes:

```
<!-- xq167.xsl: converts xq168.xml into xq169.xml. -->
<xsl:template match="verse">
<line status="done" hue="{@color}" number="{amount}"
        sourceElement="src{generate-id()}"/>
</xsl:template>
```

This template rule will convert the following verse element

```
<verse color="red">
  <amount>5</amount>
</verse>
```

to this:

```
<line status="done" hue="red" number="5" sourceElement="srcb2a"/>
```

(The generate-id() function may create a different value with your XSLT processor.) The template rule reads a verse element and outputs it as a line element with four attributes, which get their values from four different sources:

- The template's status attribute is just the hard-coded string of text "done" that will appear just as it's shown in the stylesheet in all line elements created from verse elements.

- The template's hue attribute takes its value from the color attribute value of the source tree's verse element.

- The template's number attribute has the contents of the verse element's amount child as its value.

- The template's sourceElement attribute makes a function call (to generate-id(), which generates a unique ID for the source node) and adds three characters of text before the result to create the attribute value node for the result tree.

  TIP   The template rule uses curly braces for all but the first attribute value. These tell the XSLT processor that their contents are expressions to be evaluated and not plain text like the string "done" in the first attribute. If the second attribute specification didn't have the curly braces and said hue="@color", that's exactly what would have shown up in the output, like this:

```
<line status="done" hue="@color" number="5"  sourceElement="srcb2a"/>
```

This use of curly braces in attribute values is known as attribute value templates.

Instead of putting the attributes right in the element start-tags in the stylesheet, you can specify them using the xsl:attribute element. The following template does the same thing as the previous "verse" template, using this specialized element for each attribute specification. (Note that the xsl:attribute elements are inside an xsl:element element. See section 3.1, "Adding new elements to the result tree," page 47, for more on these.)

```
<!-- xq171.xsl: converts xq168.xml into xq169.xml -->
<xsl:template match="verse">
  <xsl:element name="line">
   <xsl:attribute name="status">done</xsl:attribute>
    <xsl:attribute name="hue">
      <xsl:value-of select="@color"/>
    </xsl:attribute>
    <xsl:attribute name="number">
      <xsl:value-of select="amount"/>
    </xsl:attribute>
  <xsl:attribute name="sourceElement">
    <xsl:text>src</xsl:text><xsl:value-of select="generate-id()"/>
  </xsl:attribute>
  </xsl:element>
</xsl:template>
```

It's more work, so why bother? Because you have more control over *how* the attributes are added to the result tree. For one thing, the xsl:attribute element lets you add attributes selectively—in other words, only adding a certain attribute to an element if a particular condition is true. For example, an xsl:attribute enclosed by an xsl:if element will only be added to the result tree if the condition specified in the xsl:if element's test attribute is true.

Because the names of the new attributes are specified as attributes themselves here, the xsl:attribute element offers a wider range of options for how you specify the attribute name than can attributes added as part of literal result elements. For example, a name attribute value of "src{generate-id()}" in an xsl:attribute element's start-tag tells the XSLT processor to output an attribute whose name is the string "src" followed by the position value of the matched source tree node.

You can specify the value of these inserted attributes either as the text content of the xsl:attribute element, such as the "done" value of the status attribute above, or by generating text using the xsl:value-of element, as with the other attribute values in the same example. This time, they don't need the curly braces that tell the XSLT processor "evaluate these and store the result on the result tree," because the processor already knows to do this with the value of an xsl:value-of element's select attribute.

To show which elements these attributes belong to, the xsl:attribute elements are inside the xsl:element element that adds a line element to the result tree when the XSLT processor finds a verse element in the source tree.

`xsl:attribute` elements must always be specified in an `xsl:element` *before* anything that specifies that element's content—that is, before the parts that will end up between the element's begin- and end-tags. This content might be specified using `xsl:apply-templates` elements, literal result elements and other `xsl:element` elements to show child elements, `xsl:value-of` elements, or even plain text.

3.14 CONVERTING ATTRIBUTES TO ELEMENTS

When an XSLT processor sees an `xsl:value-of` element, it evaluates the expression in its `select` attribute and replaces the element with the result of the evaluation. For example, after evaluating `<xsl:value-of select="2+2"/>` in a template, the processor adds the string "4" to the corresponding place on the result tree and in any output document created from that result tree.

This `select` attribute can take an XPath expression as a value, which gives you a lot more flexibility. For example, you can refer to an attribute value of the element serving as the context node or even of some other element. Surround one or more of these `xsl:value-of` elements with an `xsl:element` element or with the tags of a literal result element (that is, an element from outside the XSLT namespace that an XSLT processor will pass to the result tree unchanged), and you'll add a new element to the result tree whose content was an attribute value in the source tree.

For example, the following template rule

```
<!-- xq173.xsl: converts xq174.xml into xq175.xml -->

<xsl:template match="winery">
  <wine>
    <xsl:value-of select="@year"/><xsl:text> </xsl:text>
    <xsl:value-of select="../@grape"/>
  </wine>
</xsl:template>
```

will convert the `winery` element in the following

```
<wine grape="Cabernet Sauvignon">
  <winery year="1998">Los Vascos</winery>
</wine>
```

into this wine element:

```
<wine>1998 Cabernet Sauvignon</wine>
```

Here's how the template creates the new `wine` element:

- The "@year" value in the first `xsl:value-of` element's `select` attribute starts the `wine` literal result element with the value of the `winery` element's `year` attribute.
- The "../@grape" value in the second template's `select` attribute selects the value of the `grape` attribute in the `winery` element's parent element.
- The `xsl:text` element inserts a space between them.

A `wine` start- and end-tag pair around the whole thing make a well-formed XML element for the result tree.

See section 6.11.1, "xsl:strip-space and xsl:preserve-space," page 230 for more on using the `xsl:text` element to add the single space.

3.15 GETTING ATTRIBUTE VALUES AND NAMES

Attributes are nodes of the source tree just as elements are. The most popular way to get a particular attribute value is to use the @ prefix, an abbreviation of the `attribute::` axis specifier.

For example, to get the value of the `color` attribute of the `para` element in this short document,

```
<para color="blue" flavor="mint" author="bd">
Here is a paragraph.</para>
```

the first `xsl:value-of` element in the `para` element's template rule has "@color" as the value of its `select` attribute:

```
<xsl:template match="para">

Color: <xsl:value-of select="@color"/>

<!-- List the attribute names and values. -->
<xsl:for-each select="@*">
attribute name: <xsl:value-of select="name()"/>
attribute value: <xsl:value-of select="."/>
</xsl:for-each>

</xsl:template>
```

The value "blue" shows up in that part (the first line) of the result:

```
Color: blue
attribute name: color
attribute value: blue
attribute name: flavor
attribute value: mint
attribute name: author
attribute value: bd
```

The other result tree lines are added to the result tree by the template's `xsl:for-each` element. This instruction goes through all of the `para` element's attributes, listing the name and value of each. While the template's first `xsl:value-of` element has "@color" as the value of its `select` attribute to indicate that it wants the attribute with that name, the `xsl:for-each` element has "@*" as its `select` attribute value to show that it wants attributes of any name.

Inside the loop, the template adds four nodes to the result tree for each attribute:

- the text node "attribute name:" to label the text after it
- an `xsl:value-of` element with the function call `name()` as the value of its `select` attribute. (This adds the name of the node to the result tree; in a loop iterating through attribute nodes, it adds the attribute name.)

- the text node "attribute value:" to label the text after it
- an `xsl:value-of` element with the abbreviation "." as the value of its `select` attribute. (This XPath abbreviation for `self::node()` gives you the value of the current node—in this case, the attribute value.)

The result of applying this stylesheet to the short source document shown earlier shows each attribute's name and value.

3.16 TESTING FOR ATTRIBUTE EXISTENCE AND FOR SPECIFIC ATTRIBUTE VALUES

Sometimes, when an attribute is optional for a particular element, you want to test whether the attribute was specified or not. Other times you want to check whether it has a particular value. For example, let's say that when we process the following document, we're not sure whether its `para` element has `flavor` or `font` attributes, and while we know that the `para` element has an `author` attribute, we need to check whether `author` has a value of "jm" or not.

```
<para color="blue" flavor="mint" author="jm">
Fallen cherub, to be weak is miserable</para>
```

The following template rule adds a short text message to the result tree for each attribute it finds:

```
<!-- xq182.xsl: converts xq181.xml into xq183.xml -->
<xsl:template match="para">

  <!-- Is there a flavor attribute? -->
  <xsl:if test="@flavor">
    There is a flavor attribute
  </xsl:if>

  <!-- Is there a font attribute? -->
  <xsl:if test="@font">
    There is a font attribute
  </xsl:if>

  <!-- Does author="jm"? -->
  <xsl:if test="@author = 'jm'">
    Author equals "jm"
  </xsl:if>

</xsl:template>
```

The template rule has three `xsl:if` elements. An `xsl:if` element that only has a node name as the value of its `test` attribute is testing whether that node exists or not. In the example, the first `xsl:if` element tests whether the `para` element has a `flavor` attribute. The `para` element in the example source document does, so the string "There is a flavor attribute" shows up in the result.

```
    There is a flavor attribute
    Author equals "jm"
```

The second `xsl:if` element checks for a `font` attribute. Because the `para` element doesn't have one, the string "There is a font attribute" does not show up in the result. The stylesheet's third `xsl:if` element goes a step further than merely checking for the existence of an attribute node: it checks whether the attribute has the specific value "jm". (Note how "jm" is enclosed in single quotation marks in the stylesheet because the `xsl:if` element's `test` attribute value is enclosed in double quotation marks.) Because that is the attribute's value, the string "Author equals 'jm' " does show up in the result.

For more on the `xsl:if` instruction, see section 5.1, "Control statements," page 110.

3.17   REUSING GROUPS OF ATTRIBUTES

If you need to re-use the same group of attributes in different element types in the same result document (for example, to include `revDate`, `author`, and `docID` attributes in your result document's `chapter`, `sidebar`, and `caption` elements), you can store them in an `xsl:attribute-set` element and then reference the collection with a `use-attribute-sets` attribute of the `xsl:element` instruction.

The following shows a group of `xsl:attribute` elements in an `xsl:attribute-set` element named "lineAttrs" and an `xsl:element` instruction that incorporates those attributes with a value of "lineAttrs" for its `use-attribute-sets` attribute. Note the plural form of the name `use-attribute-sets`—the value can list more than one attribute set, as long as spaces separate the names, and all the names represent existing `xsl:attribute-set` elements.

```
<!-- xq185.xsl: converts xq168.xml into xq187.xml -->
<xsl:stylesheet xmlns:xsl="http://www.w3.org/1999/XSL/Transform"
    version="1.0">

<xsl:output omit-xml-declaration="yes"/>

<xsl:attribute-set name="lineAttrs">
  <xsl:attribute name="status">done</xsl:attribute>
  <xsl:attribute name="hue">
    <xsl:value-of select="@color"/>
  </xsl:attribute>
  <xsl:attribute name="number">
    <xsl:value-of select="amount"/>
  </xsl:attribute>
  <xsl:attribute name="sourceElement">
    <xsl:text>src</xsl:text><xsl:value-of select="generate-id()"/>
  </xsl:attribute>
</xsl:attribute-set>

<xsl:template match="verse">
  <xsl:element name="line" use-attribute-sets="lineAttrs">

    <!-- Add one more attribute to the ones in the "lineAttrs"
         group and override the value of another. -->
    <xsl:attribute name="author">BD</xsl:attribute>
```

```
<xsl:attribute name="hue">NO COLOR</xsl:attribute>
    <xsl:apply-templates/>
  </xsl:element>
</xsl:template>
</xsl:stylesheet>
```

Running this with the following source document

```
<verse color="red">
  <amount>5</amount>
</verse>
```

produces this result (the `generate-id()` function may create a different value with your XSLT processor):

```
<line status="done" hue="NO COLOR" number="5"
      sourceElement="srcb2a" author="BD">
  5
</line>
```

In addition to incorporating a named attribute set, the `xsl:element` instruction in the preceding example has two more `xsl:attribute` elements that customize the line element's set of attributes:

- The first adds an `author` attribute to the result tree's `line` elements. Along with the four attributes from the `xsl:attribute` element, this additional attribute makes a total of five attributes for the `line` elements being added to the result tree.

- The second overrides the hue attribute value set in the `lineAttrs` attribute set, because an `xsl:attribute` attribute setting takes precedence over an attribute group attribute setting.

These two `xsl:attribute` instructions illustrate that, when you use an attribute set, you're not stuck with that set—you can customize the set for the element type using it (in this case, `verse`) by adding new attributes or overriding some of the attributes it declares.

C H A P T E R   4

Advanced XML markup

4.1   COMMENTS

Comments in your output documents can provide handy information about the source data and processes that created those documents. Comments in your input documents may or may not be useful, but because an XSLT processor's default behavior is to ignore comments, it's important to know which match pattern to use when you do want to read them.

4.1.1   Outputting comments

Add comment nodes to your result tree with the xsl:comment element. Using this element is fairly simple: put the text of your comment between its start- and end-tags. For example, an XSLT processor that applies the following template to a poem element

```
<!-- xq213.xsl -->

<xsl:template match="poem">
  <html>
    <xsl:comment> Created by FabAutoDocGen release 3 </xsl:comment>
    <xsl:apply-templates/>
  </html>
</xsl:template>
```

will add this comment after the `html` start-tag and before its contents in the result tree:

```
<!-- Created by FabAutoDocGen release 3 -->
```

Note the space after the `xsl:comment` start-tag and the one before its end-tag to keep the actual comment being output from bumping into the hyphens that start and end the comment.

Speaking of hyphens, a pair of hyphens within your output comment or a single hyphen at the end of your comment, as shown in the next example, are technically errors.

```
<!-- xq215.xsl -->

<xsl:stylesheet xmlns:xsl="http://www.w3.org/1999/XSL/Transform"
    version="1.0">

<xsl:template match="poem">
  <html> <!-- Hyphens in xsl:comment element make it illegal. -->
    <xsl:comment> Created by FabAutoDocGen -- rel. 3 -</xsl:comment>
  <xsl:apply-templates/>
  </html>
</xsl:template>
</xsl:stylesheet>
```

It's easy enough for an XSLT processor to recover from this error: it can insert a space between two contiguous hyphens and a space after a hyphen that ends a comment, like this, to make the comment legal:

```
<html>
<!-- Created by the FabAutoDocGen system - - rel. 3 - -->
```

While some processors may correct this for you, it's not a good idea to take this for granted. It's better to specify valid comment text as the content of your stylesheet's `xsl:comment` element.

WARNING   If an `xsl:comment` element is a top-level element—that is, if it's a child of an `xsl:stylesheet` element—an XSLT processor will ignore it. It must be a child of an element that can add something to the result tree. In the example above, the `xsl:comment` element is a child of an `xsl:template` element.

By putting a template rule's `xsl:apply-templates` or `xsl:value-of` elements between the `xsl:comment` start- and end-tags, a stylesheet can convert the source tree content represented by these elements into an output comment. For example, the following template rule converts a `documentation` element like the ones found in W3C XML Schemas into XML 1.0 comments in the output:

```
<!-- xq217.xsl: converts xq218.xml into xq219.xml -->

<xsl:template match="documentation">
  <xsl:comment><xsl:apply-templates/></xsl:comment>
</xsl:template>
```

It converts this

```
<documentation>The following is a revision.</documentation>
```

into this:

```
<!--The following is a revision.-->
```

4.1.2 Reading and using source tree comments

By default, an XSLT processor ignores comments in the input. However, a template
with the comment() node test as the value of its match attribute selects all the
comments in the source tree so that you can add them to the result tree. The following template copies comments to the result tree:

```
<!-- xq221.xsl -->
<xsl:template match="comment()">
  <xsl:comment><xsl:value-of select="."/></xsl:comment>
</xsl:template>
```

> **TIP** The XML parser isn't required to pass comments along to the applica-
> tion—in this case, the XSLT processor—so if you don't see them showing
> up, try using a different XML parser with your XSLT processor.

Once you've read comments from the source tree, you don't have to output them as
comments. Wrapping the comment() template's xsl:value-of element with a
literal result element (or putting it inside an xsl:element element) lets you convert comments into elements. For example, the first template in the following
stylesheet:

```
<!-- xq222.xsl: converts xq223.xml into xq224.xml -->

<xsl:stylesheet xmlns:xsl="http://www.w3.org/1999/XSL/Transform"
    version="1.0">

<xsl:output omit-xml-declaration="yes"/>

<xsl:template match="comment()">
    <doc><xsl:value-of select="."/></doc>
  </xsl:template>

  <xsl:template match="verse">
   <p><xsl:apply-templates/></p>
  </xsl:template>
</xsl:stylesheet>
```

converts the comments in this document

```
<!-- Poem starts here. -->
<verse>Of Man's First Disobedience, and the Fruit</verse>
<!-- Poem ends here. -->
```

to the doc elements shown here:

```
<doc> Poem starts here. </doc>
<p>Of Man's First Disobedience, and the Fruit</p>
<doc> Poem ends here. </doc>
```

4.2 ENTITIES

In XML, entities are named units of storage. Their names are assigned and associated with storage units in a DTD's entity declarations. These units may be internal entities, whose contents are specified as a string right in their declaration, or they may be external entities, whose contents are outside the entity with the entity declaration. Typically, this means that the external entity is a file outside of the DTD file with the entity declaration, but we don't say "file" in the general case because all of XML and XSLT still work on operating systems that don't use the concept of files.

A DTD might declare an internal entity to play the same role as a constant in a programming language. For example, if a document has many copyright notices that refer to the current year, declaring an entity cpdate to store the string "2001" and then putting the entity reference "&cpdate;" throughout the document means updating the year value to "2002" for the whole document will only mean changing the declaration.

Internal entities are especially popular to represent characters not available on computer keyboards. For example, while you could insert the "ñ" character in your document using the numeric character reference "ñ" (or the hexadecimal version "ñ"), storing this character reference in an entity called ntilde lets you put "España" in an XML document as "Espanña", which is much easier to read than "España" or "España". (It has the added bonus of being familiar to those who used the same entity reference in HTML—perhaps without even knowing that it was an entity reference!)

An external entity can be a file that stores part of a DTD, which makes it an external parameter entity, or it can store part of a document, which makes it an external general entity. For example, the following XML document declares and references the external general entity ext1:

```
<!-- xq226.xml -->
<!DOCTYPE poem [
<!ENTITY ext1 SYSTEM "lines938-939.xml">
]>
<poem>
<verse>I therefore, I alone first undertook</verse>
<verse>To wing the desolate Abyss, and spy</verse>
&ext1;
<verse>Better abode, and my afflicted Powers</verse>
<verse>To settle here on Earth or in mid-air</verse>
</poem>
```

An XML parser reading this document in will look for an external entity named lines938-939.xml and report an error if it doesn't find it. If it does find a file named lines938-939.xml that looks like this,

```
<!-- xq227.xml (lines938-939.xml) -->
<verse>This new created World, whereof in Hell</verse>
<verse>Fame is not silent, here in hope to find</verse>
```

the parser will pass something like the following to the application using that XML parser (for example, an XSLT processor):

```
<poem>
<verse>I therefore, I alone first undertook</verse>
<verse>To wing the desolate Abyss, and spy</verse>
<verse>This new created World, whereof in Hell</verse>
<verse>Fame is not silent, here in hope to find</verse>
<verse>Better abode, and my afflicted Powers</verse>
<verse>To settle here on Earth or in mid-air</verse>
</poem>
```

Because an XSLT stylesheet is an XML document, you can store and reference pieces of the stylesheet using the same technique, but you'll find that the `xsl:include` and `xsl:import` instructions give you more control over how your pieces fit together. (See section 5.2, "Combining stylesheets with include and import," on page 126.

All these categories of entities are known as "parsed" entities because an XML parser reads them in, replaces each entity reference with the entity's contents, and parses them as part of the document. XML documents use unparsed entities, which aren't used with entity references but as the value of specially declared attributes, to incorporate non-XML entities. (See section 4.4, "Images, multimedia elements, and other unparsed entities," on page 104.)

When you apply an XSLT stylesheet to a document, if entities are declared and referenced in that document, your XSLT processor won't even know about them. An XSLT processor leaves the job of parsing the input document (reading it in and figuring out what's what) to an XML parser. That's why the installation of some XSLT processors requires you to identify the XML parser you want them to use. (Others include an XML parser as part of their installation.) An important part of an XML parser's job is to resolve all entity references, so that, if the input document's DTD declares a `cpdate` entity as having the value "2001", and the document has the line "copyright &cpdate; all rights reserved", the XML parser will pass along the text node "copyright 2001 all rights reserved" to put on the XSLT source tree. Newcomers to XSLT often ask how they can check for entity references such as " " or "<" in the source tree. The answer is: you can't. By the time the document's content reaches the source tree, it's too late.

How about entities in your result tree? You can't add entity declarations there, because although the `doctype-system` attribute of XSLT's `xsl:output` element can add a document type declaration to a result tree, it can't add one with an internal DTD subset, which is the only way to add DTD declarations to a document entity. (See section 6.9, "Valid XML output: including DOCTYPE declarations," on page 225 for more on this.)

There are ways to add entity references. If you create an XML document in your result tree, and you add references to any entities other than the five that all XML processors are required to handle whether they're declared or not (`lt`, `gt`, `apos`, `quot`, and amp), then your document must have a document type declaration that points to a DTD with declarations for your entities. If you're creating an HTML document, entity declarations aren't required. Most Web browsers understand a wide variety of entity references for special characters such as "é" for the "é" character and "ñ" for the "ñ" character.

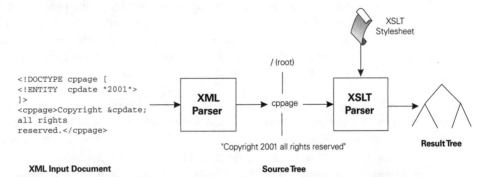

Figure 4.1 An XSLT processor's XML parser resolves all input document entity references when it builds the source tree, so when the XSLT processor looks through the source tree as it builds the result tree, it doesn't know which entity references were ever in the input document.

Let's look at approaches to creating an entity reference in a result tree. We'll use the following one-line document as a source document and try to add a text node that includes the entity reference "ñ" for the "ñ" character:

```
<test>Dagon his Name, Sea Monster</test>
```

If the stylesheet document has the appropriate entity declaration, the XML parser that feeds the stylesheet and source document to the XSLT processor will replace this entity reference in the stylesheet with the replacement text declared for it. For this stylesheet, it will replace "ñ" with the Unicode value for the "ñ" character:

```
<!-- xq230.xsl: converts xq229.xml into xq231.xml -->

<!DOCTYPE stylesheet [
<!ENTITY ntilde  "&#241;" ><!-- small n, tilde -->
]>

<xsl:stylesheet xmlns:xsl="http://www.w3.org/1999/XSL/Transform"
    version="1.0">

  <xsl:template match="test">
    <testOut>
      The Spanish word for "Spain" is "Espa&ntilde;a".
      <xsl:apply-templates/>
    </testOut>
  </xsl:template>

</xsl:stylesheet>
```

The actual "ñ" character (and not an entity reference to it) shows up in the result:

```
<?xml version="1.0" encoding="utf-8"?><testOut>
    The Spanish word for "Spain" is "España".
    Dagon his Name, Sea Monster</testOut>
```

WARNING Normally, your stylesheet doesn't need a DOCTYPE declaration, but if the stylesheet has references to any entities besides the five predeclared ones listed previously, you must declare them yourself inside a DOCTYPE declaration. The XML parser that reads in the stylesheet for your XSLT processor will replace any entity references with their entity values *before* giving the stylesheet to the XSLT processor.

This is handy, but not what we're looking for. We want to see an entity reference, and not the referenced entity, in the result document. XSLT offers no way to tell the XML processor not to make entity replacements. (Certain XSLT processors such as Xalan offer this option as a nonstandard feature). However, XSLT does offer a way to turn off its automatic "escaping" of certain characters—that is, an XSLT processor's substitution of the entity reference "&" for ampersands and "<" for less-than characters in result tree text nodes. You can turn it off for your entire result tree with an `xsl:output` instruction that has a `method` attribute value of "text" (see section 6.5, "Non-XML output," on page 202). And you can turn it off for a single `xsl:text` element by setting its `disable-output-escaping` attribute to equal "yes."

WARNING The disabling of output escaping is used too often in situations where it shouldn't be. In particular, it's used to create a less-than character that starts a tag or a declaration that could be added to a result tree with a more appropriate XSLT instruction. Because it's essentially turning off something that the XSLT processor is supposed to do, use this sparingly.

The following version of the stylesheet resembles the previous one except for the replacement text specified in the `ntilde` declaration. It's an `xsl:text` instruction with "&ntilde;" as its contents:

```
<!-- xq232.xsl: converts xq229.xml into xq233.xml -->

<!DOCTYPE stylesheet [
<!ENTITY ntilde
"<xsl:text
disable-output-escaping='yes'>&amp;ntilde;</xsl:text>">
]>

<xsl:stylesheet xmlns:xsl="http://www.w3.org/1999/XSL/Transform"
    version="1.0">

  <xsl:output doctype-system="testOut.dtd"/>

  <xsl:template match="test">
```

```
    <testOut>
      The Spanish word for "Spain" is "Espa&ntilde;a".
      <xsl:apply-templates/>
    </testOut>
  </xsl:template>

</xsl:stylesheet>
```

The XML parser that reads in the stylesheet and hands it off to the XSLT processor will replace that "&" with a "&", but because the xsl:text element has its disable-output-escaping attribute set to "yes," the XSLT processor will pass along the "ñ" string to the result tree without trying to resolve it. (If the processor did try to resolve the string, it would cause an error, because having "ñ" as the replacement text for the ntilde entity would be an illegal recursive entity declaration.) With the same test document, the new stylesheet creates this output:

```
<?xml version="1.0" encoding="UTF-8"?>
<!DOCTYPE testOut SYSTEM "testOut.dtd">
<testOut>
      The Spanish word for "Spain" is "Espa&ntilde;a".
      Dagon his Name, Sea Monster</testOut>
```

The new stylesheet has one more difference from the earlier one: it includes an xsl:output element. This element doesn't need a method attribute, because the default value of "xml" is fine. The doctype-system attribute is important, because if the result document has an "ñ" entity reference, that entity must be declared somewhere. XSLT doesn't offer a way to include such declarations in an internal DTD subset of the document's DOCTYPE declaration, although some stylesheet developers have hacked this to add these declarations using disable-output-escaping kludges. The best way to ensure that these declarations are properly declared is to give the result tree a DOCTYPE declaration with a SYSTEM identifier that points to a DTD with that declaration. The preceding example adds a SYSTEM declaration that points to a testOut.dtd file, which should include a declaration for the ntilde entity.

This trick works for any general entity reference you want in your result tree, whether it references an internal entity whose contents are included in the declaration (such as the ntilde entities in the examples above) or an external entity whose contents are stored in an external file such as the ext1 one at the beginning of the section.

To review, you can add any kind of entity reference you want to your result tree by

- adding an entity reference to your result tree
- declaring the entity's contents in the stylesheet's DOCTYPE declaration to be an ampersand, the entity name, and a semicolon all inside of an xsl:text element with its disable-output-escaping attribute set to "yes"

4.3 NAMESPACES

In XML, a namespace is a collection of names used for elements and attributes. A URI (usually, a URL) is used to identify a particular collection of names. Instead of adding an `xmlns` attribute showing a full URI to every element in order to show which namespace it comes from, you'll find it more convenient to name a short abbreviation when a namespace is declared and to then use that abbreviation to identify an element or attribute's namespace.

For example, in the following document (figure 4.2), the `table` element explicitly declares that it's from the HTML 4.0 namespace by putting the appropriate URI in an `xmlns` attribute. This makes this namespace the default for everything inside of this element as well. In other words, an XML processor will treat all of its contents (the `tr` elements and their contents) as elements from the HTML namespace unless they have namespace declarations or prefixes from other namespaces.

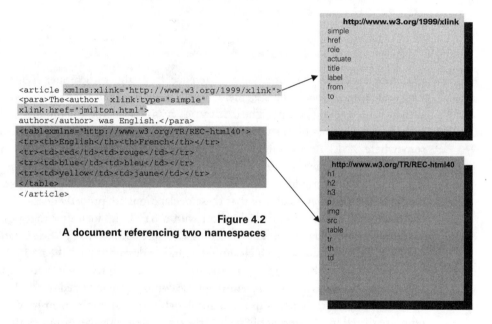

Figure 4.2
A document referencing two namespaces

The `author` element has two attributes that reference a namespace declared in the `article` element's start-tag. It shows this by adding the "xlink" prefix declared with the http://www.w3.org/1999/xlink namespace to those attribute names. An XLink-aware application will find those `type` and `href` attributes and know what to do with them.

Many simple XML applications never need to declare and use namespaces. If they don't, the XML processor treats all elements and attributes as being in the default namespace. This may be the case with some of your source documents, but it's certainly not the case with your stylesheets: the declaring and referencing of the XSLT namespace is how we tell an XSLT processor which elements and attributes in a stylesheet to treat as XSLT instructions. For example, the document element's start-tag in the following stylesheet declares a namespace for the http://www.w3.org/1999/XSL/Transform URI and assigns the prefix xsl to represent it:

```
<!-- xq236.xsl: converts xq237.xml into xq238.xml -->

  <xsl:stylesheet xmlns:xsl="http://www.w3.org/1999/XSL/Transform"
    version="1.0">

  <xsl:output method="xml" omit-xml-declaration="yes"/>

  <xsl:template match="xdata">
    <heading>xdata</heading><xsl:text>
    </xsl:text>
   <text><xsl:apply-templates/></text>
  </xsl:template>

</xsl:stylesheet>
```

When this stylesheet's single template rule sees an xdata element in the source tree, it adds two elements to the result tree: a heading element with the string "xdata" as its contents and a text element with the source tree xdata element's contents as its contents. The template turns this

```
<xdata>With Opal Towers and Battlements adorned</xdata>
```

into this:

```
<heading>xdata</heading>
<text>With Opal Towers and Battlements adorned</text>
```

The template also adds a carriage return between the result tree's heading and text elements. It does so with an xsl:text element that has a carriage return as its contents. The XSLT processor knows the difference between the text element that has the carriage return and the text element with the xsl:apply-templates instruction as its contents because the one with the carriage return has that xsl: prefix to show that it's part of the http://www.w3.org/1999/XSL/Transform namespace. The second of these two text elements has no prefix, so the XSLT processor doesn't treat it as a special XSLT element—it's just another literal result element.

WARNING The use of "xsl" as the prefix to identify XSLT elements is just a convention. (It's a pretty confusing convention, considering that the XSL convention is to use fo for "formatting objects.") In other words, XSL documents typically don't use "xsl" as their namespace prefix; XSLT stylesheets do. See section 6.13, "XSL and XSLT: creating Acrobat files and other formatted output," on page 247, for more on XSLT's relationship to XSL.

The following stylesheet, which assigns and uses harpo as the prefix for the XSLT namespace, works identically to the one above:

```
<!-- xq239.xsl: converts xq237.xml into xq238.xml -->

<harpo:stylesheet
       xmlns:harpo="http://www.w3.org/1999/XSL/Transform"
       version="1.0">

<harpo:output method="xml" omit-xml-declaration="yes"/>

<harpo:template match="xdata">
  <heading>xdata</heading><harpo:text>
  </harpo:text>
  <text><harpo:apply-templates/></text>
</harpo:template>

</harpo:stylesheet>
```

Some XSLT processors support special instructions known as "extensions" that are not part of the W3C XSLT specification. To use these instructions, you declare the namespace mentioned in that processor's documentation and then refer to those instructions using whatever prefix you declared for that namespace. (See section 5.5, "Extensions to XSLT," on page 143, for more on these.)

4.3.1   Namespaces and your result document

What if you want your result document to include elements from a specified namespace? Simply declare and use the namespace you need in your stylesheet and the XSLT processor will

- put that namespace declaration in the start-tag of the result document's document element and
- put the prefix for that namespace in the tags for any result tree elements from that namespace

(If you want it to include elements from the http://www.w3.org/1999/XSL/Transform namespace—that is, if you want your result document to be an XSLT stylesheet—it's a little trickier than the general case; we'll cover that later in this chapter.) For example, to convert the following HTML document to an XLink document, the result needs an XLink namespace declaration and each of the special XLink attributes need a prefix that references that declaration:

```
<html><body>
<p>The poem's <a href="jmilton.html">author</a> was English.</p>
</body></html>
```

The stylesheet declares the http://www.w3.org/1999/xlink namespace in the xsl:stylesheet element's start-tag along with the declaration of the http://www.w3.org/1999/XSL/Transform namespace:

```
<!-- xq242.xsl: converts xq241.html into xq243.xml -->

<xsl:stylesheet xmlns:xsl="http://www.w3.org/1999/XSL/Transform"
                xmlns:xlink="http://www.w3.org/1999/xlink"
                version="1.0">
<xsl:output method="xml" omit-xml-declaration="yes"/>
```

```
<xsl:template match="a">
  <author xlink:type="simple" xlink:href="{@href}">
    <xsl:apply-templates/></author>
</xsl:template>

<xsl:template match="p">
  <para><xsl:apply-templates/></para>
</xsl:template>

</xsl:stylesheet>
```

A document element's start-tag is where you'll usually find a namespace declaration, and the XSLT processor passes this declaration along to the start-tag of the result document's document element. It also passes all references to that namespace along to the result tree, making the result document a working XLink document:

```
<para xmlns:xlink="http://www.w3.org/1999/xlink">
The poem's <author xlink:type="simple" xlink:href="jmilton.html">
author</author> was English.</para>
```

In XSLT terms, the XSLT processor has added a namespace node to the result tree. (Six kinds of nodes may show up in source and result trees: elements, attributes, text nodes, processing instructions, comments, and namespace nodes.) You can prevent this from happening with the xsl:stylesheet element's exclude-result-prefixes attribute. This attribute's name can be confusing, because the namespace prefixes will still show up in the result tree. It doesn't mean "exclude the prefixes in the result." it means, "exclude the namespaces with these prefixes."

For example, the following stylesheet looks just like the preceding one with the addition of the attribute to tell the XSLT processor to exclude the namespace node represented by the "xlink" prefix. You can list multiple namespace prefixes as the value of the exclude-result-prefixes attribute, as long as they have spaces between them and they're all declared namespaces:

```
<!-- xq244.xsl: converts xq241.html into xq245.xml -->

<xsl:stylesheet xmlns:xsl="http://www.w3.org/1999/XSL/Transform"
                xmlns:xlink="http://www.w3.org/1999/xlink"
                exclude-result-prefixes="xlink"
                version="1.0">
  <xsl:output method="xml" omit-xml-declaration="yes"/>

  <xsl:template match="a">
   <author xlink:type="simple" xlink:href="{@href}">
    <xsl:apply-templates/></author>
  </xsl:template>

  <xsl:template match="p">
   <para><xsl:apply-templates/></para>
  </xsl:template>

</xsl:stylesheet>
```

Processing the same source document with this stylesheet creates a similar result, except that the document element's start-tag doesn't have the declaration for the XLink namespace:

```
<para>
The poem's <author xlink:type="simple" xlink:href="jmilton.html">
author</author> was English.</para>
```

You can also assign result tree elements and attributes to specific namespaces by adding a `namespace` attribute to the `xsl:element` instruction or to an `xsl:attribute` instruction. For example, the second `xsl:element` instruction in the following template and the two `xsl:attribute` elements inside the first `xsl:element` each include a `namespace` attribute along with their name attributes. These identify the two namespaces where the element and attribute names belong: the HTML and XLink namespaces:

```
<!-- xq246.xsl: converts xq237.xml into xq247.xml -->

<xsl:template match="xdata">

  <section>

    <xsl:element name="author">
      <xsl:attribute namespace="http://www.w3.org/1999/xlink"
        name="type" >simple</xsl:attribute>
      <xsl:attribute namespace="http://www.w3.org/1999/xlink"
        name="href" >jmilton.html</xsl:attribute>
      John Milton
    </xsl:element>

    <xsl:element name="img"
      namespace="http://www.w3.org/TR/REC-html40">
      <xsl:attribute name="src">milton.jpg</xsl:attribute>
    </xsl:element>
    <xsl:apply-templates/>

  </section>

</xsl:template>
```

When applied to the same source document as the earlier examples, this stylesheet creates a result document that has an `author` element with two attributes from the XLink namespace and an `img` element from the HTML namespace. The XSLT processor can make up any namespace prefixes it wants; in this case, they're "ns0" and "ns1":

```
<section>
<author xmlns:ns0="http://www.w3.org/1999/xlink"
        ns0:type="simple" ns0:href="jmilton.html">
      John Milton
      </author>
<ns1:img xmlns:ns1="http://www.w3.org/TR/REC-html40"
      src="milton.jpg"/>
With Opal Towers and Battlements adorned</section>
```

To review: the XSLT processor looks through a stylesheet for elements belonging to the XSLT namespace and executes their instructions. The processor also searches for any elements outside that namespace (that aren't from a namespace declared for extension elements), and it passes them along to the result with namespace declarations if necessary. You can even assign a specific namespace for an element or attribute by adding a namespace attribute to an `xsl:element` or `xsl:attribute` element.

If the elements from the XSLT namespace don't get passed to the result document, what do you do if you really want XSLT elements in your result element? For example, what if we want to convert the following document to a working XSLT stylesheet?

```
<ssheet>

  <elementHandler element="para">
    <p><elementContents/></p>
  </elementHandler>

</ssheet>
```

You use the `xsl:namespace-alias` element. If you use another temporary namespace (in the example below, "xslAlt") in place of the one you really want (below, "xsl"), `xsl:namespace-alias` lets you tell the XSLT processor to substitute the one you want for the temporary one when it creates the result tree:

```
<!-- xq249.xsl: converts xq248.xml into xq250.xsl -->
<xsl:stylesheet xmlns:xsl="http://www.w3.org/1999/XSL/Transform"
            xmlns:xslAlt="http://www.snee.com/xml/dummy"
        version="1.0">

  <xsl:namespace-alias stylesheet-prefix="xslAlt"
      result-prefix="xsl"/>

  <xsl:template match="elementHandler">
    <xslAlt:template match="{@element}">
      <xsl:apply-templates/>
    </xslAlt:template>
  </xsl:template>

  <xsl:template match="elementContents">
    <xslAlt:apply-templates/>
  </xsl:template>

  <xsl:template match="ssheet">
    <xslAlt:stylesheet  version="1.0">
      <xsl:apply-templates/>
    </xslAlt:stylesheet>
  </xsl:template>

  <!-- Just copy any other elements, attributes, etc. -->
  <xsl:template match="@*|node()">
    <xsl:copy>
      <xsl:apply-templates select="@*|node()"/>
```

```
    </xsl:copy>
  </xsl:template>

</xsl:stylesheet>
```

This stylesheet's first template rule will add an `xslAlt:template` element to the result tree each time it finds an `elementHandler` element source tree. Before this template, however, the stylesheet's `xsl:namespace-alias` instruction tells the XSLT processor to substitute the "xsl" prefix's namespace for the "xslAlt" prefix's namespace in the result document, so that the result tree has a namespace declaration assigning "xslAlt" as a prefix for the http://www.w3.org/1999/XSL/Transform namespace. This is the XSLT namespace, so the result document is a valid XSLT stylesheet:

```
<?xml version="1.0" encoding="utf-8"?>
<xslAlt:stylesheet
    xmlns:xslAlt="http://www.w3.org/1999/XSL/Transform"
    xmlns:xsl="http://www.w3.org/1999/XSL/Transform" version="1.0">

  <xslAlt:template match="para">
    <p><xslAlt:apply-templates/></p>
  </xslAlt:template>

</xslAlt:stylesheet>
```

When applied to this source document,

```
<para>Fallen cherub, to be weak is miserable</para>
```

the stylesheet created by the transformation with the `xsl:namespace-alias` element creates this result:

```
<?xml version="1.0" encoding="UTF-8"?>
<p>Fallen cherub, to be weak is miserable</p>
```

Creating XSLT instructions in your result document is only the most obvious application of the `xsl:namespace-alias` element. Whenever you have elements that you don't want recognized as belonging to a certain namespace until later in the process, `xsl:namespace-alias` can put the prefix you want on those elements. Or, it can take them out: a result-prefix value of "#default" assigns the relevant result-tree elements to the default namespace, which means they get no namespace prefix at all.

4.3.2   Namespaces and stylesheet logic

The preceding section shows how to control the namespaces that are declared and referenced in your result document. If your stylesheet needs to know details about the namespaces used in your source document, and to perform tasks based on which namespaces certain elements or attributes came from, XSLT offers a variety of ways to find out.

To experiment with these techniques, we'll use the following document. It has one `title` element and one `verse` element from the http://www.snee.com/red namespace, two `verse` elements from the "http://www.snee.com/blue" namespace, and one `verse` element from the default namespace:

```
<poem xmlns:red="http://www.snee.com/red"
      xmlns:blue="http://www.snee.com/blue">
<red:title>From Book IV</red:title>
<blue:verse>The way he went, and on the Assyrian mount</blue:verse>
<red:verse>Saw him disfigured, more then could befall</red:verse>
<blue:verse>Spirit of happy sort: his gestures fierce</blue:verse>
<verse>He marked and mad demeanor, then alone</verse>
</poem>
```

Our first stylesheet has template rules that act on element nodes based on several conditions. Each adds a text node to the result tree indicating what it found (for example, "Found a red node:"), followed by information about the node found. Note that for the http://www.snee.com/blue namespace, the stylesheet uses a prefix different from the one that the preceding document uses—instead of "blue", the stylesheet uses the German word for "blue" ("blau"):

```
<!-- xq255.xsl: converts xq254.xml into xq256.txt -->
<xsl:stylesheet xmlns:xsl="http://www.w3.org/1999/XSL/Transform"
                xmlns:red="http://www.snee.com/red"
                xmlns:blau="http://www.snee.com/blue"
                version="1.0">
<xsl:output method="text"/>

  <xsl:template match="poem">
   Namespace nodes:
    <xsl:for-each select="namespace::*">
      <xsl:value-of select="name()"/><xsl:text> </xsl:text>
    </xsl:for-each>
    <xsl:apply-templates/>
  </xsl:template>

  <xsl:template match="blau:verse">
   Found a blue verse.
   name           <xsl:value-of select="name()"/>
   local-name     <xsl:value-of select="local-name()"/>
   namespace-uri  <xsl:value-of select="namespace-uri()"/>
   contents       <xsl:apply-templates/>
  </xsl:template>

  <xsl:template match="red:*">
   Found a red node:
   name           <xsl:value-of select="name(.)"/>
   local-name     <xsl:value-of select="local-name(.)"/>
   namespace-uri  <xsl:value-of select="namespace-uri(.)"/>
   contents       <xsl:apply-templates/>
  </xsl:template>
```

```
<xsl:template match="verse">
  Found a verse element from the default namespace:
  name          <xsl:value-of select="name(.)"/>
  local-name    <xsl:value-of select="local-name(.)"/>
  namespace-uri <xsl:value-of select="namespace-uri(.)"/>
  contents      <xsl:apply-templates/>
</xsl:template>

<xsl:template match="*"/>

</xsl:stylesheet>
```

Let's first look at the result of applying this stylesheet to the document above before we talk about how the stylesheet achieves this result:

```
Namespace nodes:
 xml blue red

Found a red node:
name          red:title
local-name    title
namespace-uri http://www.snee.com/red
contents      From Book IV

Found a blue verse.
name          blue:verse
local-name    verse
namespace-uri http://www.snee.com/blue
contents      The way he went, and on the Assyrian mount

Found a red node:
name          red:verse
local-name    verse
namespace-uri http://www.snee.com/red
contents      Saw him disfigured, more then could befall

Found a blue verse.
name          blue:verse
local-name    verse
namespace-uri http://www.snee.com/blue
contents      Spirit of happy sort: his gestures fierce

Found a verse element from the default namespace:
name          verse
local-name    verse
namespace-uri
contents      He marked and mad demeanor, then alone
```

When the first template rule finds a poem element, it lists all the namespace nodes for that element. It does so by using an `xsl:for-each` instruction to count through the names in the `namespace` axis with any name ("*"), adding each name to the result tree by calling the `name()` function in an `xsl:value-of` instruction's `select` attribute. The template rule then puts a single space after each name with an

es don't run together. In addition to the "blue"
the poem element's start-tag, note the "xml"
result. An XSLT processor assumes that this
in all XML documents. (Well, it's supposed to,
ll processors really do make this assumption.)
for verse elements in the "blau" namespace.
namespace name. As we can see in the
the prefix assigned in the stylesheet to refer to
//www.snee.com/blue. The sample source doc-
he http://www.snee.com/blue namespace, and
documents refer to this namespace with differ-
same namespace, so the XSLT processor rec-
two "Found a blue verse" text nodes to the

is four lines to tell us about the element node

ction to show us the element's full name. For
://www.snee.com/blue namespace, this name
st template rule used the same function to
nd not element names, because that was the
ame() function inside the xsl:for-each
the namespace nodes.) A template rule look-
ttp://www.snee.com/blue namespace hands
nespace nodes, so it adds the element names

2 The second line uses the local-name() function to show us the local part of the element's name—that is, the name that identifies it within that particular namespace. For an element with a full name of "blue:verse", the local name is "blue".

3 The third line uses the namespace-uri() function to get the full URI of the element's namespace. As we saw with the http://www.snee.com/blue namespace, documents may assign any prefix to a namespace; it's the corresponding URI that really identifies the namespace. For example, you can use "xsl" or "potrze-bie" or "blue" as the prefix for your stylesheet's XSLT instructions, as long as the prefix is declared with the http://www.w3.org/1999/XSL/Transform URI so that your XSLT processor recognizes those elements as the special ones from the XSLT namespace.

4 The fourth line shows the contents of the selected element node with an xsl:apply-templates instruction.

The stylesheet's third template rule looks for any element in the "red" namespace and adds the same information to the result tree that the "blue:verse" template rule added.

Because the source document included both a `title` element and a `verse` element from the http://www.snee.com/red namespace, both get a four-line report in the result. Their corresponding element type names show up in their "name" and "local-name" parts of the result tree. The stylesheet's final template rule suppresses any elements not accounted for in the first three template rules.

We've seen how a template can select all the elements with a specific name from a specific namespace (in the example above, the `verse` elements from the http://www.snee.com/blue namespace) and how it can select all the elements, regardless of their names, from a particular namespace (in the example, those from the http://www.snee.com/red namespace). The next template shows how to select all the elements of a particular name regardless of their namespace: it has a match pattern for all the `verse` elements from any namespace.

```
<!-- xq257.xsl: converts xq254.xml into xq258.txt -->

  <xsl:template match="*[local-name()='verse']">

    Found a verse:
    name          <xsl:value-of select="name()"/>
    local-name    <xsl:value-of select="local-name()"/>
    namespace-uri <xsl:value-of select="namespace-uri()"/>
    contents      <xsl:apply-templates/>
  </xsl:template>
```

Technically speaking, this match pattern is really looking for all the elements for which the local part of their name is "verse". It does this by looking for elements of any name ("*") that meet the condition in the predicate: the `local-name()` function must return a value of "verse". When we apply this stylesheet to the document used in the earlier examples, the result shows two `verse` elements from the "blue" namespace, one from the "red" namespace, and one from the default namespace (that is, one with no specific namespace assigned to it—the last `verse` element in the source document):

```
    Found a verse:
    name          blue:verse
    local-name    verse
    namespace-uri http://www.snee.com/blue
    contents      The way he went, and on the Assyrian mount

    Found a verse:
    name          red:verse
    local-name    verse
    namespace-uri http://www.snee.com/red
    contents      Saw him disfigured, more then could befall

    Found a verse:
    name          blue:verse
    local-name    verse
    namespace-uri http://www.snee.com/blue
    contents      Spirit of happy sort: his gestures fierce
```

```
Found a verse:
name          verse
local-name    verse
namespace-uri
contents      He marked and mad demeanor, then alone
```

For a more realistic example, we'll convert certain elements of an XLink document, regardless of their element names, to HTML. The first template rule in the following stylesheet applies to elements with any name ("*") that meet both of the two conditions in the predicate:

1 They must have a `type` attribute in the XLink namespace with a value of "simple".

2 They must have an `href` attribute in the XLink namespace. The value of this attribute doesn't affect whether the XSLT processor applies this template to the node.

```
<!-- xq259.xsl: converts xq260.xml into xq261.html -->
<xsl:stylesheet xmlns:xsl="http://www.w3.org/1999/XSL/Transform"
                xmlns:xlink="http://www.w3.org/1999/xlink"
                exclude-result-prefixes="xlink"
                version="1.0">
  <xsl:output method="html"/>

  <xsl:template match="*[@xlink:type = 'simple' and @xlink:href]">
   <a href="{@xlink:href}"><xsl:apply-templates/></a>
  </xsl:template>

  <xsl:template match="recipe">
   <html><body>
    <xsl:apply-templates/>
   </body></html>
  </xsl:template>

</xsl:stylesheet>
```

If both of these conditions are true, the element—regardless of its element name—gets converted to an HTML a element in the result tree with the source tree XLink element's `href` attribute value used for the HTML `href` attribute in the result tree version. The template rule will do this to both the `author` and `ingredient` elements of the following document:

```
<recipe xmlns:xlink="http://www.w3.org/1999/xlink">
  <author xlink:href="http:/www.jcookie.com"
          xlink:type="simple">Joe "Cookie" Jones</author>
  <ingredients>
    <ingredient xlink:href="http:/www.snee.com/food/flour.html"
                xlink:type="simple">flour</ingredient>
    <ingredient xlink:href="http:/www.snee.com/food/sugar.html"
                xlink:type="simple">sugar</ingredient>
  </ingredients>
  <steps/>
</recipe>
```

Because of the example's simplicity, the result won't look fancy in a browser, but it does demonstrate how two different element types can both be converted to HTML a elements with one template rule because of the namespace of their attributes:

```
<html>
   <body>
      <a href="http://www.jcookie.com">Joe "Cookie" Jones</a>

      <a href="http://www.snee.com/food/flour.html">flour</a>
      <a href="http://www.snee.com/food/sugar.html">sugar</a>

   </body>
</html>
```

The example also demonstrates the use of the exclude-result-prefixes attribute in the xsl:stylesheet element to keep the original elements' namespace declaration and prefixes out of the result. This helps to make the result something that any Web browser would understand.

> **TIP** XSLT's ability to base processing logic on namespace values makes it a great tool for developing XLink applications.

4.4 *IMAGES, MULTIMEDIA ELEMENTS, AND OTHER UNPARSED ENTITIES*

An XML document incorporates non-XML data such as images, sound files, and any file formats you wish by declaring them as unparsed entities, then referencing them from attributes declared for this purpose. (For information on the potential role of parsed entities in XSLT transformations, see section 4.2, "Entities," on page 87.)

The following XML document references two JPEG image files. We'll see how an XSLT stylesheet converts the document to an HTML file that uses img elements to incorporate those JPEG pictures. First, let's look more closely at what's going on in the XML file:

```
<!DOCTYPE  poem [
<!ELEMENT  poem  (verse | picture)+>
<!ELEMENT  verse (#PCDATA)>
<!ELEMENT  picture EMPTY>
<!ATTLIST  picture picfile ENTITY #REQUIRED>
<!NOTATION JPEG SYSTEM "Joint Photographic Experts Group">
<!ENTITY   squadron SYSTEM "../pics/asquadron.jpg" NDATA JPEG>
<!ENTITY   ceres    SYSTEM "../pics/cerespic.jpg"  NDATA JPEG>
]>
<poem>
<verse>While thus he spake, the Angelic Squadron bright</verse>
<verse>Turned fiery red, sharpening in mooned horns</verse>
<picture picfile="squadron"/>
<verse>Their Phalanx, and began to hem him round</verse>
<verse>With ported Spears, as thick as when a field</verse>
<verse>Of Ceres ripe for harvest waving bends</verse>
<picture picfile="ceres"/>
</poem>
```

The document's DTD declares an empty `picture` element with one attribute: `picfile`, which is declared to be of type ENTITY. This means that any value supplied for a `picture` element's `picfile` attribute must be a declared entity. Two such entities are declared: `squadron` and `ceres`. Each of these two entity declarations has a SYSTEM identifier pointing to the filename to which it refers and an NDATA parameter to name its format: JPEG. An XML processor doesn't know what "JPEG" means, so the DTD includes a NOTATION declaration to formally say "here's one of the unparsed formats that documents conforming to this DTD can use: JPEG."

The actual document contains two `picture` elements, each with a `picfile` attribute naming one of the declared JPEG entities. The HTML `img` elements won't know what to do with these entity names; they need to know the name and location of the actual JPEG files. Fortunately, XSLT offers the `unparsed-entity-uri()` function to get them.

In the stylesheet used to convert the preceding XML document to HTML, the "picture" template uses the entity name in the `picfile` attribute to determine the location and name of the associated file. It does this by passing the `picfile` attribute's value as an argument to the `unparsed-entity-uri()` function, which returns the URI of the unparsed entity:

```
<xsl:stylesheet xmlns:xsl="http://www.w3.org/1999/XSL/Transform"
    version="1.0">
<!-- xq264.xsl: converts xq263.xml into xq265.xml -->
<xsl:output method="html"/>

  <xsl:template match="poem">
    <html><body>
      <xsl:apply-templates/>
    </body></html>
  </xsl:template>

  <xsl:template match="verse">
    <p><xsl:apply-templates/></p>
  </xsl:template>

  <xsl:template match="picture">
    <img src="{unparsed-entity-uri(@picfile)}"/>
  </xsl:template>

</xsl:stylesheet>
```

In the resulting HTML, the path and filenames of the JPEG files show up as the values of the `img` elements' `src` attributes (some XSLT processors may replace the relative path with an absolute path):

```
<html>
  <body>

    <p>While thus he spake, the Angelic Squadron bright</p>

    <p>Turned fiery red, sharpening in mooned horns</p>
    <img src="../pics/asquadron.jpg">
```

```
    <p>Their Phalanx, and began to hem him round</p>

    <p>With ported Spears, as thick as when a field</p>

    <p>Of Ceres ripe for harvest waving bends</p>
    <img src="../pics/cerespic.jpg">

  </body>
</html>
```

As the function name unparsed-entity-uri() tells you, this function would return an entire URI if that had been specified as the entity's location. For example, if the squadron entity had been declared like this,

```
<!ENTITY squadron SYSTEM "http://www.snee.com/pics/asquadron.jpg"
        NDATA JPEG>
```

the first img element in the result would come out like this:

```
<img src="http://www.snee.com/pics/asquadron.jpg">
```

Putting a JPEG file's full path and filename into the src attribute of an HTML img element is the simplest, most obvious use of the unparsed-entity-uri() function. Unparsed entities are a part of XML because they let XML applications take advantage of a wide variety of current and future technology. This function is guaranteed to play an important role in increasingly sophisticated applications as XSLT becomes more popular.

4.5   PROCESSING INSTRUCTIONS

The most popular use of XML processing instructions is the naming of a stylesheet to use with a particular XML or HTML document. It's just one example of how the ability to pass information that doesn't fit into a document's regular structure can give processing instructions an important role in making the different parts of an application fit together. Being able to read and write processing instructions from an XSLT stylesheet gives your application more power to communicate with other applications.

4.5.1   Outputting processing instructions

Add processing instruction nodes to your result tree with the xsl:processing-instruction element. Specify the processing instruction target (a required part of the processing instruction that is supposed to name the application for which the processing instruction's information is meant) in a name attribute and put any other contents of the processing instruction between the xsl:processing-instruction element's start- and end-tags.

> **WARNING**   Because an XML processing instruction ends with the two characters "?>" the content of your processing instruction cannot include a question mark immediately followed by a greater-than sign.

The following example

```
<!-- xq270.xsl -->

<xsl:template match="article">
  <xsl:processing-instruction name="xml-stylesheet">
    <xsl:text>href="headlines.css" type="text/css"</xsl:text>
  </xsl:processing-instruction>
  <html>
    <xsl:apply-templates/>
  </html>
</xsl:template>
```

will add this processing instruction

```
<?xml-stylesheet href="headlines.css" type="text/css"?>
```

before the html element—that is, the html element that is added to the result tree when an XSLT processor finds an article element in the source tree.

Note two special things about this example:

- The example would still work without the xsl:text element surrounding the new processing instruction's contents, but the carriage returns on either side of that text would have been included in the output, splitting the processing instruction over three lines. (Carriage returns next to character data get included in the result tree; those that aren't don't.) A processing instruction containing carriage returns would still be perfectly valid.

- The processing instruction added to the result tree ends with ">" and not "?>" as do most XML processing instructions. The XSLT processor knows that the stylesheet is creating an HTML document because the result tree's document element is called "html," so it creates an HTML-style processing instruction. If the result tree's document element isn't "html" (and if you don't specifically tell it to create HTML-style output with an "html" value for an xsl:output element's method attribute), then the new processing instruction will end with "?>."

By using elements such as xsl:apply-templates and xsl:value-of between the xsl:processing-start element's start- and end-tags, you can insert the contents and the attribute values of elements from the source tree inside a processing instruction being added to the result tree. For example, the following template rule

```
<!-- xq272.xsl: converts xq273.xml into xq274.xml -->

<xsl:template match="stylesheetFile">
  <xsl:processing-instruction name="xml-stylesheet">
      href="<xsl:value-of select='.'/>"
      type="<xsl:value-of select='@type'/>"
  </xsl:processing-instruction>
</xsl:template>
```

will turn this stylesheetFile element

```
<stylesheetFile type="text/css">headlines.css</stylesheetFile>
```

into this processing instruction:

```
<?xml-stylesheet
  href="headlines.css" type="text/css"
  ?>
```

The template uses the contents of the matched stylesheetFile element node as the href parameter in the result tree's processing instruction and the value of the stylesheetFile element's type attribute for the value of the processing instruction's type parameter. (The template doesn't use xsl:text elements around its content to prevent line breaks in the resulting processing instruction because it can't. The content includes two xsl:value-of elements, and an xsl:text element cannot have any child elements. The resulting processing instruction is still perfectly legal XML.)

WARNING An xsl:processing-instruction element cannot be a top-level element. If it's a child of an xsl:stylesheet element, an XSLT processor will ignore it. As with the example shown above, xsl:processing-instruction should be a child of an element (in this case, xsl:template) that can add nodes to the result tree.

4.5.2 Reading and using source tree processing instructions

An XSLT processor's default treatment of processing instructions in the source tree is to ignore them. Using the processing-instruction() function, your stylesheet can find processing instructions and add them to the result tree. For example, this template copies all processing instructions to the output with no changes:

```
<!-- xq276.xsl -->

<xsl:template match="processing-instruction()">
  <xsl:copy/>
</xsl:template>
```

XSLT also lets you select processing instructions by the value of the processing instruction target that must begin each one. Together with XSLT's ability to pull out processing instruction content by using the xsl:value-of element, you can use this method to convert processing instructions with specific processing instruction targets into their own elements.

For example, the following XML document excerpt has two processing instructions with different processing instruction targets: xml-stylesheet and smellPlugIn:

```
<?xml-stylesheet href="headlines.css" type="text/css"?>
<verse>And hazard in the Glorious Enterprise</verse>
<?smellPlugIn scent="newCar" duration="12secs"?>
```

In addition to converting the verse element above to a p element, the following template rules convert the xml-stylesheet processing instruction to a stylesheet element and the smellPlugIn processing instruction to a smellData element.

```
<!-- xq278.xsl: converts xq277.xml into xq279.xml -->
```

```
<xsl:template match="processing-instruction('xml-stylesheet')">
  <stylesheet><xsl:value-of select="."/></stylesheet>
</xsl:template>
```

```
<xsl:template match="processing-instruction('smellPlugIn')">
  <smellData><xsl:value-of select="."/></smellData>
</xsl:template>
```

```
<xsl:template match="verse">
  <p><xsl:apply-templates/></p>
</xsl:template>
```

The preceding templates, applied to the example input, add the following to the result tree:

```
<stylesheet>href="headlines.css" type="text/css"</stylesheet>
<p>And hazard in the Glorious Enterprise</p>
<smellData>scent="newCar" duration="12secs"</smellData>
```

CHAPTER 5

Programming issues

5.1 CONTROL STATEMENTS

Control statements are the parts of a programming language that give you greater control over which parts of a program get executed when, and for how many times. This usually includes "if" statements and "case" statements, which let you specify that a series of instructions should only be carried out if a certain condition is true, and loops, which let you specify that a series of instructions should be repeated more than once. This section explores XSLT's control statements.

5.1.1 Conditional statements with "If" and "Choose" (case) statements

Most programming languages provide some means of conditional execution. This lets a program execute an instruction or block of instructions only if a particular condition is true. Many programming languages do so with something called "if" statements; the XSLT equivalent is the `xsl:if` instruction.

Ultimately, there's only one thing that can or can't happen in XSLT, based on the Boolean value of an `xsl:if` element's `test` expression: nodes get added to the result tree or they don't. The addition of nodes to the result tree is the only end result of any XSLT activity, and the `xsl:if` element gives you greater control over which nodes get added than template rule match conditions can provide. For example, an `xsl:if` instruction can base its behavior on document characteristics such as attribute values and the existence (or lack) of specific elements in a document.

Many programming languages also offer something known as "case" or "switch" statements. These list a series of conditions to check as well as the actions to perform when finding a true condition. XSLT's `xsl:choose` element lets you specify such a series of conditions and actions in your stylesheets.

xsl:if

The `xsl:if` instruction adds its contents to the result tree if the expression in its test attribute evaluates to a Boolean value of true. For example, imagine that the template rule for the following document's poem element must know specific details about that element before it can add certain text nodes to the result tree.

```
<poem author="jm" year="1667">
<verse>Seest thou yon dreary Plain, forlorn and wild,</verse>
<verse>The seat of desolation, void of light,</verse>
<verse>Save what the glimmering of these livid flames</verse>
<verse>Casts pale and dreadful?</verse>
</poem>
```

The poem template rule below has six `xsl:if` instructions. Each adds a text node to the result tree if the `test` condition is true. (These instructions could add any kind of node—elements, attributes, or whatever you like—but the example is easier to follow if we stick with simple text messages.)

```
<!-- xq286.xsl: converts xq285.xml into xq287.txt -->

<xsl:template match="poem">

  --- Start of "if" tests. ---

  <xsl:if test="@author='jm'">
    1. The poem's author is jm.
  </xsl:if>

  <xsl:if test="@author">
    2. The poem has an author attribute.
  </xsl:if>

  <xsl:if test="@flavor">
    3. The poem has a flavor attribute.
  </xsl:if>

  <xsl:if test="verse">
    4. The poem has at least one verse child element.
  </xsl:if>
```

```
<xsl:if test="shipDate">
  5. The poem has at least one shipDate child element.
</xsl:if>

<xsl:if test="count(verse) > 3">
  6. The poem has more than 3 verse child elements.
</xsl:if>

<xsl:if test="count(verse) &lt; 3">
  7. The poem has less than 3 verse child elements.
</xsl:if>

<xsl:if test="(@author = 'bd') or (@year='1667')">
  8. Either the author is "bd" or the year is "1667".
</xsl:if>

<xsl:if test="@year &lt; '1850'">
  9a. The poem is old.

  <xsl:if test="@year &lt; '1700'">
    9b. The poem is very old.
  </xsl:if>

  <xsl:if test="@year &lt; '1500'">
    9c. The poem is very, very old.
  </xsl:if>

</xsl:if>

--- End of "if" tests.

</xsl:template>
```

The first xsl:if element tests whether the poem element's author attribute has a value of "jm."

TIP   Note the use of single quotation marks around "jm" in the template to enclose the literal string within the double quotation marks of the test attribute value. You could also use the """ or "'" entity references (for example, test="@author="jm"") to delimit the string value.

When the stylesheet is applied to the source XML, the XSLT processor adds the text node beginning with "1" to the result along with several other text nodes from the stylesheet, depending on the Boolean values of each xsl:if instruction's test attribute:

```
--- Start of "if" tests. ---

 1. The poem's author is jm.

 2. The poem has an author attribute.

 4. The poem has at least one verse child element.

 6. The poem has more than 3 verse child elements.

 8. Either the author is "bd" or the year is "1667".

 9a. The poem is old
```

```
   9b. The poem is very old.

 --- End of "if" tests.
```

Some of these expressions don't look as obviously Boolean as `@author="jm"`, but the XSLT processor can still treat them as Boolean expressions. For example, the stylesheet's second `xsl:if` instruction has a test value that only says "@author". This tells the XSLT processor to add the `xsl:if` element's contents to the result tree if the context node (in this case, the poem element node listed as the `xsl:template` element's `match` attribute value) has an attribute specified with that name. The third `xsl:if` element does the same for a `flavor` attribute. Because the poem element has an `author` attribute but no `flavor` attribute, the result of applying the stylesheet to the input shown includes the text node beginning with "2," but not the one beginning "3."

A similar test can check whether an element has a particular child subelement. The fourth and fifth `xsl:if` elements check for `verse` and `shipDate` subelements of the poem element. The output shows that it has at least one verse subelement but no `shipDate` subelements.

How many `verse` subelements does the poem element have? The `count()` function makes it easy to find out. The sixth and seventh `xsl:if` elements check whether this count is more or less than 3. The sixth is true, and its text is added to the output, but the seventh is not. (If there were exactly three `verse` child elements, neither of these conditions would be true.)

WARNING   When you want to use the less-than symbol in an `xsl:if` element's `test` attribute, remember to use the entity reference "<". The actual "<" character in the `test` attribute value (or in *any* attribute value) makes the stylesheet an ill-formed XML document, so the XML parser will choke on it and not pass it along to the XSLT processor.

You can use parentheses and the Boolean operators `and` and `or` to build more complex Boolean expressions. For example, the eighth `xsl:if` element in the preceding stylesheet adds the text node string beginning with "8" if either the `author` attribute equals "bd" or the `year` attribute equals "1667." Because the latter condition is true for the sample document's poem element, an XSLT processor will add the text. The parentheses in the `test` attribute's expression are not necessary in this case, but as with similar expressions in other programming languages, they make it easier to see the expression's structure.

For more complex conditional logic, you can nest `xsl:if` elements inside of each other. In the example, the `xsl:if` element with the line beginning "9a" contains `xsl:if` elements 9b and 9c. The output shows that, because the poem element's `year` attribute has a value less than 1850, the text string beginning with "9a" gets added to the output. Because it's also less than 1700, the text string beginning with "9b" in the first nested `xsl:if` element is also added. The `date` value is not less than 1500, so the second nested `xsl:if` element's text node does not get added to the output.

Before getting too fancy with your `xsl:if` elements, note the flexibility that the `xsl:choose` instruction gives you. It offers the equivalent of an "else" or "otherwise" section, which lets you specify nodes to add to the result tree if the `test` conditions aren't true. The `xsl:if` element offers no equivalent of this, so programmers accustomed to "if-else" constructs in other programming languages may find the `xsl:choose` element better for certain situations where `xsl:if` may first seem like the obvious choice.

For related information, see

- section 2.4, "Predicates," page 43 for more on expressions that can be treated as Boolean values.

- section 3.10, "Empty elements: creating, checking for," page 67

xsl:choose

XSLT's `xsl:choose` instruction is similar to `xsl:if` but with a few key differences:

- One `xsl:choose` element can test for more than one condition and add different nodes to the result tree based on which condition is true.

- An `xsl:choose` element can have a default template to add to the result tree if none of the conditions are true. (Compare to `xsl:if`, which has no equivalent of an "else" condition.)

- The `xsl:choose` element has specific subelements necessary for it to work. You can put any well-formed elements you want inside of an `xsl:if` element.

When an XSLT processor sees an `xsl:choose` element, it checks the `test` attribute value of each `xsl:when` element that it finds as a child of the `xsl:choose` element. When it finds a true test expression, it adds that `xsl:when` element's contents to the result tree and then skips the rest of the `xsl:choose` element. If it finds no `xsl:when` element with a true test expression, it checks for the optional `xsl:otherwise` element at the end of the `xsl:choose` element. If it finds one, it adds its contents to the result tree.

For example, let's say we want a template rule to check the date of the following poem and add a message to the result tree saying whether the poem was one of Milton's early, middle period, or later works:

```
<poem author="jm" year="1667">
  <verse>Seest thou yon dreary Plain, forlorn and wild,</verse>
  <verse>The seat of desolation, void of light,</verse>
  <verse>Save what the glimmering of these livid flames</verse>
  <verse>Casts pale and dreadful?</verse>
</poem>
```

The XSLT processor will skip over the `xsl:choose` element's first two `xsl:when` elements in the following template because their test expressions are false for the year value of "1667". The processor will add the text "The poem is one of Milton's later works" to the result tree when it finds that the condition "@year < 1668" is true. (Note the use of "<" instead of a "<" to keep the xsl:when element well-formed.)

```
<!-- xq290.xsl: converts xq289.xml into xq291.txt -->

<xsl:template match="poem">

  <xsl:choose>
    <xsl:when test="@year &lt; 1638">
    The poem is one of Milton's earlier works.
    </xsl:when>

    <xsl:when test="@year &lt; 1650">
    The poem is from Milton's middle period.
    </xsl:when>

    <xsl:when test="@year &lt; 1668">
    The poem is one of Milton's later works.
    </xsl:when>

    <xsl:when test="@year &lt; 1675">
    The poem is one of Milton's last works.
    </xsl:when>

    <xsl:otherwise>
      The poem was written after Milton's death.
    </xsl:otherwise>

  </xsl:choose>

</xsl:template>
```

Although the sample poem element's year value of "1667" also makes the last xsl:when element's test expression ("@year < 1675") true, the XSLT processor will not continue checking for more true test expressions after it finds one. The result only contains the text result node from the first xsl:when element with a true test expression:

```
The poem is one of Milton's later works.
```

Like xsl:if instructions, xsl:when elements can have more elaborate contents between their start- and end-tags—for example, literal result elements, xsl:element elements, or even xsl:if and xsl:choose elements—to add to the result tree.

5.1.2   Curly braces: when do I need them?

For some stylesheet attribute values, curly braces tell the XSLT processor to evaluate the expression between them and to replace the curly braces and their contents with the result of that evaluation. The following stylesheet demonstrates the effect of the curly braces:

```
<xsl:stylesheet xmlns:xsl="http://www.w3.org/1999/XSL/Transform"
    version="1.0">
<xsl:output method="xml" omit-xml-declaration="yes"/>
<!-- xq573.xsl: converts xq573.xsl into xq574.xml -->

<xsl:template match="/">
```

```
    <test>

      <xsl:variable name="myVar">10</xsl:variable>

      A. <atvtest at1="hello world"/>
      B. <atvtest at1="3+2+$myVar"/>
      C. <atvtest at1="{3+2+$myVar}"/>
      D. <atvtest at1="u{3+2}"/>
      E. <atvtest at1="yo, substring('hello world',7)"/>
      F. <atvtest at1="yo, {substring('hello world',7)}"/>
    </test>
  </xsl:template>

</xsl:stylesheet>
```

Some of the example's `atvtest` elements use these curly braces in their `at1` attribute values, and some don't. (This stylesheet can be applied to any XML source document, even itself, because it adds its six literal result elements to the result tree as soon as it sees the root of any source document and then doesn't bother with the source document's other nodes.) Here is the result the stylesheet creates:

```
<test>

      A. <atvtest at1="hello world"/>
      B. <atvtest at1="3+2+$myVar"/>
      C. <atvtest at1="15"/>
      D. <atvtest at1="u5"/>
      E. <atvtest at1="yo, substring('hello world',7)"/>
      F. <atvtest at1="yo, world"/></test>
```

The values of the `at1` attributes that have no curly braces in the stylesheet (lines A, B, and E) look exactly the same in the result as they look in the stylesheet. For the attribute values that do have curly braces, the XSLT processor replaces the expressions and their curly braces with the result of evaluating those expressions. This happens whether the curly braces surround the entire attribute value (line C) or just part of the attribute value (lines D and F).

Sometimes the evaluation of the example's expressions involves doing math (lines C and D), and sometimes it means calling a function unrelated to math (the `substring()` function in line F). Comparing lines B and C also shows that references to variables inside of curly braces get converted to the value they represent, but when they have no curly braces around them, the reference to the variable is treated as literal text.

Between the XPath and the XSLT functions available, the math you can do, and the use of variables, attribute value templates offer many possibilities for generating result tree attribute values.

On the other hand, you don't need those curly braces in every attribute value that you want the XSLT processor to evaluate. Take for example, the following stylesheet, which can also use itself as a source tree:

```
<!-- xq575.xsl: converts xq575.xsl into xq576.xml -->
<xsl:stylesheet xmlns:xsl="http://www.w3.org/1999/XSL/Transform"
      version="1.0">
```

```
<xsl:output method="xml" omit-xml-declaration="yes"/>

<xsl:template match="/">

  <xsl:variable name="myVar">10</xsl:variable>

  <test>
    A. <xsl:value-of select="3+2+$myVar"/>
    B. <xsl:value-of select="substring('hello world',7)"/>
  </test>
</xsl:template>

</xsl:stylesheet>
```

This stylesheet creates this result document:

```
<test>
    A. 15
    B. world</test>
```

The "3+2+$myVar" was added up to "15" and the substring() function got evaluated so that the substring starting at the seventh character of its first argument was added to the result tree.

So, if you sometimes need curly braces to tell your XSLT processor to evaluate an expression in a stylesheet attribute value and other times you don't need them, how do you know when the curly braces are necessary? The XSLT specification tells you outright if each of the special XSLT stylesheet elements' attributes is an attribute value template, which means that curly braces and any expression between them will be replaced by the result of evaluating that expression. Syntax summaries in the XSLT specification show curly braces around the values of attributes treated as attribute value templates such as the one shown for xsl:sort here:

```
<xsl:sort
  select = string-expression
  lang = { nmtoken }
  data-type = { "text" | "number" | qname-but-not-ncname }
  order = { "ascending" | "descending" }
  case-order = { "upper-first" | "lower-first" } />
```

This syntax summary illustrates that you can't use curly braces in the value of the xsl:sort element's select attribute, but you can for all its other attributes. The term string-expression means that the select value could be a literal string, but it could also be a function that returns a string like the substring() function used in the earlier example. Similar terms you might see in these syntax summaries include boolean-expression, node-set-expression, and number-expression. As with string-expression, these all show places where you can put a literal value or a function that returns one of these expressions. You don't need curly braces to tell the XSLT processor to evaluate these, because it will evaluate them anyway.

WARNING   Because you can't use curly braces in a node-set-expression, you can't use them in XPath expressions or match patterns.

- See appendix A, "XSLT quick reference" on page 259 for more information on which attributes can be treated as attribute value templates;

- see section 5.6, "Numbers and math," page 149, for more on performing math from within stylesheets, and

- section 5.7, "Strings," page 153 for more on functions that manipulate strings.

5.1.3 "For" loops, iteration

Programming languages use loops to execute an action or series of actions multiple times. After performing the last action of such a series, the program "loops" back up to the first one. The program may repeat these actions a specific number of times—for example, five times or thirty times. It may repeat the actions until a specified condition is true—for example, until there's no more input to read or until a prime number greater than a million has been calculated. XSLT offers two ways to repeat a series of actions:

- The `xsl:for-each` instruction lets you perform the same group of instructions on a given set of nodes. The specification of those nodes can take full advantage of the options offered by XPath's axis specifiers, node tests, and predicate conditions. In other words, for any set of a source tree's nodes that you can describe with an XPath expression, there's a way to say "perform this set of actions on these nodes." While this provides a way to execute a set of instructions repeatedly, you're repeating them over a set of nodes, not for an arbitrary number of iterations, which is what a "for" loop does in most programming languages.

- By having a named template call itself recursively with parameters, you can execute a series of instructions for a fixed number of times or until a given condition is true. This technique comes from one of XSLT's ancestors, the LISt Processing Language (LISP) developed for artificial intelligence work in the 1960s. The technique may not be familiar to programmers accustomed to the "for" and "while" loops available in languages such as Java, C++, and Visual Basic, but it can perform the same tasks.

Iteration across nodes with xsl:for-each

When do you need `xsl:for-each`? Less often than you might think. If there's something you need to do with (or to) a particular set of nodes, an `xsl:template` template rule may be the best way to do it. Reviewing this approach will make it easier to understand what the `xsl:for-each` instruction can offer us.

In an `xsl:template` template rule, you specify a pattern in the `match` attribute that describes which nodes you want the rule to act on. For example, let's say you want to list out the figure titles in the following document:

```
<chapter>
<para>Then with expanded wings he steers his flight</para>
<figure><title>"Incumbent on the Dusky Air"</title>
<graphic fileref="pic1.jpg"/></figure>
```

```
<para>Aloft, incumbent on the dusky Air</para>
<sect1>
<para>That felt unusual weight, till on dry Land</para>
<figure><title>"He Lights"</title>
<graphic fileref="pic2.jpg"/></figure>
<para>He lights, if it were Land that ever burned</para>
<sect2>
<para>With solid, as the Lake with liquid fire</para>
<figure><title>"The Lake with Liquid Fire"</title>
<graphic fileref="pic1.jpg"/></figure>
</sect2>
</sect1>
</chapter>
```

The following stylesheet adds only these `title` elements to the result tree. It suppresses the `para` elements, which are the only other elements that have character data:

```
<!-- xq296.xsl: converts xq295.xml into xq297.txt -->
<xsl:stylesheet xmlns:xsl="http://www.w3.org/1999/XSL/Transform"
    version="1.0">
<xsl:output method="xml" omit-xml-declaration="yes" indent="no"/>

<xsl:template match="figure/title">
   <xsl:apply-templates/>
  </xsl:template>

  <xsl:template match="para"/>

</xsl:stylesheet>
```

This stylesheet creates the following result from the document above:

```
"Incumbent on the Dusky Air"

"He Lights"

"The Lake with Liquid Fire"
```

Simple template rules aren't always enough to perform a series of actions on a specified set of nodes. What if you want to list the figure titles at the top of the result document and then output the rest of the source document under that list? A stylesheet like the one above, which goes through the document adding only the figure's `title` elements to the result tree, won't do this. The `para` elements need to be added as well. Our new stylesheet needs to add all the figure titles to the result tree as soon as it reaches the beginning of the source tree's `chapter` element, then it must continue on through the rest of the source tree, processing the remaining nodes.

The `xsl:for-each` instruction is great for this. The following template rule has four children:

- a text node with the string "Pictures"

- an `xsl:for-each` instruction to add the `figure` elements' `title` subelements to the result tree

- a text node with the string "Chapter"

- an `xsl:apply-templates` element to add the `chapter` element's contents to the result tree

```
<!-- xq298.xsl: converts xq295.xml into xq299.txt -->

<xsl:template match="chapter">
  <!-- Odd indenting to make result line up better -->
Pictures:
<xsl:for-each select="descendant::figure">
<xsl:value-of select="title"/><xsl:text>
</xsl:text>
  </xsl:for-each>
Chapter:<xsl:apply-templates/>
</xsl:template>
```

The `xsl:for-each` element's `select` attribute indicates which nodes to iterate over. The XPath expression used for this attribute value has an axis specifier of "descendant" and a node test of "figure". So, taken together, the expression means "all the descendants of the `chapter` node (the one named in the template's match pattern) with 'figure' as their node name." Here we can see a key advantage of the `descendant` axis over the default `child` one: the `descendant::figure` XPath expression gets the `title` element nodes from the `chapter` element's child, grandchild, and great-grandchild `figure` elements.

The contents of the `xsl:for-each` element consists of two things to add to the result tree for each node that `xsl:for-each` iterates over:

- The `xsl:value-of` element adds the contents of each `figure` element's `title` child
- The `xsl:text` element with a single carriage return as its contents adds that carriage return after each `title` value

Following is the result:

```
Pictures:
"Incumbent on the Dusky Air"
"He Lights"
"The Lake with Liquid Fire"

Chapter:
Then with expanded wings he steers his flight
"Incumbent on the Dusky Air"

Aloft, incumbent on the dusky Air

That felt unusual weight, till on dry Land
"He Lights"

He lights, if it were Land that ever burned

With solid, as the Lake with liquid fire
"The Lake with Liquid Fire"
```

Rearranging a document's structure as you copy the document to the result tree is one of the most popular uses of XSLT. The xsl:for-each element is a particularly valuable tool here because of its ability to grab a copy of a set of nodes that aren't located together in the source tree, perform any changes you require on those nodes, and then put them together in the result tree wherever you like.

Another advantage of acting on a set of nodes with an xsl:for-each element instead of with an xsl:template element lies in a limitation to template rules that XSLT novices often don't notice: while it may appear that you can use XPath expressions in an xsl:template element's match attribute, you're actually limited to the subset of XPath expressions known as patterns. In the xsl:for-each element's select attribute, however, you have the full power of XPath expressions available.

For example, you can't use the ancestor axis specifier in match patterns, but you can do so in an xsl:for-each element's select attribute. The following template uses the ancestor axis specifier to list the names of all a title element's ancestors:

```
<!-- xq300.xsl: converts xq295.xml into xq301.txt -->

<xsl:template match="title">
  <xsl:text>title ancestors:</xsl:text>
  <xsl:for-each select="ancestor::*">
   <xsl:value-of select="name()"/>
    <!-- Output a comma if it's not the last one in
         the node set that for-each is going through. -->
   <xsl:if test="position() != last()">
   <xsl:text>,</xsl:text>
   </xsl:if>
  </xsl:for-each>
</xsl:template>

<xsl:template match="para"/>
```

The second template rule suppresses para elements from the result tree. The first template's "title ancestors:" and "," text nodes are inside xsl:text elements to prevent the adjacent carriage returns from being copied to the result. This way, each title element's ancestor list is on one line directly after the title introducing it.

This stylesheet outputs the following when applied to the document we saw on page 118:

```
title ancestors:chapter,figure

title ancestors:chapter,sect1,figure

title ancestors:chapter,sect1,sect2,figure
```

Like the xsl:value-of instruction, xsl:for-each is a great way to grab a set of nodes from the source tree while the XSLT processor is applying a template to any other node. The xsl:value-of element has one crucial limitation that highlights the value of xsl:for-each: if you tell xsl:value-of to get a set of nodes, it only returns a string version of the first node in that set. If you tell xsl:for-each to get a set of nodes, it gets the whole set. As you iterate across that set of nodes, you can do anything you want with them. (The `xsl:copy-of` instruction can also grab nearly any set of nodes, but with `xsl:for-each`, you can do something with them before copying them to the result tree, such as the addition of the text nodes in the example above.)

> **TIP** The `xsl:sort` instruction lets you sort the node set through which your `xsl:for-each` element is iterating. (See section 6.7, "Sorting," page 215, for more on this.)

Arbitrary repetition with named template recursion

XSLT offers no specific element for repeating a group of instructions a set number of times or until a given condition is true. To understand why XSLT doesn't provide a specific element requires a little historical background.

Just as XML got its start as a simplified version of SGML, XSLT and XSL began as simplified, XML-based versions of the stylesheet language developed for SGML called Document Style Semantics and Specification Language (DSSSL—pronounce it to rhyme with whistle). Like SGML, DSSSL is an ISO standard, but its actual use in the real world has been limited.

Why didn't DSSSL catch on? One problem was its roots in Scheme, a programming language that evolved from the LISP language. As mentioned earlier, "LISP" stands for "LISt Processing" language, but many say that it stands for "Lots of Irritating Silly Parentheses." LISP, Scheme, and DSSSL use parentheses for nearly all their punctuation, and the parenthesized expressions get nested at such deep levels that expressions ending with ")))))" are common in all three languages. Both data structures and control structures are parenthesized expressions in these languages, which makes their code difficult to follow.

XSL and XSLT remedy this by applying many of DSSSL's principles using XML. Expressions can be deeply nested, but instead of being nested within dozens of parentheses, they're nested inside regular XML elements that have names describing their purpose right in their tags—for example, `xsl:if`, `xsl:number`, and `xsl:comment`. This makes XSLT stylesheets much easier to follow than DSSSL stylesheets. XSLT still inherited a related aspect of its ancestors that some view as a blessing and others as a curse: there's no concept of an instruction series being executed sequentially. (The technical term is "side effect free" language.) A stylesheet gets applied to a source tree to create a result tree. While the structure of the result tree is important, the order in which it's created is irrelevant. Since you can't have a series of instructions, you certainly don't have a way to repeat a series of instructions.

However, this doesn't prevent you from doing something a specific number of times or until a given condition is true in XSLT. You just have to use the LISP/Scheme/DSSSL technique for doing so: recursion. Using recursive named templates, you can get the benefits of both "for" loops and "while" loops.

To demonstrate, we'll use this simple input document:

```
<sample>the facile gates of hell too slightly barred</sample>
```

The following template illustrates how to repeat something a specific number of times. It has a named template called "hyphens", that can call itself as many times as necessary to add the specified number of hyphens to the result tree. To demonstrate the use of this named template, the "sample" template calls the "hyphens" template four times, asking it to add a different number of hyphens to the result tree each time. First, the "sample" template calls the "hyphens" template with no value overriding the howMany parameter so that we can see the template's default behavior, and then it calls the template three more times with the values 3, 20, and 0 to override the parameter's default value of 1. (If you're not familiar with the use of named templates with parameters that can be set by the instruction calling them, see section 5.3, "Named templates," page 132, and section 5.8.2, "Parameters," page 169.)

```
<!-- xq304.xsl: converts xq303.xml into xq305.txt -->

<xsl:template name="hyphens">
  <xsl:param name="howMany">1</xsl:param>
  <xsl:if test="$howMany &gt; 0">

    <!-- Add 1 hyphen to result tree. -->
    <xsl:text>-</xsl:text>

    <!-- Print remaining ($howMany - 1) hyphens. -->
    <xsl:call-template name="hyphens">
    <xsl:with-param name="howMany" select="$howMany - 1"/>
    </xsl:call-template>
  </xsl:if>
</xsl:template>

<xsl:template match="sample">

  Print 1 hyphen:
  <xsl:call-template name="hyphens"/>

  Print 3 hyphens:
  <xsl:call-template name="hyphens">
    <xsl:with-param name="howMany" select="3"/>
  </xsl:call-template>

  Print 20 hyphens:
  <xsl:call-template name="hyphens">
    <xsl:with-param name="howMany" select="20"/>
  </xsl:call-template>

  Print 0 hyphens:
  <xsl:call-template name="hyphens">
    <xsl:with-param name="howMany" select="0"/>
  </xsl:call-template>

</xsl:template>
```

This creates the following result:

```
  Print 1 hyphen:
  -
```

```
Print 3 hyphens:
---

Print 20 hyphens:
--------------------

Print 0 hyphens:
```

The "hyphens" named template first declares the howMany parameter with an xsl:param element that sets this parameter's default value to 1. The rest of the template is a single xsl:if element whose contents get added to the result tree if how-Many is set to a value greater than zero. If howMany passes this test, a single hyphen is added to the result tree and an xsl:call-template instruction calls the "hyphens" named template with a value of howMany one less than its current setting. If howMany is set to 1, xsl:call-template calls it with a value of 0, so no more hyphens will be added to the result tree. If howMany is set to 3, the named template will be called with a howMany value of 2 after adding the first of the 3 requested hyphens. The process is repeated until the template is called with a value of 0.

This technique is what we mean by "recursion." When a template calls itself, it's a recursive call. You don't want the "hyphens" named template to call itself forever, so the recursive template needs a stopping condition—in the case above, an xsl:if element that won't perform the recursive call unless howMany is greater than 0 (See figure 5.1).

You must also be sure that this stopping condition will eventually be true. If the stopping condition was "$howMany = 0", and the recursive call subtracted 2 from the current value of howMany before calling the "hyphens" template again, calling the template with a value of 3 would then mean making subsequent calls with howMany values of 1, –1, –3, –5, and so forth without ever hitting 0. The recursive calls would never stop. (The actual outcome of such an endless loop depends on the XSLT processor being used.)

WARNING   The fancier the condition you use to control recursion, the more careful you must be to make absolutely sure that the stopping condition will eventually be true. Otherwise, the execution of your stylesheet could get stuck there.

```
Print 3 hyphens:
<xsl:call-template name="hyphens">
  <xsl:with-param name="howMany" select="3"/
>
</xsl:call-template>
--------------------------- 3 --------------
<xsl:template name="hyphens">
  <xsl:param name="howMany">1</xsl:param>
  <xsl:if test="$howMany &gt; 0">

    <!-- Add 1 hyphen to result tree. -->
    <xsl:text>-</xsl:text>

    <!-- Print remaining ($howMany - 1) hyphens. -->
    <xsl:call-template name="hyphens">
      <xsl:with-param name="howMany" select="$howMany - 1"/>
    </xsl:call-template>
  </xsl:if>
</xsl:template>
--------------------------- 2 --------------
<xsl:template name="hyphens">
  <xsl:param name="howMany">1</xsl:param>
  <xsl:if test="$howMany &gt; 0">

    <!-- Add 1 hyphen to result tree. -->
    <xsl:text>-</xsl:text>

    <!-- Print remaining ($howMany - 1) hyphens. -->
    <xsl:call-template name="hyphens">
      <xsl:with-param name="howMany" select="$howMany - 1"/>
    </xsl:call-template>
  </xsl:if>
</xsl:template>
--------------------------- 1 --------------
<xsl:template name="hyphens">
  <xsl:param name="howMany">1</xsl:param>
  <xsl:if test="$howMany &gt; 0">

    <!-- Add 1 hyphen to result tree. -->
    <xsl:text>-</xsl:text>

    <!-- Print remaining ($howMany - 1) hyphens. -->
    <xsl:call-template name="hyphens">
      <xsl:with-param name="howMany" select="$howMany - 1"/>
    </xsl:call-template>
  </xsl:if>
</xsl:template>
--------------------------- 0 --------------
<xsl:template name="hyphens">
  <xsl:param name="howMany">1</xsl:param>
  <xsl:if test="$howMany &gt; 0">

    <!-- Add 1 hyphen to result tree. -->
    <xsl:text>-</xsl:text>

    <!-- Print remaining ($howMany - 1) hyphens. -->
    <xsl:call-template name="hyphens">
      <xsl:with-param name="howMany" select="$howMany - 1"/>
    </xsl:call-template>
  </xsl:if>
</xsl:template>
```

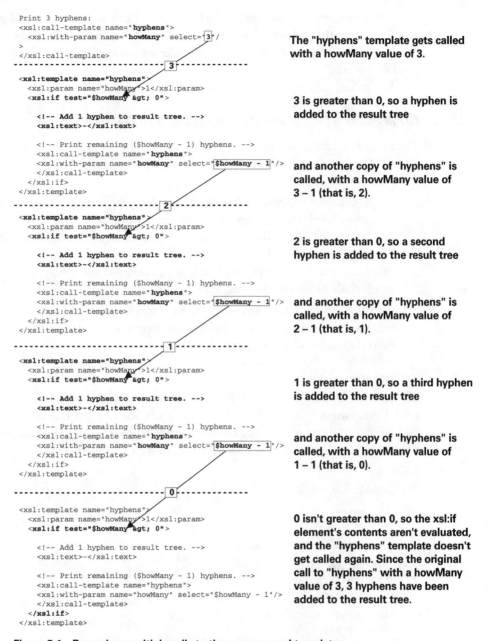

The "hyphens" template gets called with a howMany value of 3.

3 is greater than 0, so a hyphen is added to the result tree

and another copy of "hyphens" is called, with a howMany value of 3 – 1 (that is, 2).

2 is greater than 0, so a second hyphen is added to the result tree

and another copy of "hyphens" is called, with a howMany value of 2 – 1 (that is, 1).

1 is greater than 0, so a third hyphen is added to the result tree

and another copy of "hyphens" is called, with a howMany value of 1 – 1 (that is, 0).

0 isn't greater than 0, so the xsl:if element's contents aren't evaluated, and the "hyphens" template doesn't get called again. Since the original call to "hyphens" with a howMany value of 3, 3 hyphens have been added to the result tree.

Figure 5.1   Recursion: multiple calls to the same named template

The preceding example simulates the "for" loops used by many other programming languages, because the recursive template in the example performs an action a specific number of times, with the exact number passed to it at runtime. A "while" loop typically repeats an action or actions as long as a certain condition is true. And guess what? The example above is really a "while" loop. The condition is the "$howMany > 0" test in the named template's `xsl:if` start-tag. You can put any condition you want in there, and the template will make recursive calls to itself as long as the condition is true.

For related information, see section 5.3, "Named templates," page 132.

5.2 COMBINING STYLESHEETS WITH INCLUDE AND IMPORT

The `xsl:include` and `xsl:import` instructions give you ways to say "get a certain XSLT stylesheet and incorporate it into this one." There are two situations where these are useful:

- Large, complex stylesheets, like large complex programs, are easier to maintain when you break them down into modules with specific roles to play. In XSLT, the `xsl:include` and `xsl:import` instructions let you assemble the pieces. This modular approach also makes it easier to share parts of a stylesheet with other stylesheets that only want certain features, not the whole thing; they can just include or import the parts they need.

- Customizing an existing stylesheet without actually editing that stylesheet is easy, because you incorporate it and then separately override any template rules that don't do exactly what you want.

5.2.1 xsl:include

The `xsl:include` instruction is similar to the "include" instruction available in several programming languages. The XSLT processor replaces this instruction with the contents of the stylesheet named in its `href` attribute. For example, the following `makehtml.xsl` stylesheet names the `inlines.xsl` stylesheet in order to incorporate that stylesheet:

```
<!-- xq191.xsl (makehtml.xsl) -->

<xsl:stylesheet xmlns:xsl="http://www.w3.org/1999/XSL/Transform"
     version="1.0">

  <xsl:include href="inlines.xsl"/>

  <xsl:template match="chapter">
   <html><xsl:apply-templates/></html>
  </xsl:template>

  <xsl:template match="para">
   <p><xsl:apply-templates/></p>
  </xsl:template>

  <xsl:template match="chapter/title">
   <h1><xsl:apply-templates/></h1>
  </xsl:template>
</xsl:stylesheet>
```

If inlines.xsl looks like this,

```
<!-- xq192.xsl (inlines.xsl) -->

<xsl:stylesheet xmlns:xsl="http://www.w3.org/1999/XSL/Transform"
     version="1.0">

  <xsl:template match="emphasis">
   <b><xsl:apply-templates/></b>
  </xsl:template>

  <xsl:template match="literal">
   <tt><xsl:apply-templates/></tt>
  </xsl:template>

</xsl:stylesheet>
```

the XSLT processor will treat makehtml.xsl as if it looked like this:

```
<!-- xq193.xsl -->

<xsl:stylesheet xmlns:xsl="http://www.w3.org/1999/XSL/Transform"
     version="1.0">

  <xsl:template match="emphasis">
   <b><xsl:apply-templates/></b>
  </xsl:template>

  <xsl:template match="literal">
   <tt><xsl:apply-templates/></tt>
  </xsl:template>

  <xsl:template match="chapter">
   <html><xsl:apply-templates/></html>
  </xsl:template>

  <xsl:template match="para">
   <p><xsl:apply-templates/></p>
  </xsl:template>

  <xsl:template match="chapter/title">
   <h1><xsl:apply-templates/></h1>
  </xsl:template>

</xsl:stylesheet>
```

The complete inlines.xsl stylesheet didn't get inserted; its contents did. In other words, everything between its `xsl:stylesheet` tags (the stylesheet's "emphasis" and "literal" template rules) was inserted where the `makehtml.xsl stylesheet` had its `xsl:include` instruction.

The included stylesheet must still be a complete stylesheet. Unlike the "include" mechanisms offered by some programming languages, the part you're including can't just be a piece of something—it must be a complete stylesheet. (If you really do want to incorporate a fragment of a stylesheet into another one, you can use XML general entities, because, after all, XSLT stylesheets are XML documents. See section 4.2, "Entities," page 87, for more on these.)

An included stylesheet may in turn include other stylesheets, and, they too, may include other stylesheets. There's no limit to the levels of inclusion that you can use, although the more you add, the more complexity you have to keep track of.

WARNING   If inclusion levels lead to a file including itself, it's an error.

The xsl:include element can go anywhere you want in a stylesheet, as long as it's a top-level element—that is, a child of the xsl:stylesheet element that makes up the main body of the stylesheet. Putting an xsl:include instruction inside another element, such as an xsl:template template rule, wouldn't make sense, anyway. There would be no point to inserting another stylesheet's complete contents inside of a template rule.

The preceding example is fairly simple. A large, complex stylesheet like the one that turns DocBook files into HTML uses xsl:include on a larger scale. Of the sixty-two XSLT instructions in version 1.2's main docbook.xsl file, thirty-eight of them are xsl:include instructions that incorporate components such as division.xsl and titlepage.xsl.

TIP   Using xsl:include doesn't change XSLT's attitude about multiple template rules that apply to the same node. If the XSLT processor can't find a more specific and therefore more appropriate template for a particular source tree node, it's an error. Using xsl:include does increase the chance of this error happening, especially if you include stylesheets that include other stylesheets, because it's harder to keep track of the full collection of template rules being grouped together.

5.2.2   xsl:import

The xsl:import instruction is similar to xsl:include except that instructions in the imported stylesheet can be overridden by instructions in the importing stylesheet and in any included stylesheet. For example, the following makehtml2.xsl stylesheet tells the XSLT processor to import the inlines.xsl stylesheet. The syntax is nearly identical to the use of xsl:include—you name the imported stylesheet with the href attribute:

```
<!-- xq195.xsl (makehtml2.xsl) -->

<xsl:stylesheet xmlns:xsl="http://www.w3.org/1999/XSL/Transform"
    version="1.0">

<xsl:import href="inlines.xsl"/>

<xsl:template match="chapter">
 <html><xsl:apply-templates/></html>
</xsl:template>

<xsl:template match="para">
 <p><xsl:apply-templates/></p>
</xsl:template>

<xsl:template match="chapter/title">
```

```
  <h1><xsl:apply-templates/></h1>
  </xsl:template>

  <xsl:template match="emphasis">
   <i><xsl:apply-templates/></i>
  </xsl:template>

</xsl:stylesheet>
```

If inlines.xsl looks like this,

```
<!-- xq196.xsl (inlines.xsl) -->

<xsl:stylesheet xmlns:xsl="http://www.w3.org/1999/XSL/Transform"
    version="1.0">

  <xsl:template match="emphasis">
   <b><xsl:apply-templates/></b>
  </xsl:template>

  <xsl:template match="literal">
   <tt><xsl:apply-templates/></tt>
  </xsl:template>

</xsl:stylesheet>
```

the XSLT processor will treat makehtml2.xsl as if it looked like this:

```
<!-- xq197.xsl -->

<xsl:stylesheet xmlns:xsl="http://www.w3.org/1999/XSL/Transform"
    version="1.0">

  <xsl:template match="emphasis">
   <i><xsl:apply-templates/></i>
  </xsl:template>

  <xsl:template match="literal">
   <tt><xsl:apply-templates/></tt>
  </xsl:template>

  <xsl:template match="chapter">
   <html><xsl:apply-templates/></html>
  </xsl:template>

  <xsl:template match="para">
   <p><xsl:apply-templates/></p>
  </xsl:template>

  <xsl:template match="chapter/title">
   <h1><xsl:apply-templates/></h1>
  </xsl:template>

</xsl:stylesheet>
```

The inlines.xsl stylesheet's "literal" template rule was added to the normalized makehtml2.xsl stylesheet, but the same stylesheet's "emphasis" template rule was ignored. Both makehtml2.xsl and inlines.xsl have template rules with a match pattern of "emphasis", and because inlines.xsl was imported and not included, an XSLT processor will use the "emphasis" template rule in makehtml2.xsl and not the one in inlines.xsl. The XSLT processor will add `emphasis` element nodes to the result tree, surrounded by the `i` start- and end-tags shown in makehtml2.xsl and not by the `b` tags in the imported "emphasis" template rule in inlines.xsl.

WARNING   If the example above had used `xsl:include` instead of `xsl:import`, the presence of two `xsl:template` elements with a match pattern of "emphasis" would have been an error.

As with inclusion, there's no limit to the levels of importing you may use. Your imported stylesheets may import other stylesheets, which may import a fourth level of stylesheets, and so on—as long as no file ultimately tries to include itself.

Any `xsl:import` element must come before any other elements from the XSLT namespace in a stylesheet. This way, the XSLT processor knows that, when it finds a template rule with the same match pattern as one in an imported template rule, it can forget about the imported one and use the most recently found one.

For a more industrial-strength demonstration of the difference between `xsl:include` and `xsl:import`, here's a real-life example—the stylesheet I use to create HTML versions of this book when I want a nicely formatted hard copy to proofread. Because I'm using the DocBook DTD, I use Norm Walsh's DocBook stylesheets (http://www.nwalsh.com/docbook/xsl/), but I wanted to make changes to my own copy of the stylesheets. For example, Norm's stylesheets italicize all `emphasis` elements, but I want emphasized text within `literallayout` elements to be bolded and not italicized so that readers can more easily see the important parts of the book's sample stylesheets and XML documents. (The previous sample stylesheets all include sections tagged as `emphasis` elements.) To make these changes, I edited the files included as part of Norm's stylesheet and added a comment with my name in them so that I could locate these changes if I ever had to make them again to a newer version of the stylesheet.

Since I sometimes write using a notebook computer running Linux and sometimes on a desktop computer running Windows, I had to remember which stylesheet files I edited and then copy them to the other computer. I just zipped up all the stylesheet files and unzipped them on the other machine. While this is a simple procedure, it still leaves too much room for error, and the more changes I made, the more trouble it would be to upgrade to a newer version of the DocBook stylesheets.

By using `xsl:import` and `xsl:include`, most of these problems go away. Here's the complete main stylesheet that I use when I want to create an HTML version of this book now:

```
<!-- xq198.xsl -->

<xsl:stylesheet xmlns:xsl="http://www.w3.org/1999/XSL/Transform"
    version="1.0">

 <xsl:import href="/usr/local/lib/xml/xsl/docbook/html/docbook.xsl"/>
```

```
  <xsl:include href="dbMods.xsl"/>

</xsl:stylesheet>
```

All this stylesheet does is *import* the main DocBook stylesheet file (a stylesheet that, as I mentioned, includes many component files) and then *include* a stylesheet that I wrote called dbMods.xsl. Now, when I want to change something in my copy of the DocBook stylesheet, I copy the appropriate `xsl:template` element from the source file in the /usr/local/lib/xml/xsl/docbook/html/ directory to my dbMods.xsl stylesheet and make my changes there. Here are two edited `xsl:template` elements:

```
<!-- xq199.xsl (dbMods.xml excerpt) -->

<xsl:template match="literallayout/emphasis">
  <b><xsl:apply-templates/></b>
</xsl:template>

<xsl:template match="ulink">
  <a>
    <xsl:attribute name="href">
      <xsl:value-of select="@url"/>
    </xsl:attribute>
    <!-- bd added following line -->
    <tt><xsl:value-of select="@url"/></tt>
    <xsl:apply-templates/>
  </a>
</xsl:template>
```

The first adds b tags around any emphasis element that is a child of a `literallayout` element. When you download Norm's DocBook stylesheet, it contains a template rule with a pattern of "emphasis" that adds i tags around emphasis elements. Because the dbMods.xsl "literallayout/emphasis" template is more specific than that (it doesn't match all emphasis nodes, but only the ones that are children of `literallayout` elements), an XSLT processor will use that template for those emphasis elements.

The second template above overrides one in the imported DocBook stylesheet. The regular DocBook version of the template for the `ulink` element type adds an a element that uses the source tree `ulink` element's `url` attribute as its `href` attribute value. However, it doesn't add any contents between the result tree's a tags, and I wanted the `url` value to show up there, so I added the line that puts the value between tt ("teletype") tags for the HTML result tree version. The comment about adding that line helps me to remember the difference between the original template and my altered version.

My dbMods.xsl file has many more template rules that I copied from the original DocBook stylesheet files and then revised. Taking these revisions from my Linux notebook to my Windows desktop machine is easy: I just bring the dbMods.xsl file. (The actual stylesheet file that includes docbook.xsl and imports dbMods.xsl is slightly different on the Windows machine from the one you see above because docbook.xsl is not in a directory named /usr/local/lib/xml/xsl/docbook/html/ on the Windows machine.)

When a new version of the DocBook stylesheet comes out, I just install it into a new directory, edit the value of the href attribute in my xsl:import element to point at the new version's docbook.xsl file, and I'm all set.

5.3   NAMED TEMPLATES

Most xsl:template elements get applied to nodes because their match attribute names a certain kind of node. An XSLT processor that finds one of those nodes applies a particular template to it if no other template applies more directly to that node. If an xsl:template element has a name attribute, you can use this name to call the template whenever you want instead of waiting for the XSLT processor to decide that it's the most appropriate template to apply to a particular node. In practice, few xsl:template elements have both a match and name attribute. Most templates are designed to use one or the other.

How would you use a template that only had a name attribute? Imagine that we're converting the following to HTML, and we want to bold the result tree version of the winery and product elements.

```
<wine grape="Cabernet">
  <winery>Duckpond</winery>
  <product>Merit Selection</product>
  <year>1996</year>
  <price>11.99</price>
</wine>
```

The first xsl:template element in the following stylesheet has no match attribute, so the XSLT processor will never apply that template to any node unless it's explicitly told to do so. The second and third templates do exactly that by using the xsl:call-template element.

```
<!-- xq202.xsl: converts xq201.xml into xq203.xml -->

<xsl:template name="boldIt">
  <b><xsl:apply-templates/></b>
</xsl:template>

<xsl:template match="winery">
  <p><xsl:call-template name="boldIt"/></p>
</xsl:template>

<xsl:template match="product">
  <p><xsl:call-template name="boldIt"/></p>
</xsl:template>

<xsl:template match="year | price">
  <p><xsl:apply-templates/></p>
</xsl:template>
```

With the sample document above, the stylesheet gives us this result:

```
<p><b>Duckpond</b></p>
<p><b>Merit Selection</b></p>
<p>1996</p>
<p>11.99</p>
```

(Keep in mind that there are more efficient ways to bold this source document's `winery` and `product` elements. The above is just a simple demonstration of how named templates work.) The content of both the "winery" and "product" template rules is a p element with an `xsl:call-templates` element inside it. The `xsl:call-template` elements' required name attribute identifies the template to call: the "boldIt" template defined above them.

> **TIP**   This difference between letting the XSLT processor call templates as needed and explicitly calling them with the `xsl:call-template` instruction is viewed by XSLT developers as a philosophical difference in the approach to stylesheet structure. The former is known as the "push" approach because the XSLT processor pushes the source tree's nodes through the stylesheet; the latter is called the "pull" approach because the stylesheet pulls the source tree nodes as needed.

Because named templates can store a collection of code that you can use from various points in the stylesheet (even from inside other named templates), they can take the role of subroutines or functions used by many other programming languages. When you declare a parameter in a named template with the `xsl:param` element, the calling template can pass a new value for the parameter by using the `xsl:with-param` instruction, making the named template more versatile. (See section 5.8.2, "Parameters," page 169, for more on passing parameters to named templates.)

This ability to function as subroutines which accept passed parameters makes named templates useful as building blocks in large, complex stylesheets. Many large stylesheets have a library of named templates that call each other. In fact, a named template can even call itself. This plays a key role in the recursion that stands in for the "for" and "while" loops found in many other programming languages. (See "Arbitrary repetition with named template recursion," on page 122 for more on this.)

5.4   *DEBUGGING*

When your stylesheet doesn't do exactly what you want it to, and you don't know why, what resources are available to figure it out? In other words, how do you debug a buggy stylesheet?

For now, I know of no XSLT equivalent to the kind of integrated debugger commonly used with C++, Java, and Visual Basic development. These typically let you pause the execution of a program to look at the values of specific variables at the stopping point as well as the steps that lead to that point. Still, XSLT coding tricks and features of certain processors do exist that help to do what these integrated debuggers do: let you know what's really going on when a stylesheet doesn't behave the way you expected.

The techniques in this chapter are grouped by the categories of XSLT areas that can cause confusion. (For a discussion of one particularly confusing aspect of XSLT, see section 6.11, "Whitespace: preserving and controlling," page 229.)

5.4.1 Runtime messages, aborting processor execution

The xsl:message instruction is supposed to send a message to somewhere other than the result tree. Exactly where depends upon the processor. A command line processor typically displays the message on the screen, even if the XSLT processor's output is been redirected to a file.

> **WARNING** Some processors such as the msxml3.dll version of Microsoft's XML/XSLT processor don't do anything with the xsl:message elements, so check the documentation of your processor to see what to expect.

Like the most primitive method of debugging in any language (that is, a lot of extra "print" statements outputting variable names and values during execution), the xsl:message instruction can be used to give some insight into the inner workings of your stylesheet.

For example, let's look at a stylesheet that converts this wine element to HTML:

```
<wine grape="Cabernet">
  <winery>Duckpond</winery>
  <product>Merit Selection</product>
  <year>1996</year>
  <price>11.99</price>
</wine>
```

The stylesheet has an xsl:message element inside an xsl:if element that only lets the xsl:message instruction do its job if the bodyTextSize parameter is set to something other than the default value. (See section 5.1.1, "Conditional statements with 'If' and 'Choose' (case) statements," page 110, and section 5.8.2, "Parameters," page 169, if you're unfamiliar with these.)

```
<!-- xq578.xsl: converts xq580.xml into xq583.html. -->
<xsl:stylesheet xmlns:xsl="http://www.w3.org/1999/XSL/Transform"
    version="1.0">

  <xsl:output method="html"/>

  <xsl:param name="bodyTextSize">10pt</xsl:param>

  <xsl:template match="/">
    <xsl:if test="$bodyTextSize != '10pt'">
      <xsl:message>bodyTextSize default value overridden
      with value of <xsl:value-of select="$bodyTextSize"/>.
      </xsl:message>
    </xsl:if>
    <xsl:apply-templates/>
  </xsl:template>
```

```
<xsl:template match="winery">
  <b><font size="{$bodyTextSize}"><xsl:apply-templates/>
  <xsl:text> </xsl:text>
  <xsl:value-of select="../@grape"/></font></b><br/>
</xsl:template>

<xsl:template match="product">
  <i><font size="{$bodyTextSize}">
    <xsl:apply-templates/></font></i><br/>
</xsl:template>

<xsl:template match="year | price">
  <font size="{$bodyTextSize}"><xsl:apply-templates/></font><br/>
</xsl:template>

</xsl:stylesheet>
```

The following example shows this stylesheet being run with the `wine` document above using the Sablotron XSLT processor. The stylesheet includes an `xsl:param` element named `bodyTextSize` that gets overridden at the command line with a value of "8pt".

```
C:\dat>sabcmd xq578.xsl xq580.xml $bodyTextSize=8pt > xq583.html

Warning [code:460] [URI:file://C:/dat/xq578.xsl] [line:11]
[node:element '<xsl:message>']
   xsl:message (bodyTextSize default value overridden
       with value of 8pt.
       )
```

Because the `bodyTextSize` value is not "10pt" for this run of the stylesheet, the `xsl:if` instruction's test is true, so its contents gets evaluated: An `xsl:message` instruction sends the user a message about the default `bodyTextSize` value being overridden. Although the command line redirects the XSLT processor's output to a file called xq583.html, the message still appears on the screen. (Sablotron happens to enclose it in parentheses after some introductory text. Other processors may handle it differently.) The xq583.html file was created without the message in it:

```
<b><font size="8pt">Duckpond Cabernet</font></b><br/>
<i><font size="8pt">Merit Selection</font></i><br/>
<font size="8pt">1996</font><br/>
<font size="8pt">11.99</font><br/>
```

The insertion of a parameter value ("8pt") in the text output by the `xsl:message` instruction illustrates how handy this element can be for reporting on the state of the system as the processor applies the stylesheet.

The `xsl:message` instruction's `terminate` attribute lets the stylesheet abort the execution of the processor. Its default value is "no"; the following stylesheet sets it to "yes". Except for the `xsl:if` instruction's test condition and the `xsl:message` element inside that `xsl:if` element, the stylesheet is identical to the previous one:

```
<!-- xq581.xsl: converts xq580.xml. -->

<xsl:stylesheet xmlns:xsl="http://www.w3.org/1999/XSL/Transform"
    version="1.0">

  <xsl:output method="html"/>

  <xsl:param name="bodyTextSize">10pt</xsl:param>

  <xsl:template match="/">
    <xsl:if test="not(contains($bodyTextSize,'pt'))">
      <xsl:message terminate="yes">bodyTextSize must be specified
      in points (pt).</xsl:message>
    </xsl:if>
    <xsl:apply-templates/>
  </xsl:template>

  <xsl:template match="winery">
    <b><font size="{$bodyTextSize}"><xsl:apply-templates/>
    <xsl:text> </xsl:text>
    <xsl:value-of select="../@grape"/></font></b><br/>
  </xsl:template>

  <xsl:template match="product">
    <i><font size="{$bodyTextSize}">
      <xsl:apply-templates/></font></i><br/>
  </xsl:template>

  <xsl:template match="year | price">
    <font size="{$bodyTextSize}"><xsl:apply-templates/></font><br/>
  </xsl:template>

</xsl:stylesheet>
```

The test condition in this stylesheet's xsl:if instruction uses the not() and contains() functions to check whether the value of bodyTextSize is missing the string "pt". If so, the message about the need to specify bodyTextSize in points is output, and because of the terminate value of "yes" in the xsl:message element, the XSLT processor halts after outputting the message. (The xq585.html file created by this command line is 0 bytes.)

```
C:\dat>sabcmd xq581.xsl xq580.xml $bodyTextSize=2feet > xq585.xml
Error [code:255] [URI:file://C:/dat/xq581.xsl] [line:11]
 [node:element '<xsl:message>']
  xsl:message (bodyTextSize must be specified
       in points (pt).) - terminating
```

Despite XSLT's lack of interactivity, this ability to output messages about the state of the stylesheet's execution and to even halt that execution gives you a tool for checking what's going on under the hood when the results aren't what you expected. It also lets you make your stylesheets more bulletproof, because an application that can check whether something went wrong (especially something with the data) and then deliver a sensible message to the user about the problem is a much more robust application.

5.4.2   Keeping track of your elements

As the size and complexity of your source documents and stylesheets get larger, you have more to keep track of and more potential for losing track of something. One technique for troubleshooting is to make sure that every element type is accounted for in the stylesheet by never relying on the default template rules for processing elements.

We'll use the following document as a sample source document to demonstrate the identification of elements that a stylesheet might miss. Imagine that its `chapter` and `appendix` elements are much, much bigger and that it has many more than those shown here:

```
<book>
  <chapter><title>From Book I</title>
<para>Then with expanded wings he steers his flight</para>
<para>Aloft, incumbent on the dusky Air</para>
</chapter>

<chapter><title>More From Book I</title>
<para>For who can yet believe, though after loss</para>
<para>That all these puissant Leginos, whose exile</para>
</chapter>

<afterword>
<para>That was some poem, huh?</para>
</afterword>

<appendix><title>The Author</title>
<para>John Milton was born in London in 1608.</para>
<para>He died in 1674.</para>
</appendix>

<appendix><title>Glossary</title>
<para>puissant</para>
<para>Leginos</para>
</appendix>

</book>
```

The following stylesheet converts this document to an HTML file. Its first template rule covers all element types needing no special handling, sending their contents to the result tree. In other words, this template rule makes explicit what the default XSLT element handling template rule makes implicit:

```
<!-- xq587.xsl: converts xq586.xml into xq588.html -->
<xsl:stylesheet xmlns:xsl="http://www.w3.org/1999/XSL/Transform"
    version="1.0">
  <xsl:output method="html"/>

  <xsl:template match="chapter | appendix | afterword">
    <xsl:apply-templates/>
  </xsl:template>

  <xsl:template match="*">
    <h1><xsl:value-of select="name()"/> ELEMENT UNACCOUNTED
      FOR BY STYLESHEET: <xsl:apply-templates/></h1>
```

```
</xsl:template>

<xsl:template match="book">
  <html><body><xsl:apply-templates/></body></html>
</xsl:template>

<xsl:template match="title">
  <h1><xsl:apply-templates/></h1>
</xsl:template>

<xsl:template match="chapter/para">
  <p><font face="times"><xsl:apply-templates/></font></p>
</xsl:template>

<xsl:template match="appendix/para">
  <p><font face="arial"><xsl:apply-templates/></font></p>
</xsl:template>

</xsl:stylesheet>
```

The second template rule overrides the default element handling rule by specifying
"*" as its match condition. This template rule's job is to draw attention to any elements not addressed by any other template rules in the stylesheet. After an
`xsl:value-of` instruction to add the stray element's name to the result tree, the
template has a message to add to the result tree about why that template was called.
The message is in all capital letters, and the whole thing is enclosed by an `h1` element
to really draw attention to the problem. (You wouldn't want a production version of
your stylesheet creating such output. The `xsl:message` instruction described in
the previous section is a better way to draw attention to something like this.) Running this stylesheet against the sample input shows that a `para` element exists that
has no template with which to address it:

```
<html><body>
  <h1>From Book I</h1>
<p><font face="times">Then with expanded wings he steers his flight</
font></p>
<p><font face="times">Aloft, incumbent on the dusky Air</font></p>

<h1>More From Book I</h1>
<p><font face="times">For who can yet believe, though after loss</font></p>
<p><font face="times">That all these puissant Leginos, whose exile</font></
p>

<h1>para ELEMENT UNACCOUNTED
        FOR BY STYLESHEET: That was some poem, huh?</h1>

<h1>The Author</h1>
<p><font face="arial">John Milton was born in London in 1608.</font></p>
<p><font face="arial">He died in 1674.</font></p>

<h1>Glossary</h1>
<p><font face="arial">puissant</font></p>
<p><font face="arial">Leginos</font></p>

</body></html>
```

Where was this `para` element? A quick glance at the source document would show that it was in the `afterword` element, but remember that we're pretending that this sample source document has many huge chapters and appendixes—it's too big to quickly glance through. So how do we find the `para` element if we can't glance through the document? We know from looking at the stylesheet that it's not in a `chapter` element and it's not in an `appendix` element, or the catch-all template rule wouldn't have caught it. So how can we find out this stray `para` element's ancestry? We can do it by listing out its ancestors.

The following template rule, when added to the previous stylesheet, lists the names of all the element types enclosing any `para` elements not caught by more specific template rules:

```
<!-- xq589.xsl: converts xq586.xml into xq590.html -->
  <xsl:template match="para">
    <h1>Unaccounted for para element</h1>
    <h2>Ancestors</h2>
    <xsl:for-each select="ancestor::*">
      <xsl:value-of select="name()"/>
      <xsl:if test="position() != last()">
        <xsl:text>, </xsl:text>
      </xsl:if>
    </xsl:for-each>
    <h2>Content</h2>
    <xsl:apply-templates/>
  </xsl:template>
```

Along with the `para` elements contents (under the h2 element at the end) and headers for the contents and ancestor list, this template has an `xsl:for-each` instruction that lists the names of all the nodes in the `ancestor` axis of the `para` element. (The template performs another nice trick along the way: instead of adding a comma after every element type name in the list, it adds commas after every one but the last one. The "position() != last()" condition prevents the last ancestor's name from getting the `xsl:text` node with the comma after it.) The result shows that the `para` element's ancestors are `book` and `afterword` elements.

```
<html><body>
  <h1>From Book I</h1>
<p><font face="times">Then with expanded wings he steers his flight</font></p>
<p><font face="times">Aloft, incumbent on the dusky Air</font></p>

<h1>More From Book I</h1>
<p><font face="times">For who can yet believe, though after loss</font></p>
<p><font face="times">That all these puissant Leginos, whose exile</font></p>

<h1>Unaccounted for para element</h1>
<h2>Ancestors</h2>
book, afterword
<h2>Content</h2>
```

```
That was some poem, huh?

<h1>The Author</h1>
<p><font face="arial">John Milton was born in London in 1608.</font></p>
<p><font face="arial">He died in 1674.</font></p>

<h1>Glossary</h1>
<p><font face="arial">puissant</font></p>
<p><font face="arial">Leginos</font></p>

</body></html>
```

WARNING   The xsl:apply-templates instruction after the <h2>Content</h2>
part might add too much text if you use this template rule to catch large
elements, so save it for elements whose content you know will be a reason-
able length.

With a more complex document, the ancestor list would be longer, and this template's usefulness would be more apparent. As with many debugging techniques, this
is hardly worth the trouble when you can read through your entire program and
input in a minute or two, but the larger your project, the more you'll appreciate this
automated way to zero in on elements not caught by your stylesheet.

5.4.3   Tracing a processor's steps

The XSLT specification doesn't require XSLT processors to offer any features that let
you trace their progress as they apply a stylesheet to a document, but many processors
include these features anyway. When you release software whose job is to conform to
a public standard (that is, to perform all the same tasks as other software in the same
category), you want to offer something to get people to choose your software over the
competition's. Debugging features are an obvious choice.

These features can give you so much information about the XSLT processor's
progress that it's easiest to demonstrate them with a simple stylesheet and source document. We'll apply this stylesheet

```
<!-- xq594.xsl: converts xq595.xml into xq597.html -->
<xsl:stylesheet xmlns:xsl="http://www.w3.org/1999/XSL/Transform"
    version="1.0">
  <xsl:output method="html"/>

  <xsl:template match="story">
    <html><body>
    <xsl:apply-templates/></body></html>
  </xsl:template>

  <xsl:template match="title">
    <h1><xsl:apply-templates/></h1>
  </xsl:template>

  <xsl:template match="para">
    <p><xsl:apply-templates/></p>
   </xsl:template>

</xsl:stylesheet>
```

to this document

```
<story><title>Chapter 1</title>
   <para>A Dungeon horrible, on all sides round</para>
   <para>More unexpert, I boast not: them let those</para>
</story>
```

to create this result document:

```
<html>
   <body>
      <h1>Chapter 1</h1>

      <p>A Dungeon horrible, on all sides round</p>

      <p>More unexpert, I boast not: them let those</p>

   </body>
</html>
```

To get a sample of what kind of extra debugging information XSLT processors may make available, this section looks at two processors: Xalan and Saxon. By the time you read this, Xalan and Saxon may have more debugging features than those listed here. Check the "command line help" section of each entry in appendix B, which describes how to tell each processor, whether Saxon, Xalan, or another, to list its command line options. This is a good place to see what's available for any processors you have installed.

Xalan's Java and C++ XSLT processors offer several command line switches to request information about the processor's activity. The -TT switch tells the processor to trace the templates as they are being called. For the preceding stylesheet and source document, the following is the trace output:

```
Line #0, Column #0: xsl:template match="/"
Line #7, Column #31: xsl:template match="story"
Line #12, Column #31: xsl:template match="title"
Line #16, Column #30: xsl:template match="para"
Line #16, Column #30: xsl:template match="para"
```

The trace output lists the name of each template and its location in the stylesheet as it gets called. As the first line shows, the output even lists default templates when they are called. (The stylesheet has no "/" template rule, so "Line #0, Column #0" refers to a default XSLT template.)

Xalan's -TG switch traces each event, generated by the reading of the input to which the processor may react:

```
STARTDOCUMENT
STARTELEMENT: html
STARTELEMENT: body
STARTELEMENT: h1
CHARACTERS: Chapter 1
ENDELEMENT: h1
IGNORABLEWHITESPACE
```

```
STARTELEMENT: p
CHARACTERS: A Dungeon horrible, on all sides round
ENDELEMENT: p
IGNORABLEWHITESPACE
STARTELEMENT: p
CHARACTERS: More unexpert, I boast not: them let those
ENDELEMENT: p
IGNORABLEWHITESPACE
ENDELEMENT: body
ENDELEMENT: html
```

This is a near-complete listing of *exactly* what the processor sees in the source document, which can give you a clearer picture of why the processor performs the actions that it does as it goes through the source tree.

The Saxon Java parser offers a -T option that sets a TraceListener class to output trace information. When used with the stylesheet and source document above, the following (with some carriage returns added) is only the beginning of the information it outputs:

```
<trace>
<Top-level element="xsl:output" line="5" file="file:/home/dat/listing
s/xq594.xsl" precedence="0"/>
<Top-level element="xsl:template" line="7"
  file="file:/home/dat/listings/xq594.xsl" precedence="0"/>
<Top-level element="xsl:template" line="12"
  file="file:/home/dat/listings/xq594.xsl" precedence="0"/>
<Top-level element="xsl:template" line="16"
  file="file:/home/dat/listings/xq594.xsl" precedence="0"/>
<Instruction element="xsl:output" line="5">
</Instruction> <!-- xsl:output -->
<Source node="/story[1]" line="1" mode="*default*">
 <Instruction element="xsl:template" line="7">
   <Instruction element="html" line="8">
    <Instruction element="body" line="8">
     <Instruction element="xsl:apply-templates" line="9">
      <Source node="/story[1]/title[1]" line="1" mode="*default*">
       <Instruction element="xsl:template" line="12">
```

In addition to being detailed, this trace information is also well-formed XML, which means that you can write XSLT stylesheets to do anything you want with it. Considering the level of detail available in this trace output, one obvious application of XSLT stylesheets to this information would be the extracting and summarizing of specific subsets of it.

5.4.4 Listing the nodes in an XPath expression

XPath expressions and match patterns offer so many ways to describe a given set of nodes that the assembled pieces of your XPath expression may not always describe the exact set of nodes that you intended. When you think that a template is sending one set of nodes to the result tree (or iterating through that set of nodes to look for something) while it's actually addressing a different set of nodes, the results can be disorienting.

Fortunately, the `xsl:for-each` instruction lets you list the nodes described by a given XPath expression, showing you exactly who this node set's members are. Some examples in section 2.1, "Location paths, axes, node tests, and predicates," page 24, especially near the end of that section, demonstrate how to list out all the nodes represented by a given XPath expression.

5.5   EXTENSIONS TO XSLT

If the specialized elements of the XSLT namespace and the combined functions of XSLT and XPath aren't enough to perform the transformations you need, XSLT provides ways to incorporate additional instruction elements and functions into your stylesheets. Most XSLT processors offer several extra extension elements and functions to distinguish themselves from the competition. This section describes how a stylesheet can gracefully handle the possibility that the XSLT processor doesn't recognize an extension designed for use with another processor.

5.5.1   Extension elements

There are three categories of elements that you can find in an XSLT stylesheet:

- elements from the XSLT namespace that tell the processor how to transform the source tree into the result tree

- literal result elements of any namespace you like that get added to the result tree just as they are shown in the stylesheet

- extension elements: customized instruction elements that can be used along with the instructions from the XSLT namespace

WARNING   Elements from the XSLT namespace fall into two categories: top-level elements, which are children of the `xsl:stylesheet` element with general instructions about handling the source document, and the children of the `xsl:template` elements known as instructions, which give specific instructions about nodes to add to the result tree. Extension elements cannot be top-level elements; they are always new instructions.

It's an important part of an XSLT processor's job to recognize all elements in a stylesheet from the XSLT namespace and to carry out their instructions. If literal result elements can be from any namespace (see section 4.3, "Namespaces," page 92, for more on this), letting you add elements from the HTML, XLink, or any other namespace to the result tree, how will a processor know which elements are extension elements? The processor knows because the stylesheet must explicitly list which namespaces are to be treated as extension element namespaces in the `extension-element-prefixes` attribute.

Let's look at an example. Remember how, once you assign a value to a variable in an XSLT stylesheet, you can't change the value of that variable? Michael Kay added an assign extension element to his Saxon processor that lets you change a variable's value all you want. In the following stylesheet, the http://icl.com/saxon namespace (the one his processor expects to find for Saxon extension elements) is declared as a namespace with a prefix of "saxon", and this "saxon" namespace prefix is included in the value of the xsl:stylesheet element's extension-element-prefixes attribute:

```
<!-- xq610.xsl: converts xq610.xsl into xq611.txt -->
<!-- Must be run with the Saxon processor. -->
<xsl:stylesheet xmlns:xsl="http://www.w3.org/1999/XSL/Transform"
     xmlns:saxon="http://icl.com/saxon"
     extension-element-prefixes="saxon"
     version="1.0">
<xsl:output method="xml" omit-xml-declaration="yes"/>

  <xsl:variable name="color"
       saxon:assignable="yes">red</xsl:variable>

  <xsl:template match="/">

    <saxon:assign name="color">blue</saxon:assign>

    The color variable has the following value:
    <xsl:value-of select="$color"/>
  </xsl:template>

</xsl:stylesheet>
```

TIP The extension-element-prefix attribute is usually included with the xsl:stylesheet element, but can be added to any literal result element or extension element. If it's an attribute of an element other than the stylesheet's root xsl:stylesheet element, then it's only effective within the element where it's an attribute—in other words, any extension elements from the specified namespace can only be used in that element or in one of its descendants. That's why it's more convenient to declare any extension namespaces in an extension-element-prefixes attribute of the xsl:stylesheet element, because then you can use the extension elements anywhere you want in the document.

The preceding stylesheet, which you can run using any XML document as input, doesn't do much. First, it declares a variable named "color" and assigns it the value "red". Next, the single template rule in the stylesheet adds the phrase "The color variable has the following value:" to the result tree, followed by the variable's value as put there by the xsl:value-of instruction. The special part comes inside that template rule just before this text gets added to the result tree: the saxon:assign extension element assigns the value "blue" to the "color" variable. (XSLT also allows extension attributes as well as extension elements, and the special Saxon attribute saxon:assignable is added to XSLT's xsl:variable element to let the saxon:assign element know that changing this variable's value is Okay.) The output, when run with the Saxon processor, shows that the variable's value was successfully changed:

```
    The color variable has the following value:
    blue
```

When run with the Xalan Java processor, or any others besides Saxon, the `saxon:assign` element has no effect:

```
    The color variable has the following value:
    red
```

A lack of error messages might be considered a good thing, but in this case it's a bad thing: a stylesheet instruction failed to execute, so a message about this failure would make for a more robust system. Fortunately, XSLT offers two ways to check whether an extension element will work or not: `fallback` and the `element-available()` function.

If an XSLT processor doesn't implement a particular extension element, it must look for an `xsl:fallback` child of that element and add its contents to the result tree. In the following revision of the preceding stylesheet, the `xsl:fallback` element has no contents to add to the result tree, but instead sends an `xsl:message` text string to wherever such strings go for the processor in question. (See section 5.4.1, "Runtime messages, aborting processor execution," page 134, for more on the `xsl:message` element.)

```
<!-- xq617.xsl: converts xq617.xsl to xq637.txt  -->
<xsl:stylesheet xmlns:xsl="http://www.w3.org/1999/XSL/Transform"
    xmlns:saxon="http://icl.com/saxon"
    extension-element-prefixes="saxon"
    version="1.0">
  <xsl:output method="xml" omit-xml-declaration="yes"/>

  <xsl:variable name="color"
      saxon:assignable="yes">red</xsl:variable>

  <xsl:template match="/">

    <saxon:assign name="color">blue<xsl:fallback>
        <xsl:message>This XSLT processor doesn't support saxon:assign.
        </xsl:message></xsl:fallback></saxon:assign>

    The color variable has the following value:
    <xsl:value-of select="$color"/>
  </xsl:template>

</xsl:stylesheet>
```

When run with the Saxon processor, the stylesheet creates the same result as the earlier Saxon run. No `xsl:message` text appears at the command line, because the `saxon:assign` element enclosing the `xsl:fallback` element executed successfully. When run with the Xalan Java parser, however, the stylesheet creates the same result as with the earlier Xalan run and sends the following message to the command line window:

```
This XSLT processor doesn't support saxon:assign.
```

While the xsl:fallback element gives you a way to handle the failure of an extension element, the Boolean element-available() function offers a way to check whether the extension element is supported before even trying to execute it.

The following revision of the previous stylesheet has an xsl:choose element that uses this function to test whether the saxon:assign element is supported. If so, the saxon:assign element inside the xsl:when element gets evaluated. If not, the message "This XSLT processor doesn't support saxon:assign" gets sent wherever that XSLT processor sends such messages:

```
<!-- xq619.xsl: converts xq619.xsl  -->
<xsl:stylesheet xmlns:xsl="http://www.w3.org/1999/XSL/Transform"
     xmlns:saxon="http://icl.com/saxon"
     extension-element-prefixes="saxon"
     version="1.0">
<xsl:output method="xml" omit-xml-declaration="yes"/>

  <xsl:variable name="color"
       saxon:assignable="yes">red</xsl:variable>

  <xsl:template match="/">

    <xsl:choose>
      <xsl:when test="element-available('saxon:assign')">
        <saxon:assign name="color">blue</saxon:assign>
      </xsl:when>
      <xsl:otherwise>
        <xsl:message>This XSLT processor doesn't support saxon:assign.
        </xsl:message>
      </xsl:otherwise>
    </xsl:choose>
    The color variable has the following value:
    <xsl:value-of select="$color"/>
  </xsl:template>

</xsl:stylesheet>
```

The results, when run with Saxon and then Xalan Java, are the same as with the previous version of the stylesheet. With Saxon, the result tells us that the color variable was successfully set to "blue", and no extra messages appear in the command prompt window. When run with Xalan Java, the result tells us that the color variable remains at the original setting of "red" and the xsl:message element sends the message about the lack of support for saxon:assign to the command prompt window.

5.5.2 Using built-in extension functions

An XSLT processor can add functions to the selection required of it by the XSLT and XPath specifications. To use one of these extension functions, you only have to declare the namespace and then reference that namespace when calling the function. (When using extension elements, you need the extension-element-prefixes attribute to tell the processor that extension elements from certain namespaces will be used in the stylesheet, but there's no need for this when using extension functions.)

To demonstrate the use of an extension function available in an XSLT processor, we'll look at Xalan Java's `tokenize()` function, which is similar to the Perl programming language's `split()` function in that it splits up a string whenever it finds a certain character. If you tell the function to split up "red,green,light blue" at the commas, you'll get "red", "green" and "light blue". Xalan's `tokenize()` function accepts two parameters: a string of text delimited by a certain character, and an optional string showing the characters used as the delimiter (the default delimiters are the whitespace characters). The function then splits up the string wherever it finds the delimiting character, creating a node list that your stylesheet can iterate across using an `xsl:for-each` instruction.

Our stylesheet will use the `tokenize()` function to split up the fields in the employee elements of the following document:

```
<employees>
<employee>Herbert,Johnny,09/01/1998,95000</employee>
<employee>Hill,Graham,08/20/2000,89000</employee>
<employee>Hill,Phil,04/23/1999/100000</employee>
<employee>Moss,Sterling,10/16/2000,97000</employee>
</employees>
```

The following stylesheet converts these `employee` elements into a table. The two parameters passed to the `tokenize()` function are "." (an abbreviation of `"self::node()"`, thereby passing the contents of the employee context node), and a comma enclosed in single quotes to show that it's the delimiting character in the first string. The stylesheet also uses the `function-available()` function that must be supported by all XSLT processors to check whether the `tokenize()` function is available for use by the stylesheet. If it is, the contents of the `xsl:when` element are added to the result tree. The `tokenize()` function splits up the employee contents into a node list, and the `xsl:for-each` instruction goes through that list, adding the contents of each node to the result tree enclosed by an `entry` element. If the function isn't available, the `xsl:otherwise` instruction just adds the contents of the source tree `employee` element inside the `row` element as one big `entry` element.

```
<!-- xq620.xsl: converts xq621.xml into xq622.xml, xq623.xml -->
<xsl:stylesheet xmlns:xsl="http://www.w3.org/1999/XSL/Transform"
    xmlns:xalan="http://xml.apache.org/xalan"
    exclude-result-prefixes="xalan"
    version="1.0">
<xsl:output method="xml" omit-xml-declaration="yes"/>

  <xsl:template match="employees">
    <table>
      <xsl:apply-templates/>
    </table>
  </xsl:template>

  <xsl:template match="employee">
```

```
    <row>
      <xsl:choose>
        <xsl:when test="function-available('xalan:tokenize')">
          <xsl:for-each select="xalan:tokenize(.',')">
            <entry><xsl:value-of select="."/></entry>
          </xsl:for-each>
        </xsl:when>
        <xsl:otherwise>
          <entry><xsl:value-of select="."/></entry>
        </xsl:otherwise>
      </xsl:choose>
    </row>
  </xsl:template>

</xsl:stylesheet>
```

For the processor to recognize the function as an extension function, the stylesheet calls `tokenize()` using the namespace prefix ("saxon") that goes with the declaration identifying the namespace. An XSLT processor passes along namespace declarations for any referenced namespaces to the result tree, but we don't want this declaration in our result document, so the stylesheet has an `exclude-result-prefixes` attribute in the `xsl:stylesheet` element to prevent the declaration.

When run with the Xalan Java processor, the stylesheet splits up each `employee` element into separate `entry` elements in each row.

```
<table>
<row><entry>Herbert</entry><entry>Johnny</entry>
<entry>09/01/1998</entry><entry>95000</entry></row>
<row><entry>Hill</entry><entry>Graham</entry>
<entry>08/20/2000</entry><entry>89000</entry></row>
<row><entry>Hill</entry><entry>Phil</entry>
<entry>04/23/1999/100000</entry></row>
<row><entry>Moss</entry><entry>Sterling</entry>
<entry>10/16/2000</entry><entry>97000</entry></row>
</table>
```

When run with the Saxon XSLT processor, which doesn't support Xalan's `tokenize()` function, each `employee` element is added to the result tree as one big `entry` element.

```
<table>
<row><entry>Herbert,Johnny,09/01/1998,95000</entry></row>
<row><entry>Hill,Graham,08/20/2000,89000</entry></row>
<row><entry>Hill,Phil,04/23/1999/100000</entry></row>
<row><entry>Moss,Sterling,10/16/2000,97000</entry></row>
</table>
```

Saxon actually does have a `tokenize()` function, but because it is Saxon's own extension function, you have to use it by declaring the appropriate namespace and using that namespace to identify the function when calling it. If the stylesheet above was used in a production environment in which Xalan Java and Saxon were both available, the `xsl:choose` element could include another `xsl:when` element to check whether `saxon:tokenize()` is available and, if so, to use it.

Take a look through your XSLT processor's documentation to see what extension functions are available. Along with debugging features, this is another area where processor developers strive to stand out from the competition, because it's an obvious place to add features unavailable in other processors. It's also a place where developers can address any deficiencies they see in XSLT by adding features they feel should have been there in the first place.

5.6   NUMBERS AND MATH

XSLT itself doesn't offer much for manipulating numbers, but it is full of support for XPath's math capabilities that let you do all the basic kinds of arithmetic and a little more. Let's look at a stylesheet that demonstrates these capabilities by using the values from this document:

```
<numbers>
  <x>4</x>
  <y>3.2</y>
  <z>11</z>
</numbers>
```

Lines A through N of the stylesheet each make (or attempt to make) a different calculation. These calculations use the numbers in the document above and other numbers either hardcoded in the stylesheet or retrieved from functions that return numbers:

```
<!-- xq312.xsl: converts xq311.xml into xq313.txt -->
<xsl:stylesheet xmlns:xsl="http://www.w3.org/1999/XSL/Transform"
     version="1.0">
<xsl:output method="xml" omit-xml-declaration="yes"/>

<xsl:template match="numbers">
  A. 4 + 3.2       = <xsl:value-of select="x + y"/>
  B. 3.2 - 4       = <xsl:value-of select="y - x"/>
  C. 4 * 3.2       = <xsl:value-of select="x * y"/>
  D. 11/3.2        = <xsl:value-of select="z div y"/>
  E. 4 + 3.2 * 11  = <xsl:value-of select="x+y*z"/>
  F. (4 + 3.2) * 11 = <xsl:value-of select="(x+y)*z"/>
  G. 11 mod 4      = <xsl:value-of select="z mod x"/>
  H. 4 + 3.2 + 11  = <xsl:value-of select="sum(*)"/>
  I. floor(3.2)    = <xsl:value-of select="floor(y)"/>
  J. ceiling(3.2)  = <xsl:value-of select="ceiling(y)"/>
  K. round(3.2)    = <xsl:value-of select="round(y)"/>
  L. 11 + count(*) = <xsl:value-of select="11+count(*)"/>
  M. 3.2 + string-length("3.2") =
     <xsl:value-of select="y + string-length(y)"/>
  N. 11 + "hello"     = <xsl:value-of select="z + 'hello'"/>
</xsl:template>

</xsl:stylesheet>
```

Before we talk about what each line is doing, let's look at the result of applying the stylesheet to the `numbers` document:

```
A.  4 + 3.2         = 7.2
 B.  3.2 - 4         = -0.8
 C.  4 * 3.2         = 12.8
 D.  11/3.2          = 3.4375
 E.  4 + 3.2 * 11    = 39.2
 F.  (4 + 3.2) * 11  = 79.2
 G.  11 mod 4        = 3
 H.  4 + 3.2 + 11    = 18.2
 I.  floor(3.2)      = 3
 J.  ceiling(3.2)    = 4
 K.  round(3.2)      = 3
 L.  11 + count(*)   = 14
 M.  3.2 + string-length("3.2") =
     6.2
 N.  11 + "hello"    = NaN
```

The stylesheet has a single template rule for the source tree's `numbers` element. This template has a series of `xsl:value-of` instructions whose `select` attributes use the values of the `numbers` element's `x`, `y`, and `z` child elements to perform various mathematical tasks. Mathematical expressions like these can use the full power of XPath to say which element or attribute has a number they need. This stylesheet, however, is more concerned with demonstrating the range of mathematical operations available than with using fancy XPath expressions to retrieve elements and attributes from odd parts of a document.

Line A of the template adds the value of `x` (4) to the value of `y` (3.2) and puts their sum, 7.2, in the result tree. It's simple and straightforward, and it demonstrates that you're not limited to integers for stylesheet math.

Line B subtracts 4 from 3.2 for a result of -0.8. Negative numbers shouldn't pose any difficulties for XSLT processors.

> **WARNING** When using some XSLT processors, the use of decimal numbers may introduce a tiny error. For example, the "3.2 – 4" in this example comes out as "–0.7999999999999998" on some processors. While being off by .0000000000000002 isn't much, being off at all shows that math is not XSLT's strong point.

Line C multiplies 4 and 3.2, using the asterisk as the multiplication operator, for an answer of 12.8.

Line D divides the value of the `z` element (11), by 3.2, showing an XSLT processor's ability to perform floating-point division.

WARNING   Although most programming languages traditionally use the slash character to represent mathematical division, XPath already uses the slash to separate the steps in an XPath location path (for example, `wine/vintage` to represent the `vintage` child element of the `wine` element). Because of this, XPath and XSLT use the string "div" for division.

Lines E and F illustrate how parentheses have the same effect on operator precedence that they have in normal math notation: without them, multiplication happens before addition, so that 4 + 3.2 * 11 = 4 + 35.2. With the parentheses around the "4 + 3.2", addition happens first, so that (4 + 3.2) * 11 = 7.2 * 11.

Line G demonstrates the `mod` operator, which shows the remainder if you divide the first term by the second. The example shows that 11 modulo 4 equals 3, because 4 goes into 11 twice with 3 left over. This operator is great for checking whether one number divides into another evenly. Just check whether the larger number modulo the smaller equals zero.

Line H demonstrates the `sum()` function. With a node list as an argument, this function sums up all the numbers in that list. In the example, the asterisk means "all the children of the context node"—the numbers element's x, y, and z children.

Lines I and J demonstrate the `floor()` and `ceiling()` functions. If you pass either of these an integer, they return that integer. If you pass `floor()` a noninteger, it returns the highest integer below that number. In the example, `floor(3.2)` is 3. The `ceiling` function returns the smallest integer above a noninteger number; in the example, `ceiling(3.2)` equals 4.

Line K's `round()` function rounds off a noninteger by returning the closest integer. When 3.2 is passed to this function, it returns 3. Passing 3.5 or 3.6 to it would cause it to return a 4.

Line L incorporates another XPath function: `count()`, which returns the number of nodes in the set passed to it as an argument. (See section 3.7, "Counting elements and other nodes," page 61, for more on this function.) XPath offers several functions that, while not overtly mathematical, return numbers and can be used for any calculations you like: `count()`, `last()`, `position()`, and `string-length()`. Line M demonstrates this last one, which returns the length of a string.

Line N shows what happens when you try to perform math with something that isn't a number. When 11 gets added to the string "hello", the result is the string "NaN", an abbreviation for "Not a Number." When you pull a number out of an element's content or attribute value and then use it for a calculation, you can't always be sure that what you pulled is really a number, so XSLT's clearly defined behavior for the unworkable case makes it easier to check for and cope with in your code.

XSLT is about manipulating text, not numbers, but you can build on the mathematical operations provided as part of XSLT to perform more complicated calculations. For example, the following stylesheet, which accepts any document as input, computes the value of pi. The precision of the result depends on the value of the `iterations` variable:

```
<!-- xq314.xsl -->
<xsl:stylesheet xmlns:xsl="http://www.w3.org/1999/XSL/Transform"
     version="1.0">
<xsl:output method="text"/>

<!-- Compute pi. Based on Leibniz's algorithm that
        pi/4 = 1 - 1/3 + 1/5 - 1/7 + 1/9 - 1/11... which I did as
        pi = 4 - 4/3 + 4/5 - 4/7 + 4/9 - 4/11...
-->

<xsl:variable name="iterations" select="80000"/>

<xsl:template name="pi">
  <!-- named template called by main template below -->
  <xsl:param name="i">1</xsl:param>
  <xsl:param name="piValue">0</xsl:param>

  <xsl:choose>
  <!-- If there are more iterations to do, add the passed
       value of pi to another round of calculations. -->
  <xsl:when test="$i &lt;= $iterations">
    <xsl:call-template name="pi">
      <xsl:with-param name="i" select="$i + 4"/>
      <xsl:with-param name="piValue"
          select="$piValue + (4 div $i) - (4 div ($i + 2))"/>
    </xsl:call-template>
  </xsl:when>

  <!-- If no more iterations to do, add
       computed value to result tree. -->
  <xsl:otherwise>
   <xsl:value-of select="$piValue"/>
  </xsl:otherwise>

  </xsl:choose>

</xsl:template>

<xsl:template match="/">
  <xsl:call-template name="pi"/>
</xsl:template>

</xsl:stylesheet>
```

The repetition is implemented using a recursive named template (see "Arbitrary repetition with named template recursion," on page 122, for information about how these work). With the iterations setting shown, the stylesheet creates this result:

```
3.1415676535897985
```

With that many iterations, the answer is only accurate up to the first four digits after the decimal. Of course, if you seriously want to compute the value of pi, there are many more appropriate languages, but it's nice to know that you can push XSLT to do some fairly complex math when necessary.

5.7 STRINGS

XSLT is a language for manipulating XML documents. XML documents are text. When you're manipulating text, functions for searching strings and pulling out substrings are indispensable for rearranging documents to create new documents. The XPath string functions incorporated by XSLT give you a lot of power when you're manipulating element character data, attribute values, and any other strings of text that your stylesheet can access.

5.7.1 Extracting and comparing strings

To demonstrate XSLT's string manipulation functions, we'll use the following simple document:

```
<poem>
  <verse>Seest thou yon dreary Plain, forlorn and wild,</verse>
  <verse>


      The seat of desolation, void of light,


  </verse>
</poem>
```

(Note how the second verse element begins and ends with extra spaces and carriage returns. We'll learn about a function that tells the XSLT processor to ignore them.) The following template adds the complete contents of each verse element in the sample document above to the result tree at line 1 and then demonstrates ways to pull substrings out of them. Curly braces in the result make it easier to see exactly which substrings are getting pulled out of the verse elements:

```
<!-- xq319.xsl: converts xq318.xml into xq320.txt -->

<xsl:template match="verse">
  1. By itself: {<xsl:value-of select="."/>}
  2. {<xsl:value-of select="substring(.,7,6)"/>}
  3. {<xsl:value-of select="substring(.,12)"/>}
  4. {<xsl:value-of select="substring-before(.,'dreary')"/>}
  5. {<xsl:value-of select="substring-after(.,'desolation')"/>}
</xsl:template>
```

Before talking about individual functions, let's look at what this stylesheet does to the sample document:

```
  1. By itself: {Seest thou yon dreary Plain, forlorn and wild,}
  2. {thou y}
  3. {yon dreary Plain, forlorn and wild,}
  4. {Seest thou yon }
  5. {}

  1. By itself: {

      The seat of desolation, void of light,
```

```
}
   2. {   The}
   3. {e seat of desolation, void of light,
}
   4. {}
   5. {, void of light,
}
```

The source document has two verse elements, so the "verse" template rule adds two sets of lines 1 through 5 to the result. Each line 1 in the result shows the complete contents of the verse element. For the second verse element, line 1 includes the extra whitespace around the source document's text.

Lines 2 and 3 of the stylesheet demonstrate the substring() function. In line 2, the function call substring(.,7,6) takes the verse element's contents (because "." abbreviates self::node()) and, starting at its seventh character, gets six characters. For the first verse element, it skips the first six characters ("Seest ") to start at the seventh and get the six-character string "thou y". For the second verse element, the six characters to skip on the way to that seventh character are two carriage returns and four spaces, so that the six-character string starting at the seventh character is "   The" (three spaces followed by the three letters you see). Line 3 of the stylesheet has no third parameter to specify the length of the substring to extract, so the substring(.,12) function call starts at the twelfth character and gets everything to the end of the string. For the second verse element, this includes the two carriage returns that end it.

The function call substring-before(.,'dreary') in line 4 of the stylesheet looks for the string passed as the second argument in the string passed as the first argument (., or self::node()). If it finds that string, it returns everything in the first string before that occurrence of the second string. When looking for "dreary" in the first verse element, the function finds it and returns the string "Seest thou yon "; in the second verse element, it doesn't find it, and nothing appears between the curly braces of the fourth line for that element.

The function call substring-after(.,'desolation') resembles substring-before except that if it finds the second argument in the first argument's text, it returns the string *after* that text. The first verse element doesn't have the string "desolation", so nothing appears between the curly braces of the first line 5. The second verse element does contain this string, and the XSLT processor puts the characters after it (the string ", void of light," followed by two carriage returns) between the curly braces of the result document's second line 5.

The next stylesheet demonstrates a more diverse group of XPath string functions.

```
<!-- xq321.xsl: converts xq318.xml into ,.txt -->

<xsl:template match="verse">
   1. {<xsl:value-of select="concat('length: ',string-length(.))"/>}
   2. <xsl:if test="contains(.,'light')">
```

```
          <xsl:text>light: yes!</xsl:text>
        </xsl:if>
  3.  <xsl:if test="starts-with(.,'Seest')">
          <xsl:text>Yes, starts with "Seest"</xsl:text>
        </xsl:if>
  4.  {<xsl:value-of select="normalize-space(.)"/>}
  5.  {<xsl:value-of select="translate(.,'abcde','ABCD')"/>}

</xsl:template>
```

With the same source document as the previous example, this new stylesheet creates this result:

```
  1.  {length: 46}
  2.

  3.  Yes, starts with "Seest"

  4.  {Seest thou yon dreary Plain, forlorn and wild,}
  5.  {Sst thou yon DrAry PlAin, forlorn AnD wilD,}

  1.  {length: 49}
  2.  light: yes!

  3.

  4.  {The seat of desolation, void of light,}
  5.  {

      Th sAt of DsolAtion, voiD of light,

}
```

Line 1 of this stylesheet demonstrates two functions: `string-length()`, which returns the number of characters in the string passed as an argument, and `concat()`, which concatenates its argument strings into one string. The function call `concat ('length: ',string-length(.))` shows that its arguments don't have to be literal strings; you can use functions that return strings (or can easily be converted into strings, like the integer returned by the `string-length()` function) as arguments as well. This, along with its ability to accept any number of arguments greater than one, make `concat()` a very flexible function.

Lines 2 and 3 of the stylesheet (which each take up more than one line of the stylesheet) each have an `xsl:if` instruction that uses a Boolean string function—that is, a function that evaluates a certain condition about a string or strings and returns a Boolean value of true or false. The first function call, `contains(.,'light')`, checks whether its first argument contains the string passed as the second argument and returns a Boolean true if it does. For the source document's first `verse` element the argument doesn't contain this string, so nothing appears after the first "2" in the result. The second `verse` element does, so the message "light: yes!" appears in the result.

Line 3's `xsl:if` instruction has a similar function call in its `test` attribute: `starts-with(.,'Seest')`, which only returns true if the string in its first argument starts with the string in its second. This is true for the first `verse` element, so the message "Yes, starts with 'Seest'" appears on the result tree, but the second `verse` element doesn't, so nothing appears after its "3."

Line 4's `normalize-space(.)` function call accepts one argument, strips whitespace at its beginning and end, replaces any sequence of whitespace in the string with a single space character, and returns the resulting string. In English, the targeted whitespace characters are the spacebar space, the tab character, and the carriage return. The first `verse` element's text looks the same when processed by this function, but the second is definitely different: all the leading and trailing space characters have been removed. An XML processor does this to the spaces in most kinds of attributes, and it's handy to be able to do it to element character data as well—especially when you want to compare two strings of element character data whose only difference may be the spacing around them in their source document.

Line 5's `translate()` function provides a way to map one set of characters to another. It goes through the string in the first argument and replaces any characters also in the second argument with the corresponding character in the third argument. If the third argument has no corresponding character, then the XSLT processor deletes the one found in the first string. In the example, the function call `translate(., 'abcde', 'ABCD')` maps the letters "a", "b", "c", and "d" to their uppercase equivalents. Because the letter "e" is in that second argument but not the third, it's mapped to nothing—that is, any occurrences of it are removed from the copy of the first argument's string that the function returns.

Let's look at a more realistic example of string manipulation functions. In the following, the `binCode` element represents a wine brand's location on the wine store shelf. The first two characters are its row; the third character is its shelf; and the text after the hyphen is its product number:

```
<winelist>
    <wine>
        <winery>Lindeman's</winery>
        <product>Bin 65</product>
        <year>1998</year>
        <price>6.99</price>
        <binCode>15A-7</binCode>
    </wine>
    <wine>
        <winery>Benziger</winery>
        <product>Carneros</product>
        <year>1997</year>
        <price>7.55</price>
        <binCode>15C-5</binCode>
    </wine>
    <wine>
        <winery>Duckpond</winery>
        <product>Merit Selection</product>
        <year>1996</year>
```

```
      <price>14.99</price>
      <binCode>12D-1</binCode>
   </wine>
</winelist>
```

The following template rule separates the three components of the binCode element type into separate elements: row, shelf, and prodNum, all inside a productLocation container element:

```
<!-- xq324.xsl: converts xq323.xml to xq318.xml -->

  <xsl:template match="binCode">
    <productLocation>
      <row><xsl:value-of select="substring(text(),1,2)"/>
    </row>
      <shelf><xsl:value-of select="substring(.,3,1)"/>
    </shelf>
      <prodNum><xsl:value-of select="substring-after(text(),'-')"/>
    </prodNum>
    </productLocation>
  </xsl:template>
```

The call to substring() that creates the row element has text() as its first argument. For the purposes of this stylesheet, this means the same thing as ".". (Technically, text() refers to the text node child of the context node, and "." refers to a string representation of the node's contents when used as the first parameter to the substring() function.) The resulting XML looks like the input, except that the XSLT processor has replaced each binCode element with the productLocation element and its three child elements:

```
<?xml version="1.0" encoding="UTF-8"?>
<winelist>
    <wine>
      <winery>Lindeman's</winery>
      <product>Bin 65</product>
      <year>1998</year>
      <price>6.99</price>
      <productLocation><row>15</row><shelf>A</shelf>
      <prodNum>7</prodNum></productLocation>
   </wine>
   <wine>
      <winery>Benziger</winery>
      <product>Carneros</product>
      <year>1997</year>
      <price>7.55</price>
      <productLocation><row>15</row><shelf>C</shelf>
  <prodNum>5</prodNum></productLocation>
   </wine>
   <wine>
      <winery>Duckpond</winery>
      <product>Merit Selection</product>
      <year>1996</year>
```

```
      <price>14.99</price>
      <productLocation><row>12</row><shelf>D</shelf>
   <prodNum>1</prodNum></productLocation>
    </wine>
</winelist>
```

To see if two elements are the same, XSLT compares their string values using the equals sign ("="). To demonstrate several variations on this, our next stylesheet compares the a element in the following with its sibling elements:

```
<poem>
  <a>full of Pomp and Gold</a>
  <b>full of Pomp and Gold</b>
  <c>full of pomp and gold</c>
  <d>
full of Pomp     and   Gold

</d>
</poem>
```

The stylesheet contains a template rule for the a element with a series of xsl:if instructions. Each instruction compares the a element's content with something and reports whether or not the test is true:

```
<!-- xq327.xsl: converts xq326.xml into xq328.txt -->

<xsl:template match="a">

  <xsl:if test=". = 'full of Pomp and Gold'">
    1. a = "full of Pomp and Gold"
  </xsl:if>

  <xsl:if test=". = ../b">
    2. a = ../b
  </xsl:if>

  <xsl:if test=". = ../c">
    3. a = ../c
  </xsl:if>

  <xsl:if test=". != ../c">
    4. a != ../c
  </xsl:if>

  <xsl:if
   test="translate(.,'abcdefghijklmnopqrstuvwxyz',
                    'ABCDEFGHIJKLMNOPQRSTUVWXYZ') =
        translate(../c,'abcdefghijklmnopqrstuvwxyz',
                    'ABCDEFGHIJKLMNOPQRSTUVWXYZ')">
    5. a = ../c (ignoring case)
  </xsl:if>

  <xsl:if test=". = ../d">
    6. a = ../d
  </xsl:if>

  <xsl:if test=". = normalize-space(../d)">
```

```
    7. a = normalize-space(../d)
  </xsl:if>

</xsl:template>
```

As the result shows, `xsl:if` elements 1, 2, 4, 5, and 7 are true for the preceding document:

```
1. a = "full of Pomp and Gold"

2. a = ../b

4. a != ../c

5. a = ../c (ignoring case)

7. a = normalize-space(../d)
```

Test number 1 in this stylesheet compares the a element (represented by ".") with the literal string "full of Pomp and Gold". They're equal, as the message added to the result tree tells us. Test 2 compares the a element with its sibling b element, and as the result shows, they, too, are equal. (If you're unfamiliar with the `../b` notation to point to the b sibling, see chapter 2, "XPath," on page 23)

Test 3 compares element a with element c, and they're not equal—two characters are in a different case. XML is case-sensitive, so this `xsl:if` instruction adds nothing to the result.

Test 4 compares elements a and c again, but using the `!=` comparison operator to check for inequality. This test is true, so a message about test 4 gets added to the result.

The fifth test uses the `translate()` function to map the a and c elements to upper-case versions, then compares those. Because upper-case versions of these two elements are the same, test 5 is true, and the appropriate message gets added to the result.

XSLT offers no built-in way to automatically convert a string's case because the mapping is often dependent upon the language being used—and sometimes, even dependent upon where the language is being used. For example, an upper-case "é" at the start of a word is "É" in France but "E" in Canada.

Test 6 compares element a with element d, which has the same text and some additional whitespace (a few carriage returns and either spacebar spaces or tabs to indent the text). As the result document shows, the two elements are not equal.

Test 7 compares a and d again, but a element is compared to a version of the d element returned by the `normalize-space()` function. This time, the equality test is true.

The `normalize-space()` function has been the savior of many string equality tests. XML's treatment of whitespace can be a complex topic, because it's not always clear which whitespace an XML parser ignores and which it recognizes. Any automated process that creates XML elements may put whitespace between elements or it may not, so a way to say "get rid of extraneous whitespace before comparing this string to something" is very useful in XSLT. In fact, the seventh `xsl:if` instruction above would be even better if both sides of the comparison in the `xsl:if` element's `test` attribute were passed to this function, like this:

```
<!-- xq329.xsl -->

  <xsl:if test="normalize-space(.) = normalize-space(../d)">
    7. a = normalize-space(../d)
  </xsl:if>
```

Check out your particular XSLT processor's documentation to see if it offers any string manipulation functions in addition to the ones required by the XSLT specification.

5.7.2 Search and replace

XSLT offers no built-in method for globally replacing one string of text with another. The `translate()` function can replace specific characters with other characters. (See section 5.7.1, "Extracting and comparing strings," page 153, for more on this.)

Global replacement is a basic text transformation task. XSLT is a language for transforming text (that is, a language for transforming XML documents, which are text) so string replacement is closely related to the tasks that a stylesheet developer often attacks with XSLT. Fortunately, existing XSLT techniques can be combined to give a stylesheet a search-and-replace capability. The most important technique is the use of parameters with recursive named templates. (See "Arbitrary repetition with named template recursion," on page 122 if you're unfamiliar with this technique.)

As an example, we'll look at a stylesheet that converts the string "finish" to "FINISH" throughout the following XML document:

```
<winelist>

  <wine grape="Chardonnay">
    <winery>Benziger</winery>
    <product>Carneros</product>
    <year>1997</year>
    <desc>Well-textured flavors, good finish.</desc>
    <prices>
      <list>10.99</list>
      <discounted>9.50</discounted>
      <case>114.00</case>
    </prices>
  </wine>

  <wine grape="Cabernet">
    <winery>Duckpond</winery>
    <product>Merit Selection</product>
    <year>1996</year>
    <desc>Sturdy and generous flavors, long finish.</desc>
    <prices>
      <list>13.99</list>
      <discounted>11.99</discounted>
      <case>143.50</case>
    </prices>
  </wine>

</winelist>
```

The stylesheet has three template rules. The third one just copies all the source tree nodes, except for text nodes, to the result tree.

The second template rule handles text nodes. It calls the first template, the named "globalReplace" template, to add the text node template's contents to the result tree:

```
<!-- xq332.xsl: converts xq331.xml into xq333.xml -->
<xsl:stylesheet xmlns:xsl="http://www.w3.org/1999/XSL/Transform"
     version="1.0">
<xsl:output method="xml" omit-xml-declaration="yes"/>

<xsl:template name="globalReplace">
  <xsl:param name="outputString"/>
  <xsl:param name="target"/>
  <xsl:param name="replacement"/>
  <xsl:choose>
    <xsl:when test="contains($outputString,$target)">

      <xsl:value-of select=
        "concat(substring-before($outputString,$target),
              $replacement)"/>
      <xsl:call-template name="globalReplace">
        <xsl:with-param name="outputString"
            select="substring-after($outputString,$target)"/>
        <xsl:with-param name="target" select="$target"/>
        <xsl:with-param name="replacement"
            select="$replacement"/>
      </xsl:call-template>
    </xsl:when>
    <xsl:otherwise>
      <xsl:value-of select="$outputString"/>
    </xsl:otherwise>
  </xsl:choose>
</xsl:template>

<xsl:template match="text()">
  <xsl:call-template name="globalReplace">
  <xsl:with-param name="outputString" select="."/>
  <xsl:with-param name="target" select="'finish'"/>
  <xsl:with-param name="replacement" select="'FINISH'"/>
  </xsl:call-template>
</xsl:template>

<xsl:template match="@*|*">
  <xsl:copy>
    <xsl:apply-templates select="@*|node()"/>
  </xsl:copy>
</xsl:template>

</xsl:stylesheet>
```

The "globalReplace" named template is a general purpose string replacement template based on one posted to the XSL-List mailing list by Mike J. Brown. As the example shows, it gets called with three parameters:

1 `outputString` is the string on which it will perform the global replacement.

2 `target` is the string that it will look for in `outputString`—the string that will be replaced.

3 `replacement` is the new string that will be substituted for any occurrence of `target` in outputString.

The template must add `outputString` to the result tree unchanged if it has no occurrence of the target string, so, first, it checks whether the target string is there or not. An if-else construction would be great for this, but XSLT offers no equivalent of an "else" condition to go with its `xsl:if` instruction. However, an `xsl:choose` instruction can perform the same logic with a single `xsl:when` element, followed by an `xsl:otherwise` element. In the template, the `xsl:when` condition uses the `contains()` function to check whether `outputString` has `target` in it. If it does, an `xsl:value-of` instruction uses a `concat()` function to put together two strings for the result tree: everything in `outputString` before the first `target` and then the `replacement` string.

What about the rest of `outputString`, after the `target` that was found and replaced by the `replacement` string? The "globalReplace" named template makes a recursive call to itself to make any additional necessary substitutions in the remaining part of the string. The template passes `substring-after($output-String, $target)` (that is, everything in `outputString` after the found occurrence of `target`) as the value of `outputString` for this new invocation of the function. If that new invocation finds another occurrence of the target string, it will add everything up to it and the replacement string to the result tree, then call the function again for the remainder of that string if necessary. By making recursive calls to handle the remainder of the string, it really is a global replace, because multiple occurrences of the `target` all get replaced.

If the `xsl:when` instruction's `test` attribute doesn't find the `target` string in `outputString`, the `xsl:otherwise` element's `xsl:value-of` instruction only adds the value of `outputString` to the result tree. This is the crucial stopping condition that any recursive template needs to ensure so that it doesn't call itself forever. Whether `outputString` has zero occurrences of `target` or fifty of them, eventually this `xsl:otherwise` part of the `xsl:choose` instruction will get chosen and the "globalReplace" named template will not call itself again for this source tree text node.

The result of calling this stylesheet with the preceding document has both occurrences of the string "finish" replaced with "FINISH":

```
<winelist>

  <wine grape="Chardonnay">
    <winery>Benziger</winery>
    <product>Carneros</product>
```

```
      <year>1997</year>
      <desc>Well-textured flavors, good FINISH.</desc>
      <prices>
        <list>10.99</list>
        <discounted>9.50</discounted>
        <case>114.00</case>
      </prices>
    </wine>

    <wine grape="Cabernet">
      <winery>Duckpond</winery>
      <product>Merit Selection</product>
      <year>1996</year>
      <desc>Sturdy and generous flavors, long FINISH.</desc>
      <prices>
        <list>13.99</list>
        <discounted>11.99</discounted>
        <case>143.50</case>
      </prices>
    </wine>

</winelist>
```

One nice thing about this "globalReplace" named template is that it really is a general purpose named template: it still works when called in other situations. For example, the following template also calls the "globalReplace" named template, but note the template's match condition: It only replaces the one-character string "9" with the "0" in text nodes that are child nodes of year elements, because those are the nodes specified by the template rule's match condition:

```
<!-- xq334.xsl: converts xq331.xml into xq335.xml -->
<xsl:template match="year/text()">
  <xsl:call-template name="globalReplace">
  <xsl:with-param name="outputString" select="."/>
  <xsl:with-param name="target" select="'9'"/>
  <xsl:with-param name="replacement" select="'0'"/>
  </xsl:call-template>
</xsl:template>
```

When run with the same source document as the previous example, this template rule replaces the nines in the year elements and leaves the nines in the prices elements alone:

```
<?xml version="1.0" encoding="UTF-8"?>
<winelist>

  <wine grape="Chardonnay">
    <winery>Benziger</winery>
    <product>Carneros</product>
    <year>1007</year>
    <desc>Well-textured flavors, good finish.</desc>
    <prices>
      <list>10.99</list>
      <discounted>9.50</discounted>
```

```
      <case>114.00</case>
    </prices>
  </wine>

  <wine grape="Cabernet">
    <winery>Duckpond</winery>
    <product>Merit Selection</product>
    <year>1006</year>
    <desc>Sturdy and generous flavors, long finish.</desc>
    <prices>
      <list>13.99</list>
      <discounted>11.99</discounted>
      <case>143.50</case>
    </prices>
  </wine>

</winelist>
```

(If you really want to replace one character with another like this, the translate() function would be more efficient.) We can see that customizing the stylesheet's use of the "globalReplace" template doesn't have to mean tinkering with the template itself. Instead, being more selective about the outputString value passed to the template allows the stylesheet to focus the template's power.

5.8   VARIABLES AND PARAMETERS: SETTING AND USING

Variables and parameters add flexibility to your stylesheets. With a properly designed stylesheet, the simple resetting of a variable value (or parameter value, which is even easier to reset) can adapt your stylesheet to deal with different kinds of data and situations.

5.8.1   Variables

A variable in XSLT has more in common with a variable in algebra than with a variable in a typical programming language. A variable is a name that represents a value and, within a particular application of a template, it will never represent any other value: it can't be reset. XSLT variables actually have a lot more in common with something known as "constants" in many programming languages, and variables are used for a similar purpose as constants. If you use the same value multiple times in your stylesheet, and a possibility exists that you'll have to change them all to a different value, it's better to assign that value to a variable and use references to the variable instead. Then, if you need to change the value when re-using the stylesheet, you only change the value assigned in the creation of that variable.

For example, imagine that we want to turn this XML

```
<wine grape="Cabernet">
  <winery>Duckpond</winery>
  <product>Merit Selection</product>
  <year>1996</year>
  <price>11.99</price>
</wine>
```

into this HTML:

```
<b><font size="10pt">Duckpond Cabernet</font></b><br>
<i><font size="10pt">Merit Selection</font></i><br>
<font size="10pt">1996</font><br>
<font size="10pt">11.99</font><br>
```

The following templates would accomplish this:

```
<!-- xq340.xsl: converts xq338.xml into xq339.html -->

<xsl:template match="winery">
  <b><font size="10pt"><xsl:apply-templates/>
  <xsl:text> </xsl:text>
  <xsl:value-of select="../@grape"/></font></b><br/>
</xsl:template>

<xsl:template match="product">
  <i><font size="10pt"><xsl:apply-templates/></font></i><br/>
</xsl:template>

<xsl:template match="year | price">
  <font size="10pt"><xsl:apply-templates/></font><br/>
</xsl:template>
```

If you want to change the three font elements' size attribute to "12pt", however, it would be too easy to miss one—especially if the template rules weren't right next to each other in the stylesheet. The solution is to use a variable to represent this size value:

```
<!-- xq341.xsl: converts xq338.xml into xq339.html -->

<xsl:variable name="bodyTextSize">10pt</xsl:variable>

<xsl:template match="winery">
  <b><font size="{$bodyTextSize}"><xsl:apply-templates/>
  <xsl:text> </xsl:text>
  <xsl:value-of select="../@grape"/></font></b><br/>
</xsl:template>

<xsl:template match="product">
  <i><font size="{$bodyTextSize}">
    <xsl:apply-templates/></font></i><br/>
</xsl:template>

<xsl:template match="year | price">
  <font size="{$bodyTextSize}"><xsl:apply-templates/></font><br/>
</xsl:template>
```

TIP When referencing a variable or parameter from a literal result element's attribute, you want the XSLT processor to plug in the variable's value and not a dollar sign followed by the variable's name at that point in the template. To do this, put the variable inside curly braces to make it an attribute value template. To plug a variable's value into the content of a result tree element, instead of an attribute value, use an `xsl:value-of` instruction.

In the preceding example, if the `$bodyTextSize` variables were not enclosed by curly braces, each `font` start-tag in the result would have looked like this: `<font size= "$bodyTextSize">`.

The `xsl:variable` instruction creates a variable. Its `name` attribute identifies the variable's name. The value can be specified either as the `xsl:variable` element's contents (like the "10pt" in the example) or as the value of an optional `select` attribute in the `xsl:variable` element's start-tag.

The value of the `select` attribute must be an expression. This offers two nice advantages:

1 It shows that the `xsl:variable` element isn't as limited as the constants used by popular programming languages, because the variable's value doesn't need to be hardcoded when the stylesheet is written.

2 The attribute value doesn't need curly braces to tell the XSLT processor "This is an attribute value template, evaluate it as an expression," because it always evaluates an `xsl:variable` element's `select` attribute value as an expression.

The following two `xsl:variable` elements have the same effect as the one in the previous example: they set the `bodyTextSize` variable to a value of "10pt". The `bodyTextSize` variable has its value assigned in a `select` attribute instead of in its element content; the value assigned will be the return value of a `concat` function that concatenates the string "pt" to the result of adding `$baseFontSize+2`. What's `$baseFontSize`? It's another variable, which is defined above the `bodyText-Size` variable's `xsl:variable` element. That value of "8" is added to 2 and concatenated to "pt" to create a value of "10pt" for the `bodyTextSize` variable, which can then be used just like the `bodyTextSize` variable in the previous example.

```
<!-- xq342.xsl: converts xq338.xml into xq339.html -->

<xsl:variable name="baseFontSize" select="8"/>

<xsl:variable name="bodyTextSize"
    select="concat($baseFontSize+2,'pt')"/>
```

This example demonstrates options available when using an expression in the `select` attribute to assign a variable's value. The second `xsl:variable` element references another variable, does some math, and makes a function call. Variables aren't as limited as many XSLT newcomers might think.

The example also demonstrates another nice feature of variables: they don't have to all be strings. Once `baseFontSize` is set to "8", the `select` value of the body-

TextSize variable's xsl:variable element adds "2" to it and comes up with "10". If the XSLT processor had treated these numbers as strings, putting "8" and "2" together would get us "82". Instead, the XSLT processor treats the baseFontSize variable as a number. It can treat a variable as any type of object that can be returned by an XSLT expression: a string, a number, a Boolean value, or a node set.

WARNING   If an XSLT variable has a value assigned by an xsl:variable element's contents *and* by a select attribute, the XSLT processor uses the one in the select attribute.

The examples above show "top-level" variables. They're defined with xsl:variable elements that are children of the main xsl:stylesheet element, making them global variables that can be referenced anywhere in the stylesheet.

Variables can be "local" as well—that is, defined inside a template rule and only available for use within that template rule. For example, the following templates have the same result as the ones in the examples above, except that the font start-tag before the result winery element's content has a value of "12pt" in its size attribute instead of "10pt".

```
<!-- xq343.xsl: converts xq338.xml into xq344.html -->

<xsl:template match="wine">

  <xsl:variable name="bodyTextSize">10pt</xsl:variable>

  <xsl:apply-templates select="winery"/>
  <i><font size="{$bodyTextSize}">
    <xsl:apply-templates select="product"/>
  </font></i><br/>
  <font size="{$bodyTextSize}"><xsl:apply-templates select="year"/>
  </font><br/>
  <font size="{$bodyTextSize}"><xsl:apply-templates select="price"/>
  </font><br/>

</xsl:template>

<xsl:template match="winery">

  <xsl:variable name="bodyTextSize">12pt</xsl:variable>

  <b><font size="{$bodyTextSize}"><xsl:apply-templates/>
  <xsl:text> </xsl:text>
  <xsl:value-of select="../@grape"/></font></b><br/>

</xsl:template>
```

The way these templates assign these size values is different. Instead of one global bodyTextSize variable to use throughout the stylesheet, the two template rules each have their own bodyTextSize variables declared between their xsl:template tags. The first one sets bodyTextSize to a value of "10pt", and that's what gets plugged into the size attribute values for the font tags that start the product, year, and price elements. The second template sets bodyTextSize to

"12pt", so the winery and grape element contents copied to the result tree by that template start with font tags that have a size value of "12pt":

```
<b><font size="12pt">Duckpond Cabernet</font></b><br>
<i><font size="10pt">Merit Selection</font></i><br>
<font size="10pt">1996</font><br>
<font size="10pt">11.99</font><br>
```

That's just a toy example. The next stylesheet uses a selection of the string manipulation functions available in XSLT (see section 5.7, "Strings," page 153) to right align the result tree versions of the color elements in this document:

```
<test>
<color>red</color>
<color>blue</color>
<color>yellow</color>
</test>
```

The fieldWidth global variable stores the desired column width. The goal is to add spaces before each color value so that the spaces plus the color name add up to this value.

The color element's template rule has two local variables:

- The value-length variable stores the length of the color name using the string-length() function.

- The padding variable stores the number of spaces required to right-align the color name. It does so by subtracting the value of the local valueLength variable from the global fieldWidth variable.

Once the template rule knows how much space it needs to add to the result tree before adding the color element's contents, it adds that many spaces, using the substring() function to pull the necessary spaces out of a string of spaces passed to the substring() function as its first argument:

```
<!-- xq346.xsl: converts xq345.xml into xq478.txt -->
<xsl:stylesheet xmlns:xsl="http://www.w3.org/1999/XSL/Transform"
version="1.0">
<xsl:output omit-xml-declaration="yes"/>

  <xsl:variable name="fieldWidth">12</xsl:variable>

  <xsl:template match="color">
    <xsl:variable name="valueLength"
        select="string-length(.)"/>
    <xsl:variable name="padding"
        select="$fieldWidth - $valueLength"/>

    <xsl:value-of
        select="substring('                ',1,$padding)"/>
    <xsl:value-of select="."/>

  </xsl:template>
</xsl:stylesheet>
```

In the result, "red" has nine spaces before it, "blue" has eight, and "yellow" has six:

```
    red
   blue
  yellow
```

I could have done this without any local variables; in fact, when I originally wrote this stylesheet, I did. As with any programming language, using local variables made it easier to break down the problem into pieces and to make the relationship of those pieces easier to understand.

5.8.2   Parameters

The xsl:param instruction is just like xsl:variable, with one important difference: its value is only treated as a default value and can be overridden at runtime. All the stylesheet examples in section 5.8.1, "Variables," page 164, would work the same way if you substituted xsl:param elements for their xsl:variable elements, but you would have the option of overriding the values when calling their templates.

For instance, let's take an example from that section and make the substitution. Here is how it looks as a complete stylesheet:

```
<!-- xq348.xsl: converts xq338.xml into xq339.html.
     Compare this with xq340.xsl. -->

<xsl:stylesheet xmlns:xsl="http://www.w3.org/1999/XSL/Transform"
     version="1.0">

  <xsl:output method="html"/>

  <xsl:param name="bodyTextSize">10pt</xsl:param>

  <xsl:template match="winery">
   <b><font size="{$bodyTextSize}"><xsl:apply-templates/>
   <xsl:text> </xsl:text>
   <xsl:value-of select="../@grape"/></font></b><br/>
  </xsl:template>

  <xsl:template match="product">
   <i><font size="{$bodyTextSize}">
    <xsl:apply-templates/></font></i><br/>
  </xsl:template>

  <xsl:template match="year | price">
   <font size="{$bodyTextSize}"><xsl:apply-templates/></font><br/>
  </xsl:template>

</xsl:stylesheet>
```

If we run the stylesheet as shown with the same source document, it produces the same result as the previous section's version, which used xsl:variable instead of xsl:param:

```
<b><font size="10pt">Duckpond Cabernet</font></b><br/>
```

```
<i><font size="10pt">Merit Selection</font></i><br>
<font size="10pt">1996</font><br>
<font size="10pt">11.99</font><br>
```

However, if we pass the stylesheet a value of "8pt" to use for `bodyTextSize`, it substitutes this new value for all uses of this parameter:

```
<b><font size="8pt">Duckpond Cabernet</font></b><br/>
<i><font size="8pt">Merit Selection</font></i><br/>
<font size="8pt">1996</font><br/>
<font size="8pt">11.99</font><br/>
```

Of course, I'm skimming over one important detail here: how do you pass the alternative value for the parameter to the stylesheet? The official XSLT spec doesn't tell us. In fact, it deliberately tells us that it's not going to tell us. Just as the W3C's XSL Working Group wanted to leave the potential methods for giving input to and getting output from an XSLT processor as open as possible, they also didn't want to limit how the processors will be told of a new value for a global parameter setting. (As we'll see, not all parameters are global like the `bodyTextSize` one above. They can also be local to template rules.) So, it's up to the particular XSLT processor's designer. To pass the new value of "8pt" to the stylesheet when using the Saxon XSLT processor, the command line might look like this:

```
java com.icl.saxon.StyleSheet -x org.apache.xerces.parsers.SAXParser
  -y org.apache.xerces.parsers.SAXParser xq338.xml
  xq348.xsl bodyTextSize=8pt
```

(This is actually one command split over three lines to fit on the page here. When using Saxon or any other Java-based XSLT processor, you would make your life easier if you stored everything before the "xq338.xml" in that command line in a Windows batch file, a UNIX shell script, or your operating system's equivalent. Then, you can pass it the important parameters each time you run it, with no need to type the full Java library names for the XSLT processor and XML parser. See appendix B, "Running XSLT processors" on page 269 for more.)

The only difference between applying the xq348.xsl stylesheet to the xq338.xml document this way and running it with the `bodyTextSize` default value is the addition of the "bodyTextSize=8pt" part at the end. Other XSLT processors may require a different syntax when passing a new parameter value along from the command line, but they still create the same result when using this stylesheet and input.

Local parameters are even more useful in template rules than XSLT local variables, because the flexibility of passing one or more values to a template lets that template adapt to different situations. Named templates that don't take advantage of this can still operate as functions or subroutines, but when you use named templates that do, you can start treating XSLT like a real programming language. For example, the ability of named templates to call themselves with parameters allows recursion and all the power associated with it.

How we pass a new value to a template rule's local parameter isn't quite the open question that it is with global parameters, because XSLT provides the `xsl:with-param` instruction for just this purpose. You can use this element in an `xsl:apply-templates` element to assign a new value to a parameter in a template being applied, but it's more commonly used when calling a named template with the `xsl:call-template` instruction. For example, the first template rule in the following stylesheet has a name attribute and not a `match` attribute. Instead of the XSLT processor looking for nodes where it can apply this template, the processor will wait until the template is explicitly called with an `xsl:call-template` instruction.

```
<!-- xq352.xsl: converts xq353.xml into xq354.html -->
<xsl:stylesheet xmlns:xsl="http://www.w3.org/1999/XSL/Transform"
    version="1.0">

  <xsl:template name="titles">
    <xsl:param name="headerElement">h4</xsl:param>
    <xsl:element name="{$headerElement}">
      <xsl:apply-templates/>
    </xsl:element>
  </xsl:template>

  <xsl:template match="chapter/title">
    <xsl:call-template name="titles">
      <xsl:with-param name="headerElement">h1</xsl:with-param>
    </xsl:call-template>
  </xsl:template>

  <xsl:template match="section/title">
    <xsl:call-template name="titles">
      <xsl:with-param name="headerElement" select="'h2'"/>
    </xsl:call-template>
  </xsl:template>

  <xsl:template match="para">
    <p><xsl:apply-templates/></p>
  </xsl:template>

  <xsl:template match="chapter">
    <html><body><xsl:apply-templates/></body></html>
  </xsl:template>

</xsl:stylesheet>
```

(Note how the stylesheet has no `xsl:output` element with a `method` setting of "html." Because the document element of the result tree is `html`, the XSLT processor will assume an output method of "html.") The second and third template rules, which have match patterns of "chapter/title" and "section/title", call the first template by its name of "titles", using `xsl:call-templates` elements. These `xsl:call-templates` elements don't need any children, but they have them here: `xsl:with-param` elements to pass parameter values to the named templates. The "titles" template rule will use these values to override the default value of "h4" when it's called. The `with-param` instruction in the "chapter/title" template rule is saying "pass along the value 'h1' for the headeElement parameter," and the one in the "section/title" template rule is passing the value "h2". For this input document,

```
<chapter><title>Chapter 1</title>
  <para>Then with expanded wings he steers his flight</para>
  <para author="ar">Aloft, incumbent on the dusky Air</para>
  <section><title>Chapter 1, Section 1</title>
    <para>That felt unusual weight, till on dry Land</para>
    <para>He lights, if it were Land that ever burned</para>
  </section>
</chapter>
```

the "titles" template rule is called when the XSLT processor finds each of the two title element nodes. The "titles" named template uses the passed values to create the h1 and h2 elements in the result:

```
<html>
  <body>
    <h1>Chapter 1</h1>
    <p>Then with expanded wings he steers his flight</p>
    <p>Aloft, incumbent on the dusky Air</p>
    <h2>Chapter 1, Section 1</h2>
    <p>That felt unusual weight, till on dry Land</p>
    <p>He lights, if it were Land that ever burned</p>
  </body>
</html>
```

Just as an xsl:param element can specify its default value as either content between its start- and end-tags or as the value of a select attribute, the xsl:with-param element can indicate the value to pass using either method. The two xsl:with-param elements in the example above use the two different methods to demonstrate this.

The XSLT processor evaluates the xsl:with-param element's select value as an expression just as it does with the xsl:param element's select attribute value. This is why the third template, shown previously, needs single quotation marks around the value of "h2" even though it's also enclosed by double quotation marks. The double quotation marks serve a different purpose: to tell the XML parser where the select attribute value starts and ends. The inner single quotation marks tell the XSLT processor that the value is a literal string and not an expression to evaluate.

WARNING   The name value specified in the xsl:call-template element cannot contain a variable reference. For example, if you declared a variable called templateName and stored the string "title" there, an xsl:call-template start-tag of <xsl:call-template name="$templateName"> would *not* work in the previous example's "chapter/title" or "section/title" template rules.

You don't have to specify a hard-coded string such as "h1" or "h2" as the value of the parameter to pass in an `xsl:with-param` element. You can put the result of one or more functions in there, or even an XPath expression that retrieves a value from somewhere in the document (or even from another document, using the `document()` function). This ability opens up an even broader range of possibilities for how you use parameter passing in XSLT.

For related information, see:

- section 5.1.3, "'For' loops, iteration," on page 118, for examples of the power of recursion using `xsl:param` elements.
- section 5.3, "Named templates," page 132
- section 5.8.1, "Variables," page 164
- appendix B, "Running XSLT processors" on page 269, for more on different ways to pass parameters to different XSLT processors.

5.9 DECLARING KEYS AND PERFORMING LOOKUPS

When you need to look up values based on some other value—especially when your stylesheet needs to do so a lot—XSLT's `xsl:key` instruction and `key()` function work together to make it easy. They can also make it fast. To really appreciate the use of keys in XSLT, however, let's first look at one way to solve this problem without them. Let's say we want to add information about the shirt elements in the following document to the result tree, with color names instead of color codes in the result.

```
<shirts>

  <colors>
   <color cid="c1">yellow</color>
   <color cid="c2">black</color>
   <color cid="c3">red</color>
   <color cid="c4">blue</color>
   <color cid="c5">purple</color>
   <color cid="c6">white</color>
   <color cid="c7">orange</color>
   <color cid="c7">green</color>
  </colors>

  <shirt colorCode="c4">oxford button-down</shirt>
  <shirt colorCode="c1">poly blend, straight collar</shirt>
  <shirt colorCode="c6">monogrammed, tab collar</shirt>

</shirts>
```

We want the output to look like this:

```
blue oxford button-down
yellow poly blend, straight collar
white monogrammed, tab collar
```

The following stylesheet has an `xsl:value-of` instruction that uses an XPath expression to retrieve the contents of the colors element's appropriate color child. It does so by finding, for each `shirt` element, the `color` element whose `cid` attribute value matches the `shirt` element's `color` attribute value. (For example, the stylesheet takes the `color` value of "c4" for the first `shirt` element and searches through the `colors` element's `color` children to find one with a `cid` attribute that has that same value: the one with "blue" as its contents.) Above that `xsl:value-of` element, an `xsl:variable` instruction sets the `shirtColorCode` variable equal to the `shirt` element's `color` attribute value. The XPath expression has a predicate of `[@cid = $shirtColorCode]` to get only the `color` element whose `cid` attribute has the same value as the `shirtColorCode` variable.

```
<!-- xq489.xsl: converts xq479.xml into xq490.txt -->
<xsl:stylesheet xmlns:xsl="http://www.w3.org/1999/XSL/Transform"
    version="1.0">
  <xsl:output method="text"/>

  <xsl:template match="shirt">

   <xsl:variable name="shirtColorCode" select="@colorCode"/>

    <xsl:value-of
        select="/shirts/colors/color[@cid = $shirtColorCode]"/>
    <xsl:text> </xsl:text><xsl:apply-templates/><xsl:text>
</xsl:text>

  </xsl:template>

  <xsl:template match="color"/>

</xsl:stylesheet>
```

This produces the desired output, but the complexity of the XPath expression means that, if you have a lot of `shirt` elements whose colors need to be looked up, creating the result tree could go slowly. Declaring and using keys can make the lookup go much faster, because an XSLT processor that sees that you've declared a key usually sets up an index in memory to speed these lookups. In this way you can produce the same result as the previous stylesheet, much more efficiently.

The next stylesheet does the same thing as the previous one by using the `xsl:key` instruction to declare the nodes and values used for the color name lookups and the `key()` function to actually perform the lookups.

```
<!-- xq481.xsl: converts xq479.xml into xq480.txt -->
<xsl:stylesheet xmlns:xsl="http://www.w3.org/1999/XSL/Transform"
    version="1.0">
  <xsl:output method="text"/>

  <xsl:key name="colorNumKey" match="color" use="@cid"/>

  <xsl:template match="colors"/>

  <xsl:template match="shirt">
   <xsl:value-of select="key('colorNumKey',@color)"/>
   <xsl:text> </xsl:text><xsl:apply-templates/>
  </xsl:template>

</xsl:stylesheet>
```

The xsl:key element has three attributes:

- The name attribute holds the name of the lookup key. The key() function uses this name to identify what kind of lookup it's doing.

- The match attribute holds a match pattern identifying the collection of nodes where the lookups will take place. In the example, the color elements are this collection. The fact that they are enclosed by a colors element gives the source document a little more structure, but it's not necessary for the key lookups to work.

- The use attribute specifies the part or parts of the match attribute's collection of nodes that will be used to find the appropriate node—in other words, the attribute specifies the index of the lookup. In the example, this index is the cid attribute of the color elements, because a lookup will pass along a color ID string to look up the corresponding color.

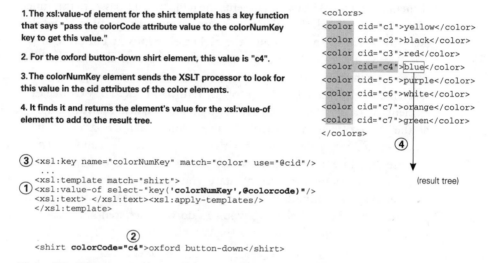

1. The xsl:value-of element for the shirt template has a key function that says "pass the colorCode attribute value to the colorNumKey key to get this value."

2. For the oxford button-down shirt element, this value is "c4".

3. The colorNumKey element sends the XSLT processor to look for this value in the cid attributes of the color elements.

4. It finds it and returns the element's value for the xsl:value-of element to add to the result tree.

```
<colors>
<color cid="c1">yellow</color>
<color cid="c2">black</color>
<color cid="c3">red</color>
<color cid="c4">blue</color>
<color cid="c5">purple</color>
<color cid="c6">white</color>
<color cid="c7">orange</color>
<color cid="c7">green</color>
</colors>
```

(result tree)

```
③ <xsl:key name="colorNumKey" match="color" use="@cid"/>
   ...
   <xsl:template match="shirt">
① <xsl:value-of select-"key('colorNumKey',@colorcode)"/>
   <xsl:text> </xsl:text><xsl:apply-templates/>
   </xsl:template>
```

②
```
<shirt colorCode="c4">oxford button-down</shirt>
```

Figure 5.2   Using an xsl:key element and key() function

Figure 5.2 shows the four steps that take place for one particular lookup:

1 The xsl:value-of element for the shirt template has a key() function that says "pass the colorCode attribute value to the colorNumKey key to get this value."

2 For the oxford button-down shirt element, this value is "c4".

3 The colorNumKey element sends the XSLT processor to look for this value in the cid attributes of the color elements.

4 It finds it and returns the element's value for the xsl:value-of element to add to the result tree.

If these color IDs and names were in a table, you could think of the table as the "colorNumKey" lookup table, the nodes named by the match attribute as the rows of the table, and the value or values named by the use attribute as the index field (or fields) of the table.

These color elements would fit nicely into a table, but the beauty of doing so with XSLT (and XML) is that the elements named by your match attribute can have much more complex structures than any relational database table row. You have the full power of XML available, and the ability to use an XPath expression in the use attribute lets you identify any part of that structure you want to use as the lookup key.

The key() function performs the actual lookup. This function takes a value, searches through the keys for one whose use value equals the one it's looking for, and returns the element or elements that have that key value. The example's template rule for the shirt elements calls this function to insert the color name before each shirt element's contents. The two arguments the template rule passes to this function are the name of the key ("colorNumKey", the name of the lookup "table"), and the value necessary to look up the needed value (the shirt element's colorCode attribute value).

Because the key() function returns the node or nodes that the lookup found, you can use the function call as part of an XPath expression to pull an attribute value, subelement, or other subnode out of the returned node. For example, if the color elements had a PMSnum attribute, and you wanted to insert this attribute value instead of the color elements' actual content, you could use a value of "key('colorNumKey',@color)/@PMSnum" for the xsl:value element's select attribute. Because the entire color node was used in the example above, its character data contents (the part between the color start- and end-tags) are added to the result tree.

Let's experiment with this color lookup table a little more. The following template demonstrates several things you can do with declared keys in XSLT using the same shirts source document as the last example:

```
<!-- xq482.xsl: converts xq479.xml into xq483.txt -->
<xsl:stylesheet xmlns:xsl="http://www.w3.org/1999/XSL/Transform"
      version="1.0">
  <xsl:output method="text"/>

  <xsl:key name="colorNumKey" match="color" use="@cid"/>
  <xsl:key name="colorKey" match="color" use="."/>

  <xsl:variable name="testVar">c4</xsl:variable>
  <xsl:variable name="keyName">colorKey</xsl:variable>

  <xsl:template match="colors">

  Looking up the color name with the color ID:

    c3's color: <xsl:value-of select="key('colorNumKey','c3')"/>

    c4's color: <xsl:value-of select="key('colorNumKey',$testVar)"/>

    c8's color: <xsl:value-of select="key('colorNumKey','c8')"/>

    c7's colors:
```

```
<xsl:for-each select="key('colorNumKey','c7')">
 <xsl:value-of select="."/><xsl:text> </xsl:text>
</xsl:for-each>

Looking up the color ID with the color name:

blue's cid: <xsl:value-of select="key('colorKey','blue')/@cid"/>

black's cid: <xsl:value-of select="key($keyName,'black')/@cid"/>

gray's cid: <xsl:value-of select="key('colorKey','gray')/@cid"/>
</xsl:template>

<!-- Don't bother outputting shirt contents for this example. -->
<xsl:template match="shirt"/>

</xsl:stylesheet>
```

Before discussing what the template does, let's look at the result it creates:

```
Looking up the color name with the color ID:

c3's color: red

c4's color: blue

c8's color:

c7's colors:
orange green

Looking up the color ID with the color name:

blue's cid: c4

black's cid: c2

gray's cid:
```

The first three xsl:value-of instructions use the same "colorNumKey" key as the previous example. The first xsl:-value-of instruction passes the literal string "c3" as the index value to look up. The result shows that "c3" is the key for the color "red". The second shows how a variable can be used for this argument to the key() function: an xsl:variable instruction near the beginning of the stylesheet declares a testVar variable with a value of "c4", and when the XSLT processor uses this variable to look up a color name, the result shows the color "blue".

The third xsl:value-of instruction in the stylesheet passes the string "c8" to use for the lookup. No color element exists here with a cid attribute value of "c8", so nothing shows up in the result tree after "c8's color:".

The next part of the template looks up the value "c7". The document has two color elements with a cid value of "c7", so the template uses an xsl:for-each instruction instead of an xsl:value-of instruction to add both to the result tree. (If the template had used xsl:value-of, only the first would have appeared in the result.) A key() function can return multiple nodes, and this one does, so the xsl:for-each instruction iterates through the "c7" nodes, printing the value and a space (using an xsl:text element for the latter) for each.

The beginning of this stylesheet declares two keys: the "colorNumKey" is the same one we saw in the previous stylesheet; and the second key, "colorKey", is used by the remaining `xsl:variable` instructions in this new stylesheet. Its use attribute names the `color` elements' contents (".") as the lookup index. Each of the three `xsl:value-of` elements pass this key a color name to look up the node instead of passing a string to match against the `color` elements' `cid` values. The entire `color` node still gets returned, and these three `xsl:value-of` elements each pull `cid` attribute value out of this node by adding a slash and "@cid" to make a second location step for the XPath expression in each `xsl:value-of` element's `select` attribute.

So, instead of passing a color ID value to get a color name, these last three lookups are each passing a color name to get a color ID. They're looking up the same type of node in the same set of nodes using a different part of those nodes as the lookup index. Getting back to the table analogy, it's similar to looking up rows in the same table as before, but using a different column as the key field.

The first of these last three lookups passes the string "blue", and the XSLT processor adds "c4" as the corresponding color ID to the result tree. The second passes the string "black", but unlike any of the lookups before, this one identifies the key name by using a variable instead of a hard-coded string: `$keyName`, which was set to "colorKey" near the beginning of the stylesheet. This causes no problems, and the "c2" color ID corresponding to "black" is added to the result tree.

The last `key()` function call tries to look up the color name "gray". None exists in the key. The function returns nothing, and nothing is added after the text node "gray's cid" in the result tree.

The lookup keys don't have to be in the same document as the elements that trigger the lookup. If the example document's `colors` element had been in a separate document in a separate file, you could still declare its contents as a key and use it for looking up the `shirt` colors in this document. This ability to look up something in an external data source lets you develop some powerful document processing systems. (See section 6.3, "Multiple input documents," page 195, for information on reading in a second file and using that file's contents as a lookup key.)

5.10   FINDING THE FIRST, LAST, BIGGEST, AND SMALLEST

If you can describe a set of nodes from a document with a *single-step* XPath expression then you can get the first of those nodes by adding a predicate of `[1]` to that expression, and you can find the last node by adding a predicate of `[last()]`.

To demonstrate, let's look at the titles in the following `chapter` document. When processing the document, the XPath expression `descendant::title` contains all of the `title` elements within the `chapter` element, whether they're children, grandchildren, or descendants of the grandchildren:

```
<chapter><title>"Paradise Lost" Excerpt</title>
  <para>Then with expanded wings he steers his flight</para>
```

```
<figure><title>"Incumbent on the Dusky Air"</title>
<graphic fileref="pic1.jpg"/></figure>
<para>Aloft, incumbent on the dusky Air</para>
<sect1>
  <para>That felt unusual weight, till on dry Land</para>
  <figure><title>"He Lights"</title>
  <graphic fileref="pic2.jpg"/></figure>
  <para>He lights, if it were Land that ever burned</para>
  <sect2>
    <para>With solid, as the Lake with liquid fire</para>
    <figure><title>"The Lake with Liquid Fire"</title>
    <graphic fileref="pic3.jpg"/></figure>
  </sect2>
</sect1>
</chapter>
```

The following template lists the first and last title elements in the chapter document by adding the [1] and [last()] predicates to that XPath expression:

```
<!-- xq358.xsl: converts xq357.xml into xq359.txt -->

<xsl:template match="chapter">
  First title in chapter:
  <xsl:value-of select="descendant::title[1]"/>
  Last title in chapter:
  <xsl:value-of select="descendant::title[last()]"/>
</xsl:template>
```

Although the first title element in the chapter is a child of the chapter element and the last title element is a great-great-grandchild (being a grandchild of the sect2 element, which is a grandchild of chapter), the template rule finds them and adds their contents to the result tree:

```
  First title in chapter:
  "Paradise Lost" Excerpt
  Last title in chapter:
  "The Lake with Liquid Fire"
```

Why doesn't this work with a multi-step XPath expression? Because a predicate in an XPath location step is only applied to the nodes in that location step. For example, let's say we want the last title of the last figure element in the chapter shown above. The XPath expression in the following template won't do it:

```
<!-- xq360.xsl: converts xq357.xml into xq361.txt -->

<xsl:template match="chapter">
  Last figure title in chapter?
    <xsl:value-of select="descendant::figure/title[last()]"/>
  No.
</xsl:template>
```

The [last()] predicate here isn't asking for the last figure title in the chapter; it's looking for the last title element within each figure element. Each figure element has only one `title`, so the expression returns a node list of all those `figure` elements' `title` elements. When the `xsl:value-of` instruction converts a node list to a text node for the result tree, it only gets the first one, so we see the first `figure` element's `title` element in the result:

```
Last figure title in chapter?
   "Incumbent on the Dusky Air"
No.
```

What if we really do want the `title` of the last `figure` element in the chapter? The secret to getting the first or last node of a node list described by a more complex XPath expression is to have an `xsl:for-each` instruction get the list of nodes in question, and then get the last (or first) one in that list.

For example, the following template rule has an `xsl:for-each` instruction going through the `title` elements of all `figure` elements descended from the context node. As the `xsl:for-each` instruction goes through them, one `xsl:if` element inside the `xsl:for-each` instruction checks whether the node is first in this list, and, if so, it adds a message about this to the result tree. A second `xsl:if` element does the same for the last node in the list:

```
<!-- xq362.xsl: converts xq357.xml into xq363.txt -->

<xsl:template match="chapter">

  <xsl:for-each select="descendant::figure/title">

    <xsl:if test="position() = 1">
      First figure title in chapter: <xsl:value-of select="."/>
    </xsl:if>

    <xsl:if test="position() = last()">
      Last figure title in chapter: <xsl:value-of select="."/>
    </xsl:if>

  </xsl:for-each>

</xsl:template>
```

The result shows just what we wanted: the `title` of the first `figure` element in the document and the `title` of the last `figure` element in the document:

```
        First figure title in chapter: "Incumbent on the Dusky Air"
        Last figure title in chapter: "The Lake with Liquid Fire"
```

What if we wanted the figure titles that were the first and last alphabetically? We simply add an `xsl:sort` instruction inside the `xsl:for-each` element:

```
<!-- xq364.xsl: converts xq357.xml into xq365.txt -->

<xsl:template match="chapter">

  <xsl:for-each select="descendant::figure/title">

    <xsl:sort/>

    <xsl:if test="position() = 1">
```

```
        First figure title in chapter: <xsl:value-of select="."/>
      </xsl:if>

      <xsl:if test="position() = last()">
        Last figure title in chapter: <xsl:value-of select="."/>
      </xsl:if>

    </xsl:for-each>

</xsl:template>
```

The result shows the first and last entries from an alphabetically sorted list of figure titles:

```
      First figure title in chapter: "He Lights"
      Last figure title in chapter: "The Lake with Liquid Fire"
```

(Because the xsl:sort instruction has no select attribute to identify a sort key, a default sort key of "." is used, which uses the string-value of the current node—in this case, the nodes that the xsl:for-each element is counting through—as the sort key. (See section 6.7, "Sorting," page 215, for more on ways to control sorting.)

In addition to using the xsl:sort instruction to find the first and last values alphabetically, you can use it to find the first and last or greatest and smallest values for any sort key. For example, let's say we want to know who has the highest and lowest salaries of all the employees in the following list:

```
<employees>

  <employee hireDate="04/23/1999">
    <last>Hill</last>
    <first>Phil</first>
    <salary>100000</salary>
  </employee>

  <employee hireDate="09/01/1998">
    <last>Herbert</last>
    <first>Johnny</first>
    <salary>95000</salary>
  </employee>

  <employee hireDate="08/20/2000">
    <last>Hill</last>
    <first>Graham</first>
    <salary>89000</salary>
  </employee>

</employees>
```

The following template rule sorts the employee elements within the employees element by their salary, with a data-type attribute telling the XSLT processor to treat the salary values as numbers and not as strings. (Otherwise, a salary of "100000" would come before a salary of "89000".) As with the previous example, two xsl:if elements add messages to the result for the first and last nodes in the list as the xsl:for-each instruction counts through the nodes:

```
<!-- xq367.xsl: converts xq366.xml into xq368.txt -->

<xsl:template match="employees">
  <xsl:for-each select="employee">
  <xsl:sort select="salary" data-type="number"/>

    <xsl:if test="position() = 1">
      Lowest salary: <xsl:apply-templates/>
    </xsl:if>

    <xsl:if test="position() = last()">
      Highest salary: <xsl:apply-templates/>
    </xsl:if>

  </xsl:for-each>
</xsl:template>
```

Because this list is sorted numerically by employee salary, the result tells us which employees have the lowest and highest salaries:

```
    Lowest salary:
  Hill
  Graham
  89000

    Highest salary:
  Hill
  Phil
  100000
```

If the employees' salary figures were stored in an attribute instead of in an element, finding the largest and smallest salary figures would be the same, except that the template would sort the `employee` elements using the `salary` attribute value as a sort key instead of the `salary` child element. For anything you can sort on, you can always find the first or last values of the sorted list. This makes it easy to find the biggest, smallest, earliest, latest, or whatever values the first and last entries of that sorted list represent.

5.11 USING THE *W3C XSLT* SPECIFICATION

The W3C's XSLT Recommendation (available at http://www.w3.org/TR/xslt) is a specification describing the XSLT language and the responsibilities of XSLT processors. If you're new to XSLT, the Recommendation can be difficult to read, especially if you're not familiar with W3C specifications in general and the XML, XPath, and Namespaces specs in particular.

This chapter summarizes some of the concepts and terms most likely to confuse an XSLT novice reading the XSLT Recommendation. Much of this material is available in other parts of the book, especially in part 1 and the glossary, but as a centralized collection of it, this section provides a companion to the W3C specification for beginners who want to tackle XSLT's primary reference.

But first, what do we mean by "Recommendation"? The W3C can't force anyone to do anything, so they call a specification that has been through their whole process of drafts, reviews, discussions, revisions, and final approval a "Recommendation."

The first step on this path is Working Draft status. A Working Draft comes from either a submission by a W3C member company or from a Working Group formed by the W3C to work on the specification. Further work is done by a Working Group that makes the draft public at various stages for comments from both within and outside of the W3C. The beginning of each specification describes where to send comments and where on the web to read comments that have been sent so far. (See http://www.w3org/TR for links to all the specs in any stage of W3C consideration.)

When the Working Group feels that the Working Draft is ready, they submit it to the W3C director for possible promotion to Candidate Recommendation status. This used to be the last stop before becoming an official Recommendation, but the W3C has recently added a new penultimate stage: Proposed Recommendation. The Candidate Recommendation stage is now the time when application developers are encouraged to implement the spec, and if all goes well, the Candidate Recommendation becomes a Proposed Recommendation. If everyone (in the W3C, that is) is happy with the Proposed Recommendation at that point, it becomes a Recommendation. XSLT 1.0 reached this point on November 16th, 1999.

W3C specs are generally specifications for software behavior aimed at programmers. They rarely include tutorials and can be tough to read whether you jump in somewhere in the middle or start from the beginning. Like most W3C specs, the XSLT Recommendation has confusing terms that get used often. Even more confusing are the pairs of terms just similar enough to make them easy to mix up.

5.11.1   Pairs of confusing related terms

document element and document root   For an XML document to be well formed, the last tag must be an end-tag corresponding to the start-tag that starts the whole thing—in other words, one single element must enclose all the other elements. We call that element the document element. If a DOCTYPE declaration exists, it names the element type of that document element. If you picture a tree of the document's elements, that element would be the root of that tree. But, remember, other kinds of trees can represent a document, such as a DOM tree or the source and result trees used in XSLT. These trees have their own root node, and the node representing the document element is a child of that root. This way, if the document has comments or processing instructions outside of the document element, they can still be represented as part of the document tree, as sibling nodes of the document element node.

expression and pattern   In XSLT, an XPath expression uses the XPath language to describe a set of nodes. Patterns, which specify a set of conditions a node must meet, use a subset of XPath expression syntax that limits you to using the `child` and `attribute` axes. Because expressions are discussed more often, it can be confusing to see something like "wine[@year='1999']" referred to as a pattern when it looks like an XPath expression. It *is* an XPath expression in addition to being a pattern, but if it's being used as the `match` value of an `xsl:template` element or an `xsl:key` element, or as the `count` or `from` attribute of an `xsl:number` element, it's acting as a match pattern.

node and element, tree and document   Computer programs use tree-like structures to represent a lot of things. In fact, several different ways exist for trees to represent the same XML document: to show its entity structure; to show its element structure; or to appear as a Document Object Model (DOM) tree. In trees used to store an XML document for processing with an XSLT stylesheet, the nodes, or components, can be element nodes, attribute nodes, text nodes, processing instruction nodes, comment nodes, or namespace nodes. For most documents, most of the nodes are element nodes, so nodes and elements can seem almost synonymous at times. For example, to find a sibling element (an element with the same parent as the context node), you'll want a sibling node (a node with the same parent as the one in question) that happens to be an element node.

template and template rule   A template rule consists of two parts: a pattern matched against the source tree nodes, and a template that gets added to the result tree for each node that matches that pattern. In an XSLT stylesheet, `xsl:template` elements represent template rules; the value of these elements' `match` attributes are the patterns to match against the source tree nodes; and the elements' content (the part between the `xsl:template` elements' start- and end-tags) are the templates. The fact that an `xsl:template` element doesn't represent an XSLT template, but instead represents a template rule, adds to the confusion.

XSLT elements and instructions   Using XSLT is about learning how to use the elements from the XSLT namespace such as `xsl:template`, `xsl:apply-templates`, and `xsl:output`. XSLT elements such as `xsl:apply-templates`, `xsl:text`, and `xsl:element` that tell the XSLT processor to add something to the result tree are sometimes called instructions. Since most XSLT elements are instructions, the terms can sometimes seem to mean the same thing, but some XSLT elements aren't instructions: "top-level" elements such as `xsl:output` and `xsl:strip-space` give more general instructions to the XSLT processor about how to perform the transformation.

URL and URI   "URI" stands for Uniform Resource Identifiers, the system for naming resources on the web. Web address URLs such as http://www.snee.com are the most common form of URIs. For now, URIs that aren't URLs are so rare that the terms "URI" and "URL" are practically synonymous.

5.11.2   Other confusing terms

context node   An XPath term. In XSLT, a context node generally refers to the source tree node currently being processed by the XSLT processor. Inside an `xsl:for-each` loop, the context node is the one currently being processed by the loop. In a template rule (and outside of an `xsl:for-each` loop), it's usually the node that matched the pattern in the `xsl:template` element's `match` attribute to trigger the template rule.

expanded-name   An expanded-name is an attribute or element's name and its namespace URI (if this namespace isn't null) taken together. For the `xsl:stylesheet` element, the expanded-name would be "http://www.w3.org/1999/XSL/Transform" and "stylesheet."

instantiate   In the world of object-oriented development, a class declaration describes the structure and behavior of a particular class of objects. When one of these objects (also known as an "instance" of that class) is created in memory, we say that it is "instantiated." In XSLT, a template describes the structure of something that may be added to the result tree, and when an instance of that template is added to the result tree, we also say that the template is "instantiated."

location step   An XPath expression consists of one or more location steps separated by slashes. Each location step can have up to three parts: an axis specifier, a required node test, and an optional predicate. The XPath expression "child::wine" has one step, and "wines/wine/attribute:year" has three. (See section 2.1, "Location paths, axes, node tests, and predicates," page 24, for more information.)

NCName   The XSLT specification describes many components of XSLT syntax as "NCNames," a term that comes from the W3C namespace specification. To simplify a little, an NCName is any name that begins with a letter or underscore and has no space or colon in it ("NC" = No Colon). It can't have a colon because it may have a namespace prefix added to its beginning. Namespace prefixes themselves are also defined as NCNames. Because the prefix and the part after it are connected by a colon, a colon within these names would confuse a processor trying to figure out where the prefix ended and the other part began, so they both must be "No Colon" names. (See also *QName* on page 186.)

NameTest   A NameTest is an XPath term used to show where you can put

- the name of an element type or attribute, with or without a namespace prefix
- an asterisk as a wildcard representing any name
- a namespace prefix followed by a colon and an asterisk, representing any name in a particular namespace

For example, when the XSLT spec tells you that the `xsl:strip-space` element has an `elements` attribute where you list the elements whose extra whitespace nodes you want stripped, it doesn't actually tell you to list elements there, but instead tells you that it's a list of NameTests to show that all the possibilities described by the list above are legal in this attribute.

node-set-expression   A node-set-expression is an XPath expression describing a set of nodes.

QName   A QName is a "Qualified Name" that includes an optional namespace prefix and colon before a required "local part," which is an NCName. For example, the value of an xsl:template element's name attribute is a QName. A QName can be a simple name, such as "indexTemplate", or it can include a namespace prefix and colon, as with "snee:indexTemplate".

token, nmtoken   To a parser (that is, to a program that reads in text and has to figure out what its pieces are and how they're related), a token is the smallest string of characters that can function as a unit. An element name, the "<?" that starts a processing instruction, a variable name, and the word "if" in a C or Java program are all tokens.

In XML, an nmtoken (name token) is a token composed of the characters that are allowed for names according to the XML spec: basically, letters, digits, the period, hyphen, underscore, and colon, with no whitespace splitting the name up. (Compare with "NCName," on page 185.) A lot of places in XML-related specs such as the XSLT Recommendation say "token" or "nmtoken" instead of saying "some name that you or someone made up goes here".

top-level   A top-level element is a special XSLT stylesheet element (an element from the http://www.w3.org/1999/XSL/Transform namespace) that is a child of the stylesheet's xsl:stylesheet document element. Except for the xsl:template element, which specifies a template rule for the stylesheet, the others specify general instructions about the stylesheet, such as global variables, other stylesheets to import, and instructions about the format of the result document. Nearly all XSLT elements that are not top-level elements are used in the templates inside the template rules.

The XSLT spec also refers to top-level variables, which are variables that are global across the stylesheet so that they can be referenced from within any stylesheet element. (A template rule can also have its own local variables that can be referenced only from within that template rule. (See section 5.8.1, "Variables," page 164, for more on using variables in stylesheets.)

C H A P T E R   6

Specialized input & output

6.1   HTML AND XSLT

If your application is reading or writing the HTML flavor known as XHTML (a W3C standard form of HTML that follows all the rules of XML—documents are well-formed, empty elements have start- and end-tags or closing slashes, and entities besides XML's five predefined ones are explicitly declared), then you have nothing to worry about. XHTML is perfectly good XML just like anything else that XSLT can read or write. If your application is reading older legacy HTML or outputting HTML for use in older browsers, however, you should keep in mind a few small problems, as well as some simple techniques for getting around these problems.

6.1.1   HTML as input

XSLT processors expect their input to be well-formed XML. HTML documents can be well-formed, but most aren't. For example, any Web browser would understand the following HTML document, but a number of things prevent the document from being well-formed:

- The `html` start-tag lacks a corresponding end-tag.
- The tags enclosing the `h1` and `body` elements are not in a consistent case.
- The value of the `IMG` element's `SRC` attribute isn't quoted.
- The `br` and `IMG` elements' tags have no closing slash or matching end-tags to show that they're empty elements.

```
<html>
<body>
<h1>My Heading</H1>
<p>Here is the first paragraph.
<P>Here is the second.<br>
Second line of the second paragraph.
<IMG SRC=somepic.jpg>
</BODY>
```

If a browsing program can still figure out what's what in this document and display it on a screen, it had to be inevitable that someone would write a utility to parse such a document and output a proper well-formed version. Dave Raggett of the W3C turned out to be that person, and, luckily, his "HTML Tidy" program is free and available for many different platforms at http://www.w3.org/People/Raggett/tidy. With the -asxml option added to this tidy program's command line, telling it to include closing slashes in empty elements, it turns the HTML document above into the well-formed XHTML document below:

```
<?xml version="1.0"?>
<!DOCTYPE html PUBLIC "-//W3C//DTD XHTML 1.0 Strict//EN"
    "http://www.w3.org/TR/xhtml1/DTD/strict.dtd">
<html xmlns="http://www.w3.org/TR/xhtml1">
<head>
<title></title>
</head>
<body>
<h1>My Heading</h1>

<p>Here is the first paragraph.</p>

<p>Here is the second.<br />
Second line of the second paragraph. <img src="somepic.jpg" /></p>
</body>
</html>
```

Writing an XSLT stylesheet to process this tidied-up version is no different from writing an XSLT stylesheet to process any other well-formed XML. One XSLT trick that comes in particularly handy when reading XHTML documents as input is the use of numeric predicates in XPath expressions or match patterns to convert HTML td elements ("table data"—that is, the cells of an HTML table) into elements with more meaningful names. For example, if you have an HTML table where you know that the first column consistently shows employee last names; the second shows first names, the third shows salaries; and the fourth shows a hire date, like this,

```
<html>
<body>
<table>
<tr>
  <td>Hill</td><td>Phil</td><td>100000</td><td>4/23/1999</td>
</tr>
<tr>
  <td>Herbert</td><td>Johnny</td><td>95000</td><td>09/01/1998</td>
</tr>
<tr>
  <td>Moss</td><td>Sterling</td><td>97000</td><td>10/16/2000</td>
</tr>
</table>
</body>
</html>
```

you can convert each of these columns of td elements to elements with names that reflect their contents better. You can do this by using a number in square brackets to point to the td element inside each tr element that serves the purpose you need:

```
<!-- xq377.xsl: converts xq376.html into xq378.xml -->
<xsl:stylesheet xmlns:xsl="http://www.w3.org/1999/XSL/Transform"
     version="1.0">
<xsl:output method="xml" omit-xml-declaration="yes" indent="no"/>

<xsl:template match="table">
  <employees><xsl:apply-templates/></employees>
</xsl:template>

<xsl:template match="tr">
  <employee hireDate="{td[4]}">
    <last><xsl:value-of select="td[1]"/></last>
    <first><xsl:value-of select="td[2]"/></first>
    <salary><xsl:value-of select="td[3]"/></salary>
  </employee>
</xsl:template>

</xsl:stylesheet>
```

This simple stylesheet, with only those two template rules, converts the HTML table above into the following more valuable XML:

```
<employees>
<employee hireDate="4/23/1999"><last>Hill</last>
<first>Phil</first><salary>100000</salary></employee>
```

```
<employee hireDate="09/01/1998"><last>Herbert</last>
<first>Johnny</first><salary>95000</salary></employee>
<employee hireDate="10/16/2000"><last>Moss</last>
<first>Sterling</first><salary>97000</salary></employee>
</employees>
```

Section 2.4, "Predicates," on page 43, and section 3.4, "Previous, next, first, third, last siblings," page 53, provide more background on referring to elements by their numeric position among their siblings.

6.1.2 HTML as output

A basic rule of XSLT is that your stylesheets must be well-formed. All tags must either be a member of a start- and end-tag pair or an empty element tag with its closing slash. Since the XSLT processor's output will reflect the structure of much of the stylesheet, this could be a problem when creating HTML to be read by older browsers. More recent browsers may have no problem with a closing slash in empty HTML elements such as br, hr, and img, but older browsers won't know what to do with elements that have this closing slash—remember, when early versions of the popular browsers were released XML hadn't been invented yet. (Because XHTML is an XML way to store HTML, XHTML documents will have this closing slash in these empty elements.)

If you're going to the trouble of converting your XML to HTML, you probably want to ensure that the widest possible array of browsers can read the Web pages that you're creating, and XSLT's xsl:output element lets you do this. By setting its method attribute to a value of "html", you're telling the XSLT processor to represent empty HTML elements (area, base, basefont, br, col, frame, hr, img, input, isindex, link, meta and param, according to the XSLT spec) as a single tag with no closing slash. For example:

```
<!-- xq380.xsl: converts xq381.xml into xq382.html -->

<xsl:stylesheet xmlns:xsl="http://www.w3.org/1999/XSL/Transform"
     version="1.0">

<xsl:output method="html"/>

<xsl:template match="poem">
  <html><body>
    <xsl:apply-templates/>
  </body></html>
</xsl:template>

<xsl:template match="title">
  <h1><xsl:apply-templates/></h1>
</xsl:template>

<xsl:template match="excerpt">
  <p><xsl:apply-templates/></p>
  <hr></hr>
</xsl:template>

<xsl:template match="verse">
```

```
    <xsl:apply-templates/><br/>
</xsl:template>

</xsl:stylesheet>
```

An XSLT processor using the stylesheet above converts this XML document

```
<poem><title>From Book I</title>
<excerpt><!-- I 225 - 229 -->
<verse>Then with expanded wings he steers his flight</verse>
<verse>Aloft, incumbent on the dusky Air</verse>
<verse>that felt unusual weight, till on dry Land</verse>
<verse>He lights, if it were Land that ever burne'd</verse>
<verse>With solid, as the Lake with liquid fire;</verse>
</excerpt>
<excerpt><!-- 632 - 635 -->
<verse>For who can yet believe, though after loss</verse>
<verse>That all these puissant Leginos, whose exile</verse>
<verse>Hath emptied Heav'n, shall fail to re-ascend</verse>
<verse>Self-rais'd, and repossess their native seat.</verse>
<verse></verse>
</excerpt>
</poem>
```

to this HTML document:

```
<html>
    <body>
        <h1>From Book I</h1>

        <p>
            Then with expanded wings he steers his flight<br>
            Aloft, incumbent on the dusky Air<br>
            that felt unusual weight, till on dry Land<br>
            He lights, if it were Land that ever burne'd<br>
            With solid, as the Lake with liquid fire;<br>

        </p>
        <hr>

        <p>
            For who can yet believe, though after loss<br>
            That all these puissant Leginos, whose exile<br>
            Hath emptied Heav'n, shall fail to re-ascend<br>
            Self-rais'd, and repossess their native seat.<br>
            <br>

        </p>
        <hr>

    </body>
</html>
```

After converting each excerpt element to a p element, the stylesheet adds an HTML hr element for a horizontal rule. When copying each verse element to the result tree, it adds an HTML `br` ("break") element after it. Because the stylesheet itself must be well-formed, it includes both the start- and end-tags for the `hr` elements, and uses a `br` element with a closing slash to show that it represents an empty element. (Both empty elements could have been represented either way in the stylesheet.)

Because of the stylesheet's `xsl:output` element, the `hr` and `br` elements in the HTML output are single tags with no closing slash, just as they were in pre-XML styles of HTML.

The `xsl:output` element with a `method` value of "html" isn't always necessary. If your stylesheet doesn't specify otherwise, the XSLT processor will know that the stylesheet is creating an HTML document if the root element of your output (or, technically, the only element child of the result tree's root) is an `html` element. The XSLT processor that sees this and isn't directed otherwise will output `hr`, `img`, and the other empty HTML elements as single tags without the closing slash. As with most system development issues, being explicit is better in the long run, because it makes your intentions that much clearer and your code therefore more understandable if you include the `xsl:output` element with a `method` attribute of "html" when you want your stylesheet to create old-fashioned HTML output.

For related information, see:

- section 4.5, "Processing instructions," page 106
- section 6.5, "Non-XML output," page 202
- section 6.8, "Stripping all markup from a document," page 224
- section 6.9, "Valid XML output: including DOCTYPE declarations," page 225

6.2   BROWSERS AND XSLT

Most XSLT processors offer some way to tell them "here is the source document and here is the stylesheet to use when processing it." For a command line XSLT processor, the document and stylesheet are usually two different parameters to specify at the command line.

Web browsers, however, usually read a document from a web server and have no way to separately be told about the stylesheet to apply. To remedy this, the W3C Recommendation "Associating Style Sheets with XML Documents" describes a processing instruction that you can put at the beginning of a document to name a stylesheet to apply to that document. For example, a processing instruction like the one in the following document tells an application to apply the stylesheet xq603.xsl to that document:

```
<?xml version="1.0"?>
<?xml-stylesheet href="xq603.xsl" type="text/xsl" ?>
<poem>
  <title>"Paradise Lost" excerpt</title>
  <verse>Him thus intent <prop>Ithuriel</prop> with his spear</verse>
  <verse>Touched lightly; for no falsehood can endure</verse>
  <verse>Touch of Celestial temper, but returns</verse>
```

```
<verse>Of force to its own likeness: up he starts</verse>
<verse>Discovered and surprised.</verse>
</poem>
```

The processing instruction needs to be at the beginning of a document, unless an XML declaration exists first, as with this example. The processing instruction in the preceding example tells the application to apply the following stylesheet to the document:

```
<!-- xq603.xsl: converts xq602.xml into xq605.html -->
<xsl:stylesheet xmlns:xsl="http://www.w3.org/1999/XSL/Transform"
    version="1.0">
  <xsl:output method="html"/>

  <xsl:template match="poem">
   <html><body>
    <xsl:apply-templates/>
   </body></html>
  </xsl:template>

  <xsl:template match="title">
   <h1><xsl:apply-templates/></h1>
  </xsl:template>

  <xsl:template match="verse">
   <p><xsl:apply-templates/></p>
  </xsl:template>

  <xsl:template match="prop">
   <i><xsl:apply-templates/></i>
  </xsl:template>

</xsl:stylesheet>
```

(If you're using XSLT to create a document that has a processing instruction in it, see Section 4.5, "Processing instructions," on page 106, for information on using XSLT's `xsl:processing-instruction` instruction.) Applying the stylesheet shown to the example document with a command line XSLT processor creates the following result document:

```
<html>
    <body>
   <h1>"Paradise Lost" excerpt</h1>
   <p>Him thus intent <i>Ithuriel</i> with his spear</p>
   <p>Touched lightly; for no falsehood can endure</p>
   <p>Touch of Celestial temper, but returns</p>
   <p>Of force to its own likeness: up he starts</p>
   <p>Discovered and surprised.</p>
  </body>
</html>
```

The best thing about specifying a document's stylesheet with this xml-stylesheet processing instruction is that it lets you use the document and designated stylesheet with a web browser.

6.2.1 Internet Explorer

When Microsoft's Internet Explorer web browser reads the preceding XML document and XSLT stylesheet, it converts the source document to HTML according to the stylesheet's instructions and displays the document as if it were the result tree HTML document, as you can see in figure 6.1

Figure 6.1
Internet Explorer displaying an XML document converted with an XSLT stylesheet

As I write this, the version of Internet Explorer that you download from Microsoft's web site won't really do this. I had to download a more recent version of one component of Internet Explorer called msxml.dll. This is the file responsible for Internet Explorer's XML and XSLT processing, and it hasn't yet been incorporated into the general distribution of their browser. As you read this, it probably is part of the standard Microsoft browser, so no special extra steps should be necessary to read in an XML document and transform it with a stylesheet named by this processing instruction.

6.2.2 Netscape Navigator

As I write this (a phrase I must apologize for over-using, but waiting for all of the browser XSLT support to fall into place seems like a long wait), Netscape Navigator has no XSLT support. The recently released Navigator 6 was based on Netscape's open source Mozilla browser effort. Certain releases of Mozilla did have XSLT support, but that support wasn't carried over to the first release of Navigator 6.

Mozilla supported XSLT by incorporating an XSLT processor called TransforMiiX. It used the same `xml-stylesheet` processing instruction as Internet Explorer to indicate an XML document's stylesheet. Even though full XSLT support from Netscape has a way to go, it's encouraging to see both Microsoft and the Netscape effort supporting the W3C's syntax for linking a document to a stylesheet.

6.3 MULTIPLE INPUT DOCUMENTS

When you run an XSLT processor, you tell the processor where to find the source tree document—probably in a disk file on a local or remote computer—as well as the stylesheet to apply to that document. You can't tell the processor to apply the stylesheet to multiple input documents at once. The document() function, however, lets the stylesheet name an additional document to read in. You can insert the whole document into the result tree or insert part of it, based on a condition described by an XPath expression. You can even use this function with the xsl:key instruction and key() function to look up a key value in a document outside your source document.

To start with a simple example, let's look at a stylesheet that copies one document and inserts another into the result document. It will read this document

```
<shirts>
  <shirt colorCode="c4">oxford button-down</shirt>
  <shirt colorCode="c1">poly blend, straight collar</shirt>
  <shirt colorCode="c6">monogrammed, tab collar</shirt>
</shirts>
```

and copy it to the result tree, inserting this xq485.xml document after the result version's shirts start-tag:

```
<!-- xq485.xml -->
<colors>
  <color cid="c1">yellow</color>
  <color cid="c2">black</color>
  <color cid="c3">red</color>
  <color cid="c4">blue</color>
  <color cid="c5">purple</color>
  <color cid="c6">white</color>
  <color cid="c7">orange</color>
  <color cid="c7">green</color>
</colors>
```

The stylesheet that does this has just two template rules. The second copies all the source tree nodes to the result tree except the one for the shirts element, which is covered by the first template rule:

```
<!-- xq486.xsl: converts xq484.xml into xq491.xml -->
<xsl:stylesheet xmlns:xsl="http://www.w3.org/1999/XSL/Transform"
    version="1.0">
  <xsl:output method="xml" omit-xml-declaration="yes"/>

  <xsl:template match="shirts">
    <shirts>
      <xsl:apply-templates select="document('xq485.xml')"/>
```

```
      <xsl:apply-templates/>
    </shirts>
  </xsl:template>

  <xsl:template match="@*|node()">
    <xsl:copy>
      <xsl:apply-templates select="@*|node()"/>
    </xsl:copy>
  </xsl:template>

</xsl:stylesheet>
```

The first template rule's second `xsl:apply-templates` instruction copies the contents of a `shirts` element to the result tree between two `shirts` tags. Before that second `xsl:apply-templates` instruction, however, is another `xsl:apply-templates` instruction with a `select` attribute. This attribute's value calls the `document()` function and names the xq485.xml document as its one argument. The function reads in this XML document and parses it as an XML document, and the `xsl:apply-templates` instruction tells the XSLT processor to apply any relevant template rules to it. The stylesheet's second template is the relevant template. It processes the xq485.xml document's contents the same way that it processes the source tree document's content: copying it all to the result tree.

> **TIP** When a stylesheet uses the `document()` function to read in another document, that stylesheet can include template rules to process this other document's nodes as easily as it can include template rules to process the source tree's nodes.

Because the `xsl:apply-templates` instruction that uses the `document()` function comes after the `shirts` start-tag and before the `xsl:apply-templates` instruction that processes the content of the source document's `shirts` element, the contents of the xq485.xml document shows up in the result after the `shirts` start-tag and before the `shirts` element's contents:

```
<shirts><!-- xq485.xml --><colors>
  <color cid="c1">yellow</color>
  <color cid="c2">black</color>
  <color cid="c3">red</color>
  <color cid="c4">blue</color>
  <color cid="c5">purple</color>
  <color cid="c6">white</color>
  <color cid="c7">orange</color>
  <color cid="c7">green</color>
</colors>
  <shirt color="c4">oxford button-down</shirt>
  <shirt color="c1">poly blend, straight collar</shirt>
  <shirt color="c6">monogrammed, tab collar</shirt>
</shirts>
```

Don't confuse the document() function with the use of xsl:include and xsl:import. Those XSLT instructions let you insert one stylesheet inside another; the document() function lets you access other documents to combine with your source documents.

You don't need to insert the entire document read by the document() function into your result document. This next stylesheet is like the last one except that the xsl:apply-templates element's select attribute selects only the elements in that document whose cid attribute value equals "c7":

```
<!-- xq488.xsl: converts xq484.xml into xq492.xml -->

<xsl:template match="shirts">
  <shirts>
  <xsl:apply-templates select="document('xq485.xml')//*[@cid='c7']"/>
  <xsl:apply-templates/>
  </shirts>
</xsl:template>

<xsl:template match="@*|node()">
  <xsl:copy>
    <xsl:apply-templates select="@*|node()"/>
  </xsl:copy>
</xsl:template>
```

The result only has those elements from the xq485.xml inserted:

```
<shirts><color cid="c7">orange</color><color cid="c7">green</color>
  <shirt color="c4">oxford button-down</shirt>
  <shirt color="c1">poly blend, straight collar</shirt>
  <shirt color="c6">monogrammed, tab collar</shirt>
</shirts>
```

One valuable use of the document() function is to read in a document that stores elements to use for lookups. (For an introduction to the declaration and use of keys, see section 5.9, "Declaring keys and performing lookups," page 173.) For example, let's say we want to add the same source document's list of shirts to the result tree, but we want each shirt listed with its color name spelled out instead of its color code. We need to take the value of the colorCode attribute in each shirt element (for example, "c4" or "c1"), find the color element in the xq485.xml document that has that value in its cid attribute, and then output that color element's contents—the actual name of the color, such as "yellow" or "blue." The result should look like this:

```
blue oxford button-down
yellow poly blend, straight collar
white monogrammed, tab collar
```

The following stylesheet does this because it references the xq485.xml document twice, the stylesheet first declares a variable named colorLookupDoc whose value uses the document() function to read the document into a tree where it can be

referenced elsewhere in the document. (This is more efficient than making the document () function call twice.)

```
<!-- xq487.xsl: converts xq484.xml into xq493.xml -->
<xsl:stylesheet xmlns:xsl="http://www.w3.org/1999/XSL/Transform"
     version="1.0">
  <xsl:output method="text"/>

<xsl:variable name="colorLookupDoc" select="document('xq485.xml')"/>

<xsl:key name="colorNumKey" match="color" use="@cid"/>

<xsl:template match="shirts">
  <xsl:apply-templates select="$colorLookupDoc"/>
  <xsl:apply-templates/>
</xsl:template>

<xsl:template match="colors"/>

  <xsl:template match="shirt">
    <xsl:variable name="shirtColor" select="@colorCode"/>
    <xsl:for-each select="$colorLookupDoc">
      <xsl:value-of select="key('colorNumKey',$shirtColor)"/>
    </xsl:for-each>
    <xsl:text> </xsl:text><xsl:apply-templates/><xsl:text>
</xsl:text>
  </xsl:template>

</xsl:stylesheet>
```

The xsl:key instruction names a colorNumKey key as a group of color elements whose cid attribute will be used an index to look up specific color elements. When an efficient XSLT processor sees this instruction, it should create a hash
table in memory or another data structure to speed these lookups.

The template rule for the shirts element resembles the one in the earlier examples. It has two xsl:apply-templates instructions: one to read in the external
xq485.xml document (referring to this document in this example using the color-
LookupDoc variable instead of the document's filename) and another to process the
shirts element's contents.

A brief template rule for the colors element suppresses this element from being
copied to the result tree. Another template rule uses the key() function to look up
the color names within the xq485.xml document's colors element.

The template rule for the shirt element looks up the color name and adds it
to the result tree, followed by a single space (added by an xsl:text element) and
the contents of that element. The lookup is performed using a key() function that
names the colorNumKey key declared at the beginning of the stylesheet and the
color ID of the shirt element being processed as the value to look for in the key.
(The color ID is stored in a shirtColorCode variable declared at the beginning of
the template.)

Wrapping an `xsl:for-each` element around the `xsl:value-of` instruction that calls the `key()` function solves a small problem with using the `key()` function to look something up in another document. This function looks for key nodes in the same document as the context node, and without that `xsl:for-each` instruction, the context node for this `xsl:value-of` element is the `shirt` element being processed by the template rule. We're looking for a `color` element in the xq485.xml document, not in the same document as the `shirt` node, so we need to make xq485.xml the context node document for the `xsl:value-of` instruction. Wrapping it with an `xsl:for-each` instruction that selects xq485.xml (again, referenced using the variable `colorLookupDoc`) accomplishes this.

6.4   USING MODES TO CREATE TABLES OF CONTENTS AND OTHER GENERATED LISTS

XSLT's modes provide a way to have more than one template rule in a stylesheet for the same set of nodes and to use all these templates in one application of the stylesheet. This allows you to process the same source tree nodes more than once, adding them to the result tree multiple times with different markup each time.

For example, a stylesheet can have two different template rules for the `title` element children of the following document's `chapter` elements:

1. One template rule adds these `title` elements to their normal place at the beginning of each chapter.

2. One template rule for these same `title` elements adds them to a table of contents at the beginning of a document with a link to the corresponding copy of the same title put there by the other template rule.

```
<story>

  <chapter><title>Chapter 1</title>
    <para>A Dungeon horrible, on all sides round</para>
    <para>More unexpert, I boast not: them let those</para>
  </chapter>

  <chapter><title>Chapter 2</title>
    <para>Contrive who need, or when they need, not now.</para>
    <para>For while they sit contriving, shall the rest</para>
  </chapter>

  <chapter><title>Chapter 3</title>
    <para>Millions that stand in Arms, and longing wait</para>
    <para>So thick a drop serene hath quenched their Orbs</para>
  </chapter>

</story>
```

A stylesheet distinguishes between the two template rules by giving at least one a mode attribute value with an identifying name, and then using that name when applying the template with an `xsl:apply-templates` instruction. For example, the first template rule in the following stylesheet has two `xsl:apply-templates` elements after some opening HTML tags and a "Table of Contents" h1 header:

```
<!-- xq550.xsl: converts xq549.xml into xq551.html -->
<xsl:stylesheet xmlns:xsl="http://www.w3.org/1999/XSL/Transform"
     version="1.0">
  <xsl:output method="html"/>

  <xsl:template match="story">
    <html><body>
    <h1>Table of Contents</h1>
    <xsl:apply-templates select="chapter/title" mode="toc"/>
    <xsl:apply-templates/></body></html>
  </xsl:template>

  <xsl:template match="chapter/title">
    <h2><a name="{generate-id()}"/><xsl:apply-templates/></h2>
  </xsl:template>

  <xsl:template match="chapter/title" mode="toc">
    <p><a href="#{generate-id()}"><xsl:apply-templates/></a></p>
  </xsl:template>

  <xsl:template match="para">
    <p><xsl:apply-templates/></p>
  </xsl:template>

  <xsl:template match="story/title">
    <h1><xsl:apply-templates/></h1>
  </xsl:template>
</xsl:stylesheet>
```

An `xsl:apply-templates` instruction usually tells the XSLT processor to apply any applicable templates to the nodes described by the value of the `select` attribute (or, if no `select` attribute exists, to any children of the context node). The first of this template rule's `xsl:apply-templates` elements, however, has a `mode` attribute with a value of "toc", which tells the XSLT processor to only apply template rules that have a mode value of "toc" themselves. The third `xsl:template` element in the stylesheet is such a template rule, and it adds the chapter title surrounded by an HTML a element with a p element enclosing that. The a element has an `href` attribute linking it to an a element in the same document with a value given by the `generate-id()` function. (See section 6.12, "Generating IDs and links," page 243, for more on using this function to create internal HTML links.)

This template's a elements will link to additional a elements added to the result document by the stylesheet's second template rule. Whenever the XSLT processor finds a `title` child of a `chapter` element, this template rule tells the processor to add the `title` element's contents to the result document inside of an h2 element with an a element whose name attribute gets its value from the `generate-id()` function.

Let's review what this stylesheet does starting with the first template rule. For each `story` element, this template rule has the following elements in its template to add nodes to the result tree:

- start-tags for the HTML `html` and `body` elements
- a "Table of Contents" header as an `h1` element
- an `xsl:apply-templates` element with a mode setting of "toc". This adds the `title` children of `chapter` elements as processed by the stylesheet's third template rule, which puts each title in its own `p` element as a link to another copy of the same title later in the document.
- an `xsl:apply-templates` element with no `select` attribute value. This processes all the children (and, assuming the existence of the XSLT default templates, all the descendants) of the `story` element, even though some have already been processed by the first `xsl:apply-templates` element
- end-tags corresponding to the HTML `html` and `body` start-tags at the beginning of the template

The result shows that the `chapter` element's `title` contents were each added twice to the result tree: once after the "Table of Contents" header and once in their appropriate place in the body of the document:

```
<html>
    <body>
        <h1>Table of Contents</h1>
        <p>
            <a href="#N5">Chapter 1</a>
        </p>
        <p>
            <a href="#N16">Chapter 2</a>
        </p>
        <p>
            <a href="#N27">Chapter 3</a>
        </p>
  <h2>
            <a name="N5"></a>Chapter 1</h2>
    <p>A Dungeon horrible, on all sides round</p>
    <p>More unexpert, I boast not: them let those</p>
  <h2>
            <a name="N16"></a>Chapter 2</h2>
    <p>Contrive who need, or when they need, not now.</p>
    <p>For while they sit contriving, shall the rest</p>
  <h2>
            <a name="N27"></a>Chapter 3</h2>
    <p>Millions that stand in Arms, and longing wait</p>
    <p>So thick a drop serene hath quenched their Orbs</p>
    </body>
</html>
```

(Values created by the `generate-id()` function may be different when you run this example.) Even without using modes, nothing can prevent you from putting as many `xsl:apply-templates` instructions inside of a single template as you like. If none have `mode` values (or if they all have the same `mode` value), they'll just add identical copies of the appropriate node contents to the result tree by calling the same template rule repeatedly. Specifying different modes for each `xsl:apply-templates` instruction and adding corresponding template rules to the stylesheet lets you process the same source tree nodes multiple times with different processing each time, letting you re-use the same input in different ways.

This is a valuable technique for creating new documents out of old ones to get multiple uses out of the same content. This chapter's example created a table of contents to add to the source document's contents. An index, a list of figures or tables, or any other re-use of a subset of a document's contents would all be equally easy to create using XSLT modes.

6.5   NON-XML OUTPUT

Section 6.8, "Stripping all markup from a document," on page 224, describes how to convert a source tree to a result tree containing no tags. For more complex non-XML output, simply add whatever markup you like inside the template rules—as long as it doesn't turn your stylesheet into an ill-formed stylesheet. For example, the following will turn the sample input document below it into an RTF file:

```
<!-- xq387.xsl: converts xq388.xml into xq389.rtf (sample.rtf) -->

<xsl:stylesheet xmlns:xsl="http://www.w3.org/1999/XSL/Transform"
    version="1.0">

<xsl:output method="text"/>

<xsl:template match="article">{\rtf1 <xsl:apply-templates/> }
</xsl:template>

<xsl:template match="title">
\par  {\b <xsl:apply-templates/>}
</xsl:template>

<xsl:template match="p">
\par  <xsl:apply-templates/>
</xsl:template>

</xsl:stylesheet>
```

Don't forget the `xsl:output` element with "text" as the value of its `method` attribute. This does two things:

- It tells the XSLT processor not to add an XML declaration to the result tree. You could have done this just as well with an `omit-xml-declaration` attribute in the `xsl:output` element, so the next point is more important.

- It disables output escaping. If your input document has the string "3 < 4", it's going to represent it as "3 < 4" so that the XML parser doesn't treat that "<" character as the beginning of a tag. If the XSLT parser is creating an XML or HTML document in the result tree, it's going to write out that less-than character as an "<" entity reference so that the application reading in the result tree document doesn't mistake it for the beginning of a tag. Specifying a `method` value of "text" in the `xsl:output` element tells the XSLT processor "The result tree document is plain text that won't be read by an XML or HTML application, so don't worry about escaping special characters like '&' and '<' in the result."

The preceding stylesheet, when run with this input document,

```
<article>
<title author="bd" ver="1.0">My Article</title>
<p>First paragraph. 3 &lt; 4.</p>
<p>Second paragraph. AT&amp;T is a big company.</p>
</article>
```

outputs this RTF document:

```
{\rtf1
\par  {\b My Article}

\par  First paragraph. 3 < 4.
\par  Second paragraph. AT&T is a big company. }
```

Microsoft Word has no problem with this RTF file, displaying it as shown in figure 6.2.

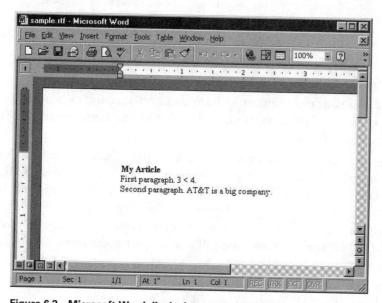

Figure 6.2   Microsoft Word displaying created RTF file

Another classic use of plain text output from XML input is the creation of comma-separated value (CSV) files. For example, to turn this input document

```
<employees>
<emp>
  <lName>Moss</lName><fName>Sterling</fName>
  <hireDate>19980323</hireDate>
</emp>
<emp>
  <lName>Hill</lName><fName>Phil</fName>
  <hireDate>19991103</hireDate>
</emp>
</employees>
```

into a comma-separated text file like this,

```
Moss,Sterling,19980323
Hill,Phil,19991103
```

the following stylesheet is all you need:

```
<!-- xq392.xsl: converts xq390.xml into xq391.txt -->

<xsl:stylesheet xmlns:xsl="http://www.w3.org/1999/XSL/Transform"
    version="1.0">

  <xsl:output method="text" indent="no"/>

  <xsl:template match="emp">
    <xsl:apply-templates select="lName"/><xsl:text>,</xsl:text>
    <xsl:apply-templates select="fName"/><xsl:text>,</xsl:text>
    <xsl:apply-templates select="hireDate"/>
  </xsl:template>

</xsl:stylesheet>
```

This stylesheet has three special features:

- The xsl:output element with the method attribute value set to "text" prevents the XSLT processor from adding an XML declaration to the beginning of the CSV output file.

- The xsl:output element's indent attribute value of "no" tells the XSLT processor not to indent the result. If you usually use XSLT to create XML output, you don't care about extra indenting, because these indentations make your output easier to read, and an XML parser reading that output will ignore the whitespace anyway. An application reading comma-separated values, however, might treat extra spaces at the beginning of a line as part of the first value on that line.

- An XSLT processor strips any whitespace between elements that isn't next to character data. If the commas in the stylesheet were not enclosed in xsl:text elements, the XSLT processor would have preserved the carriage returns you see in the stylesheet after them, because the carriage returns would have been next to character data: the commas. This would have broken up the output lines. Using the `xsl:text` elements prevented that outcome. (Another technique for avoiding carriage returns in the CSV output lines is to put everything in the `match="emp"` template rule on one line, which makes the stylesheet harder to read and prevents it from fitting on its page in this book.)

For related information, see:

- section 6.8, "Stripping all markup from a document," page 224
- section 6.11, "Whitespace: preserving and controlling," page 229

6.6   NUMBERING, AUTOMATIC

The `xsl:number` instruction makes it easy to insert a number into your result document. Its `value` attribute lets you name the number to insert, but if you really want to add a specific number to your result, it's much simpler to add that number as literal text. When you omit the `value` attribute from an `xsl:value-of` instruction, the XSLT processor calculates the number based on the context node's position in the source tree or among the nodes being counted through by an `xsl:for-each` instruction.

Eight other attributes are available to tell the XSLT processor how you want your numbers to look. Before we look at them, we'll start by numbering the color names in this simple document:

```
<colors>
  <color>red</color>
  <color>green</color>
  <color>blue</color>
  <color>yellow</color>
</colors>
```

The following template adds a number before each `color` element and puts a period and a space between the number and the element's content:

```
<!-- xq395.xsl: converts xq394.xml into xq396.txt -->

<xsl:template match="color">
  <xsl:number/>. <xsl:apply-templates/>
</xsl:template>
```

The result adds a simple number before each period:

```
1. red
2. green
3. blue
4. yellow
```

The `format` attribute gives you greater control over the numbers' appearance. The following stylesheet adds the color list to the result tree four times, using upper and lowercase Roman numerals in the `format` attribute the first two times and upper and lowercase letters the third and fourth times. In this stylesheet, the period and space are in the `format` attribute value instead of being literal text after the `xsl:number` instruction as they were in the previous example. This will be useful as we explore fancier numbering, such as "2.1.3" for a subsection:

```
<!-- xq397.xsl: converts xq394.xml into xq398.txt -->

<xsl:template match="colors">

  <xsl:for-each select="color">
    <xsl:number format="I. "/><xsl:value-of select="."/><xsl:text>
</xsl:text>
  </xsl:for-each>

<xsl:text>
~~~~~~~~~~~~~~~~~~~~~~~~
</xsl:text>

  <xsl:for-each select="color">
    <xsl:number format="i. "/><xsl:value-of select="."/><xsl:text>
</xsl:text>
  </xsl:for-each>

<xsl:text>
~~~~~~~~~~~~~~~~~~~~~~~~
</xsl:text>

  <xsl:for-each select="color">
    <xsl:number format="A. "/><xsl:value-of select="."/><xsl:text>
</xsl:text>
  </xsl:for-each>

<xsl:text>
~~~~~~~~~~~~~~~~~~~~~~~~
</xsl:text>

  <xsl:for-each select="color">
    <xsl:number format="a. "/><xsl:value-of select="."/><xsl:text>
</xsl:text>
  </xsl:for-each>

</xsl:template>
```

To output the same list from the preceding XML document four times, this stylesheet has a single template rule for the list's parent element, `colors`. Its template has four `xsl:for-each` elements, one for each pass through the list.

> **TIP**   `xsl:for-each` elements are a popular place to use the `xsl:number` instruction, because a template that needs to iterate through a list of nodes and to add nodes to the result tree may well want to add them with numbers (or letters) in front of them.

The stylesheet also has `xsl:text` nodes to add carriage returns after each color name and a line of tilde characters (~) between each set of color names. Using the same color names input document, this stylesheet creates the following result document:

```
I. red
II. green
III. blue
IV. yellow

~~~~~~~~~~~~~~~~~~~~~~~~
i. red
ii. green
iii. blue
iv. yellow

~~~~~~~~~~~~~~~~~~~~~~~~
A. red
B. green
C. blue
D. yellow

~~~~~~~~~~~~~~~~~~~~~~~~
a. red
b. green
c. blue
d. yellow
```

The next example shows how leading zeros before a "1" in a format attribute tell the XSLT processor to pad the number with zeros to make it the width shown. The "001. " in the template above will (in addition to adding a period and a space after each number) add as many zeros as necessary before each number to make it three digits wide:

```
<!-- xq399.xsl: converts xq400.xml into xq401.txt -->
<xsl:template match="color">
    <xsl:number format="001. "/><xsl:apply-templates/>
</xsl:template>
```

For example, it converts this source document

```
<colors>
  <color>red</color>
  <color>green</color>
  <color>blue</color>
  <color>yellow</color>
  <color>purple</color>
  <color>brown</color>
  <color>orange</color>
  <color>pink</color>
  <color>black</color>
  <color>white</color>
  <color>gray</color>
</colors>
```

to this:

```
001. red
002. green
```

```
003. blue
004. yellow
005. purple
006. brown
007. orange
008. pink
009. black
010. white
011. gray
```

The xsl:number element's grouping-separator and grouping-size attributes let you add punctuation to larger numbers to make them easier to read. For example, a grouping-separator value of "," and a grouping-size value of "3" put commas before each group of three digits in numbers over 999, so that 10000000 gets formatted as 10,000,000. (These two attributes work as a pair. If you use either without the other, the XSLT processor ignores it.)

If a value is specified for the xsl:number element's lang attribute, an XSLT processor may check the value and adjust the formatting of the numbers or letters to reflect the conventions of the specified language.

The xsl:number element's letter-value attribute also makes it easier to follow the numbering conventions of other languages—the attribute can have a value of either "alphabetic" or "traditional" to distinguish between the use of letters as letters and their use in some other numbering system. For example, the English language uses the letters I, V, X, C, M, and others for Roman numerals, in which case they're certainly not listed in alphabetical order. XSLT processors have built-in recognition of the difference between using these characters as alphabetic characters and as Roman numerals (see the use of the format attribute above), but for similar cases with other spoken languages, the letter-value attribute can make the stylesheet developer's intent clearer.

The level attribute specifies which source tree levels will be counted for the xsl:number element's value. Its default value is "single". A level value of "multiple" lets you count nested elements such as the color elements in this document:

```
<colors>
  <color>red</color>
  <color>green</color>
  <color>blue
    <color>robin's egg</color>
    <color>navy</color>
    <color>cerulean</color>
  </color>
  <color>yellow</color>
</colors>
```

Note how the color element with "blue" as a value contains three more color elements. To number this nested list along with the main color list, the following template rule has a value of "multiple" specified for the level attribute:

```
<!-- xq403.xsl: converts xq402.xml into xq404.xsl -->

  <xsl:template match="color">
    <xsl:number level="multiple" format="1. "/>
    <xsl:apply-templates/>
  </xsl:template>
```

When processing the XML document above, this stylesheet numbers the color "blue" as "3." and the list of colors inside of it as "3.1.", "3.2.", and "3.3.":

```
1. red
2. green
3. blue
   3.1. robin's egg
   3.2. navy
   3.3. cerulean
4. yellow
```

The level attribute can also let you do this with elements that are nested inside other kinds of elements. When you do this, the count and from attributes give you greater control over what gets counted for each level of numbering. To illustrate what these attributes can do when working together, we'll use this DocBook document:

```
<book><title>Title of Book</title>
 <chapter><title>First Chapter</title>
  <sect1><title>First Section, First Chapter</title>
    <figure><title>First picture in book</title>
      <graphic fileref="pic1.jpg"/></figure>
  </sect1>
 </chapter>
 <chapter><title>Second Chapter</title>
  <sect1><title>First Section, Second Chapter</title>
   <sect2>
    <title>First Subsection, First Section, Second Chapter</title>
    <figure><title>Second picture in book</title>
      <graphic fileref="pic2.jpg"/></figure>
   </sect2>
   <sect2>
    <title>Second Subsection, First Section, Second Chapter</title>
    <figure><title>Third picture in book</title>
      <graphic fileref="pic1.jpg"/></figure>
   </sect2>
   <sect2>
    <title>Third Subsection, First Section, Second Chapter</title>
    <figure><title>Fourth picture in book</title>
      <graphic fileref="pic1.jpg"/></figure>
   </sect2>
  </sect1>
  <sect1><title>Second Section, Second Chapter</title>
   <para>The End.</para>
  </sect1>
 </chapter>
</book>
```

This next template rule resembles the one that numbered the nested list of colors. It numbers the `sect1` elements and has a value of "multiple" for the `xsl:number` instruction's `level` attribute:

```
<!-- xq406.xsl: converts xq405.xml into xq407.txt -->

<xsl:template match="sect1">
  <xsl:number format="1. " level="multiple"/>
  <xsl:apply-templates/>
</xsl:template>
```

The result numbers the `sect1` elements, but only the `sect1` elements:

```
Title of Book
 First Chapter
   1. First Section, First Chapter
     First picture in book

 Second Chapter
   1. First Section, Second Chapter

     First Subsection, First Section, Second Chapter
     Second picture in book

     Second Subsection, First Section, Second Chapter
     Third picture in book

     Third Subsection, First Section, Second Chapter
     Fourth picture in book

   2. Second Section, Second Chapter
     The End.
```

If we want the `sect1` elements in chapter 2 to be numbered 2.1, 2.2, 2.3, the "sect1" template rule needs the `count` attribute to tell the XSLT processor which level of elements to count. The template rule for the nested `color` elements didn't need this because, when no `count` attribute is specified, the XSLT processor counts any node with the same type as the current node. In that case, the current node was a `color` element, so it counted all the `color` element nodes, even when some were inside others.

In this next template rule, the `xsl:number` instruction counts `chapter` and `sect1` elements to figure out the number to assign to each `sect1` element:

```
<!-- xq408.xsl: converts xq405.xml into xq409.txt -->
<xsl:stylesheet xmlns:xsl="http://www.w3.org/1999/XSL/Transform"
    version="1.0">
<xsl:output method="xml" omit-xml-declaration="yes"/>

<xsl:template match="sect1">
  <xsl:number format="1. " level="multiple" count="chapter|sect1"/>
  <xsl:apply-templates/>
</xsl:template>

</xsl:stylesheet>
```

Applying this template to the same source document does number the sect1 elements as 2.1 and 2.2, but it doesn't number the chapter elements:

```
Title of Book
 First Chapter
  1.1. First Section, First Chapter
    First picture in book

 Second Chapter
  2.1. First Section, Second Chapter

    First Subsection, First Section, Second Chapter
    Second picture in book

    Second Subsection, First Section, Second Chapter
    Third picture in book

    Third Subsection, First Section, Second Chapter
    Fourth picture in book

  2.2. Second Section, Second Chapter
    The End.
```

That's because it's a template rule for the sect1 element, and the stylesheet had no template rule to add numbers for the chapter elements. The next stylesheet includes a "chapter" template rule along with a sect2 template rule that counts the chapter, sect1, and sect2 elements to create three-level numbers for the sect2 elements:

```
<!-- xq410.xsl: converts xq405.xml into xq411.txt -->

<xsl:template match="chapter">
  <xsl:number format="1. "/>
  <xsl:apply-templates/>
</xsl:template>

<xsl:template match="sect1">
  <xsl:number format="1. " level="multiple" count="chapter|sect1"/>
  <xsl:apply-templates/>
</xsl:template>

<xsl:template match="sect2">
  <xsl:number format="1. " level="multiple"
              count="chapter|sect1|sect2"/>
  <xsl:apply-templates/>
</xsl:template>

</xsl:stylesheet>
```

With the same document as input, the output shows first, second, and third level numbered headers for the chapter, sect1, and sect2 elements:

```
Title of Book
 1. First Chapter
  1.1. First Section, First Chapter
    First picture in book
```

```
 2. Second Chapter
  2.1. First Section, Second Chapter
   2.1.1.
    First Subsection, First Section, Second Chapter
    Second picture in book

   2.1.2.
    Second Subsection, First Section, Second Chapter
    Third picture in book

   2.1.3.
    Third Subsection, First Section, Second Chapter
    Fourth picture in book

  2.2. Second Section, Second Chapter
    The End.
```

What if we don't want renumbering to restart with the beginning of each chapter or section? For example, if we number the `figure` elements with the following template rule,

```
<!-- xq412.xsl: converts xq405.xml into xq413.txt -->

<xsl:template match="figure">
  <xsl:number format="1. "/><xsl:apply-templates/>
</xsl:template>

</xsl:stylesheet>
```

they all come out as number 1, because each is the first `figure` element within its particular container element:

```
Title of Book
 First Chapter
  First Section, First Chapter
    1. First picture in book

 Second Chapter
  First Section, Second Chapter

    First Subsection, First Section, Second Chapter
    1. Second picture in book

    Second Subsection, First Section, Second Chapter
    1. Third picture in book

    Third Subsection, First Section, Second Chapter
    1. Fourth picture in book

  Second Section, Second Chapter
    The End.
```

We want the figures to be numbered sequentially throughout the book, so we set the `xsl:number` element's `level` attribute to "any". This tells the XSLT processor to count all the nodes that are the same as the current node (in this case, `figure` nodes) throughout the document. With this one small change in the previous template rule,

```
<!-- xq414.xsl: converts xq405.xml into xq415.txt -->

<xsl:template match="figure">
  <xsl:number format="1. " level="any"/><xsl:apply-templates/>
</xsl:template>

</xsl:stylesheet>
```

the result versions of the figure elements are numbered 1, 2, 3, and 4 throughout the document, regardless of the source tree level where each one is located:

```
Title of Book
 First Chapter
  First Section, First Chapter
    1. First picture in book

 Second Chapter
  First Section, Second Chapter

    First Subsection, First Section, Second Chapter
    2. Second picture in book

    Second Subsection, First Section, Second Chapter
    3. Third picture in book

    Third Subsection, First Section, Second Chapter
    4. Fourth picture in book

  Second Section, Second Chapter
   The End.
```

If you don't want numbering to start at the beginning of your document and keep advancing throughout that document, but you also don't want an element type's number reset to 1 each time that element shows up in a new container, you can use the xsl:number element's from attribute to constrain a level value of "any". If the from attribute names an element type (and it can name several, because you can use a pattern here), counting restarts each time—and only when—one of those named elements starts.

Using the from attribute gives you more flexibility than using a level value of multiple because the XSLT processor won't worry about the number of hierarchical levels between the elements being counted and the ones used for resetting the counting. For example, the following template rule is exactly like the last one except for its from value of "chapter":

```
<!-- xq416.xsl: converts xq405.xml into xq417.txt -->

<xsl:template match="figure">
  <xsl:number format="1. " level="any" from="chapter"/>
  <xsl:apply-templates/>
</xsl:template>

</xsl:stylesheet>
```

It numbers the figure elements sequentially, regardless of their level, restarting the count with each new chapter:

```
Title of Book
 First Chapter
  First Section, First Chapter
    1. First picture in book

 Second Chapter
  First Section, Second Chapter

    First Subsection, First Section, Second Chapter
    1. Second picture in book

    Second Subsection, First Section, Second Chapter
    2. Third picture in book

    Third Subsection, First Section, Second Chapter
    3. Fourth picture in book

  Second Section, Second Chapter
   The End.
```

You can use the from attribute with a level value of "multiple", but the XSLT processor will still reset the counting with descendants of any from elements. For example, if that xsl:number tag in the last example had said

```
<xsl:number format="1. " level="multiple" from="chapter|figure"/>
```

all the figures would have been number 1 because the level setting of "multiple" would have told the XSLT processor to reset the numbering for each sect2 element.

> **TIP** Heavy use of the xsl:number instruction slows your XSLT processor down. By heavy use, I don't necessarily mean stylesheets that use this instruction a lot—if your stylesheet only uses it once in one template and your source document has the XSLT processor calling that template 1000 times, that's heavy use. For really simple numbering, an xsl:value-of instruction that uses the position() function in its select attribute can mean a faster document transformation than you'll get using the xsl:number instruction.

The following template rule uses the position() function in an xsl:value-of element's select attribute to put numbers before each color element's content as that content is added to the result tree. The xsl:text element adds a carriage return after the contents of each color element:

```
<!-- xq418.xsl: converts xq394.xml into xq419.txt -->

  <xsl:template match="colors">
    <xsl:for-each select="color">
      <xsl:value-of select="position()"/>. <xsl:value-of select="."/>
      <xsl:text>
</xsl:text>
    </xsl:for-each>
  </xsl:template>
```

With the simple `colors` document shown at the beginning of this chapter, it creates this output:

```
1. red
2. green
3. blue
4. yellow
```

Adding numbers this way doesn't give you all the formatting control that you have with the `xsl:number` instruction, but if you only need a simple sequence of numbers in your list, doing it this way can mean much faster transformation times.

Remember that `position()` in this example refers to the node's position among the nodes selected for the `xsl:for-each` instruction—in this case, the `color` children of the `colors` element. If you had tried to number the `color` elements this way,

```
<!-- xq420.xsl: converts xq394.xml into xq421.txt -->

  <xsl:template match="color">
     <xsl:value-of select="position()"/>. <xsl:apply-templates/>
  </xsl:template>
```

the XSLT processor would have counted each `color` element's position among *all* of the `colors` element's children, including the text nodes storing the carriage returns between each `color` element in the source tree. The result would be this:

```
2. red
4. green
6. blue
8. yellow
```

The text nodes holding those carriage returns are the first, third, fifth, seventh, and ninth child nodes of the `colors` element. Numbers don't show up for them because the stylesheet only has a template rule for `color` elements and none to add the carriage returns to the result tree. Still, the `position()` function counts both the `color` children and the text node children between them to determine the numbers to put before each color name in the result document. (One thing that may be confusing is that carriage returns are whitespace, so the extra nodes being counted are nodes you can't see.) In the previous example, the `xsl:for-each` instruction ensured that the `count()` function counted only the nodes that we wanted it to count: the `color` element nodes.

6.7　SORTING

The `xsl:sort` instruction lets you sort a group of similar elements. Attributes for this element let you add details about how you want the sort done. You can sort using alphabetic or numeric ordering, sort on multiple keys, and reverse the sort order.

To demonstrate different ways to sort, we'll use the following document:

```
<employees>

  <employee hireDate="04/23/1999">
    <last>Hill</last>
    <first>Phil</first>
    <salary>100000</salary>
  </employee>

  <employee hireDate="09/01/1998">
    <last>Herbert</last>
    <first>Johnny</first>
    <salary>95000</salary>
  </employee>

  <employee hireDate="08/20/2000">
    <last>Hill</last>
    <first>Graham</first>
    <salary>89000</salary>
  </employee>

</employees>
```

This first sorting stylesheet sorts the `employee` children of the `employees` element by salary:

```
<!-- xq424.xsl: converts xq423.xml into xq425.xml -->
<xsl:stylesheet xmlns:xsl="http://www.w3.org/1999/XSL/Transform"
     version="1.0">

  <xsl:output method="text"/>

  <xsl:template match="employees">
    <xsl:apply-templates>
      <xsl:sort select="salary"/>
    </xsl:apply-templates>
  </xsl:template>

  <xsl:template match="employee">
    Last:      <xsl:apply-templates select="last"/>
    First:     <xsl:apply-templates select="first"/>
    Salary:    <xsl:apply-templates select="salary"/>
    Hire Date: <xsl:apply-templates select="@hireDate"/>
    <xsl:text>
</xsl:text>

  </xsl:template>

</xsl:stylesheet>
```

It's pretty simple. The `employees` element's template has an `xsl:apply-templates` instruction with an `xsl:sort` child to tell the XSLT processor to sort the `employees` element's child elements. The `xsl:sort` instruction's `select` attribute specifies the sort key to use: the `employee` elements' `salary` values. (If you omit the `select` attribute, the XSLT processor uses a string version of the elements to be sorted as a sort key.) The `employee` element's template adds each of its child node's values to the result tree preceded by a label. A final xsl:text element adds a carriage return after each hire date value.

TIP   Most xsl:apply-templates elements you see in XSLT stylesheets are empty. When you sort an element's children, the xsl:sort element goes between the start- and end-tags of the xsl:apply-templates element that tells the XSLT processor to process these children. The only other place you can put an xsl:sort instruction is inside the xsl:for-each instruction used to iterate across a node set.

With the preceding document, this stylesheet gives us the following output:

```
Last:      Hill
First:     Phil
Salary:    100000
Hire Date: 04/23/1999

Last:      Hill
First:     Graham
Salary:    89000
Hire Date: 08/20/2000

Last:      Herbert
First:     Johnny
Salary:    95000
Hire Date: 09/01/1998
```

The employees are sorted by salary, but they're sorted alphabetically—"1" comes before "8" and "9", so a salary of "100000" comes first. We want the salary values treated as numbers, so we make a simple addition to the template's xsl:sort instruction:

```
<!-- xq426.xsl: converts xq423.xml into xq427.xml -->

<xsl:template match="employees">
  <xsl:apply-templates>
    <xsl:sort select="salary" data-type="number"/>
  </xsl:apply-templates>
</xsl:template>
```

Now, the output is sorted by the salary element's numeric value:

```
Last:      Hill
First:     Graham
Salary:    89000
Hire Date: 08/20/2000

Last:      Herbert
First:     Johnny
Salary:    95000
Hire Date: 09/01/1998

Last:      Hill
First:     Phil
Salary:    100000
Hire Date: 04/23/1999
```

To reverse the order of this or any other sort, add an `order` attribute with a value of "descending":

```
<!-- xq428.xsl: converts xq423.xml into xq429.xml -->

<xsl:template match="employees">
  <xsl:apply-templates>
    <xsl:sort select="salary" data-type="number" order="descending"/>
  </xsl:apply-templates>
</xsl:template>
```

Whether the `data-type` attribute has a value of "number" like the stylesheet above or "text" (the default), an `order` value of "descending" reverses the order of the sort:

```
Last:      Hill
First:     Phil
Salary:    100000
Hire Date: 04/23/1999

Last:      Herbert
First:     Johnny
Salary:    95000
Hire Date: 09/01/1998

Last:      Hill
First:     Graham
Salary:    89000
Hire Date: 08/20/2000
```

If your `xsl:apply-templates` (or `xsl:for-each`) element has more than one `xsl:sort` instruction inside it, the XSLT processor treats them as multiple keys to the sort. For example, the stylesheet with this next template sorts the employees by last name and then by first name, so that any employees with the same last name will be in first name order.

```
<!-- xq430.xsl: converts xq423.xml into xq431.xml -->

<xsl:template match="employees">
  <xsl:apply-templates>
    <xsl:sort select="last"/>
    <xsl:sort select="first"/>
  </xsl:apply-templates>
</xsl:template>
```

When applied to the document above, the result shows Johnny Herbert before Phil and Graham Hill, and the secondary sort puts Graham Hill before Phil Hill:

```
Last:      Herbert
First:     Johnny
Salary:    95000
Hire Date: 09/01/1998

Last:      Hill
First:     Graham
```

```
Salary:     89000
Hire Date:  08/20/2000

Last:       Hill
First:      Phil
Salary:     100000
Hire Date:  04/23/1999
```

The sort key doesn't need to be an element child of the sorted elements. The `xsl:sort` instruction's `select` attribute can take any XPath expression as a sort key. For example, the following version sorts the employees by their `hireDate` attribute values:

```
<!-- xq432.xsl: converts xq423.xml into xq433.xml -->

<xsl:template match="employees">
  <xsl:apply-templates>
    <xsl:sort select="@hireDate"/>
  </xsl:apply-templates>
</xsl:template>
```

Treating the dates as strings doesn't do much good, because they're sorted alphabetically,

```
Last:       Hill
First:      Phil
Salary:     100000
Hire Date:  04/23/1999

Last:       Hill
First:      Graham
Salary:     89000
Hire Date:  08/20/2000

Last:       Herbert
First:      Johnny
Salary:     95000
Hire Date:  09/01/1998
```

but it's easy enough to have three sort keys based on the year, month, and day substrings of the date string:

```
<!-- xq434.xsl: converts xq423.xml into xq435.xml -->

<xsl:template match="employees">
  <xsl:apply-templates>
    <xsl:sort select="substring(@hireDate,7,4)"/> <!-- year  -->
    <xsl:sort select="substring(@hireDate,1,2)"/> <!-- month -->
    <xsl:sort select="substring(@hireDate,3,2)"/> <!-- day   -->
  </xsl:apply-templates>
</xsl:template>
```

This stylesheet sorts the dates properly:

```
Last:       Herbert
First:      Johnny
```

```
Salary:     95000
Hire Date:  09/01/1998

Last:       Hill
First:      Phil
Salary:     100000
Hire Date:  04/23/1999

Last:       Hill
First:      Graham
Salary:     89000
Hire Date:  08/20/2000
```

All the examples so far have sorted the children (the `employee` elements) of an element (`employees`) using one or more child nodes of those children (the `salary`, `first`, and `last` elements or the `hireDate` attribute) as sort keys. The previous example's use of the `hireDate` attribute showed that the expression used as the `xsl:sort` element's `select` attribute doesn't have to be a child element name, but can be an attribute name instead—or even a value returned by a function.

Your sort key can be an even more complex XPath expression. For example, the next stylesheet sorts the `wine` elements in this document's `winelist` element, but not by a child of the `wine` element. This stylesheet sorts the `wine` elements by a grandchild of the `wine` elements: the `prices` child's `discounted` element:

```
<winelist>

  <wine grape="Chardonnay">
    <winery>Lindeman's</winery>
    <product>Bin 65</product>
    <year>1998</year>
    <prices>
      <list>6.99</list>
      <discounted>5.99</discounted>
      <case>71.50</case>
    </prices>
  </wine>

<wine grape="Chardonnay">
  <winery>Benziger</winery>
  <product>Carneros</product>
  <year>1997</year>
  <prices>
    <list>10.99</list>
    <discounted>9.50</discounted>
    <case>114.00</case>
  </prices>
</wine>

  <wine grape="Cabernet">
    <winery>Duckpond</winery>
    <product>Merit Selection</product>
    <year>1996</year>
```

```
      <prices>
        <list>13.99</list>
        <discounted>11.99</discounted>
        <case>143.50</case>
      </prices>
    </wine>

    <wine grape="Chardonnay">
      <winery>Kendall Jackson</winery>
      <product>Vintner's Reserve</product>
      <year>1998</year>
      <prices>
        <list>12.50</list>
        <discounted>9.99</discounted>
        <case>115.00</case>
      </prices>
    </wine>
</winelist>
```

The sort key is only slightly more complicated than those shown in the earlier examples. It's an XPath expression saying "the discounted child of the prices element":

```
<!-- xq437.xsl: converts xq436.xml into xq438.xml -->
<xsl:stylesheet xmlns:xsl="http://www.w3.org/1999/XSL/Transform"
      version="1.0">

  <xsl:template match="winelist">
    <xsl:copy>
      <xsl:apply-templates>
        <xsl:sort   data-type="number" select="prices/discounted"/>
      </xsl:apply-templates>
    </xsl:copy>
  </xsl:template>

  <xsl:template match="*">
    <xsl:copy>
      <xsl:apply-templates/>
    </xsl:copy>
  </xsl:template>

</xsl:stylesheet>
```

The entire stylesheet is not big. It just copies the wine elements, sorted according to the sort key:

```
<?xml version="1.0" encoding="UTF-8"?>
<winelist>
<wine>
    <winery>Lindeman's</winery>
    <product>Bin 65</product>
    <year>1998</year>
    <prices>
      <list>6.99</list>
      <discounted>5.99</discounted>
```

```
        <case>71.50</case>
      </prices>
   </wine><wine>
   <winery>Benziger</winery>
   <product>Carneros</product>
   <year>1997</year>
   <prices>
      <list>10.99</list>
      <discounted>9.50</discounted>
      <case>114.00</case>
   </prices>
</wine><wine>
      <winery>Kendall Jackson</winery>
      <product>Vintner's Reserve</product>
      <year>1998</year>
      <prices>
         <list>12.50</list>
         <discounted>9.99</discounted>
         <case>115.00</case>
      </prices>
   </wine><wine>
      <winery>Duckpond</winery>
      <product>Merit Selection</product>
      <year>1996</year>
      <prices>
         <list>13.99</list>
         <discounted>11.99</discounted>
         <case>143.50</case>
      </prices>
   </wine></winelist>
```

Let's look at how the xsl:for-each instruction can use xsl:sort. The following stylesheet takes the same winelist document above and lists the wines. When the stylesheet gets to a Chardonnay, it lists all the other Chardonnays alphabetically:

```
<!-- xq439.xsl: converts xq436.xml into xq440.xml -->
<!DOCTYPE stylesheet [
<!ENTITY space "<xsl:text> </xsl:text>">
]>
<xsl:stylesheet xmlns:xsl="http://www.w3.org/1999/XSL/Transform"
     version="1.0">
  <xsl:output method="xml" omit-xml-declaration="yes" indent="no"/>

  <xsl:template match="wine">
   <xsl:apply-templates select="winery"/>&space;
   <xsl:apply-templates select="product"/>&space;
   <xsl:apply-templates select="year"/>&space;
   <xsl:apply-templates select="@grape"/>
   <xsl:if test="@grape = 'Chardonnay'">
     <xsl:text>
   other Chardonnays:
</xsl:text>
```

```
      <xsl:for-each
        select="preceding-sibling::wine[@grape = 'Chardonnay'] |
                        following-sibling::wine[@grape = 'Chardonnay']">
        <xsl:sort select="winery"/>
        <xsl:text>     </xsl:text>
        <xsl:value-of select="winery"/>&space;
        <xsl:value-of select="product"/><xsl:text>
</xsl:text>
      </xsl:for-each>
      </xsl:if>
    </xsl:template>
```

Before we examine how the stylesheet does this, let's take a look at the result:

```
Lindeman's Bin 65 1998 Chardonnay
  other Chardonnays:
    Benziger Carneros
    Kendall Jackson Vintner's Reserve

Benziger Carneros 1997 Chardonnay
  other Chardonnays:
    Kendall Jackson Vintner's Reserve
    Lindeman's Bin 65

Duckpond Merit Selection 1996 Cabernet

Kendall Jackson Vintner's Reserve 1998 Chardonnay
  other Chardonnays:
    Benziger Carneros
    Lindeman's Bin 65
```

First, notice the "&space;" entity references throughout the stylesheet. Instead of writing "<xsl:text> </xsl:text>" over and over because I needed single spaces in so many places, it was easier to declare an entity named space in the DOCTYPE declaration with this xsl:text element as content and then plug it in with an entity reference whenever I needed it.

The xsl:template template rule for the wine element has xsl:apply-templates instructions for its winery, product, and year element children followed by one for its grape attribute. Then, if the grape attribute has a value of "Chardonnay", it adds the text "other Chardonnays:" to the result tree followed by the list of Chardonnays, which are added to the result tree using an xsl:for-each instruction.

The select attribute of the xsl:for-each attribute selects all the nodes that are either preceding siblings of the current node with a grape value of "Chardonnay" or following siblings of the current node with the same grape value. (The "|" symbol is the "or" part.) For each wine element that meets this select attribute's condition, the template first adds some whitespace indenting with an xsl:text element, then the value of the wine element's winery child, a space, and the value of its product child. The first instruction in this xsl:for-each element is an xsl:sort element, which tells the XSLT processor to sort the nodes selected by the `xsl:for-each` instruction alphabetically in "winery" order. That's how the nodes look in the result: after the first "other Chardonnays:" label, "Kendall Jackson" comes after "Benziger"; after the second, "Lindeman's" comes after "Kendall Jackson"; and, after the last one, "Lindeman's" comes after "Benziger".

Because the `xsl:for-each` instruction lets you grab and work with any node set that you can describe using an XPath expression, the ability to sort one of these node sets makes `xsl:for-each` one of XSLT's most powerful features.

This chapter has only touched on the uses of `xsl:sort` in XSLT. You can combine it with other XSLT features to do even more. For example, see section 5.10, "Finding the first, last, biggest, and smallest," page 178.

For more background on other topics covered in this chapter see

- section 4.2, "Entities," page 87
- section 5.1.3, "'For' loops, iteration," page 118
- section 5.7.1, "Extracting and comparing strings," page 153
- section 5.10, "Finding the first, last, biggest, and smallest," page 178

6.8   STRIPPING ALL MARKUP FROM A DOCUMENT

How do we create a result tree with no markup? First, let's review the four ways to add XML elements to the result tree:

- putting elements from outside the XSLT namespace (or any declared extension namespace) into your stylesheet
- using the `xsl:element` instruction
- copying a source tree element node directly with `xsl:copy`
- copying a node and its children with `xsl:copy-of`

If you don't do any of these four approaches and remember to include the `xsl:output` element with a `method` attribute value of "text", your output won't even look like XML. The `xsl:output` element prevents the XSLT processor from adding an XML declaration to the result tree. If your output will be read by a non-XML application, an XML declaration will probably just confuse it. An `xsl:output` setting of "text" also tells the XSLT processor not to "escape" special characters—that is, the processor shouldn't substitute the entity reference "&" for ampersands and "<" for less-than characters in result tree text nodes. Instead, it leaves these characters alone, passing them to the result tree as plain text.

Text content of your input document's elements can be copied to the result tree with no attributes using a simple stylesheet that relies on XSLT's default template rules. The stylesheet below consists of an `xsl:stylesheet` element with an `xsl:output` element that specifies text output. It's all you need!

```
<!-- xq442.xsl -->

<xsl:stylesheet xmlns:xsl="http://www.w3.org/1999/XSL/Transform"
    version="1.0">

<xsl:output method="text"/>

</xsl:stylesheet>
```

This takes advantage of XSLT's built-in template rules, which are shown like this in the XSLT specification:

```
<!-- xq443.xsl -->

<xsl:template match="*|/">
  <xsl:apply-templates/>
</xsl:template>

<xsl:template match="text()|@*">
  <xsl:value-of select="."/>
</xsl:template>

<xsl:template match="processing-instruction()|comment()"/>
```

The first template says "for all element names and the root of the source tree, process content." The second template copies all text nodes and attributes, and the third suppresses the copying of processing instructions and comments.

For related information, see

- section 4.1, "Comments," page 84

- section 4.5, "Processing instructions," page 106

- and section 5.5, "Extensions to XSLT," page 143 for more on extension namespaces

- section 6.5, "Non-XML output," page 202

- section 6.10, "XML declarations," page 228

6.9   VALID XML OUTPUT: INCLUDING DOCTYPE DECLARATIONS

A valid XML document is one that has a document type (or "DOCTYPE") declaration and conforms to the DTD in that document type declaration.

TIP   An XML document with no DOCTYPE declaration isn't valid, but it can still be a legal XML document as long as it's well formed. "Valid" is a technical term referring to the presence of and conformance to a DOCTYPE declaration.

A DOCTYPE declaration can include DTD declarations as an internal DTD subset between square brackets, like this:

```
<!DOCTYPE chapter [
<!ELEMENT chapter (title,para+)>
<!ELEMENT title (#PCDATA)>
<!ELEMENT para (#PCDATA)>
]>
```

or it can point to a DTD declaration stored in a separate file like this:

```
<!DOCTYPE chapter SYSTEM "../dtds/chapter.dtd">
```

The SYSTEM identifier tells the XML parser where to find the DTD file on the system. An optional PUBLIC identifier can specify another string for the parser to use when locating a DTD file. These usually use a string similar to the following, which avoids any system-specific information to make the document more portable across different systems:

```
<!DOCTYPE chapter PUBLIC PUBLIC "-//OASIS//DTD DocBook XML//EN"
          "../dtds/chapter.dtd">
```

The XML parser should look up this PUBLIC identifier somewhere to find the exact location of the local copy of the DTD file. (Proposals exist for the format and location of the lookup table, but none has caught on enough to be a widespread standard in the XML world.) If it can't, it uses the SYSTEM identifier following the PUBLIC identifier. (In the example above, the SYSTEM identifier doesn't need the word "SYSTEM". Because it's a required parameter. The XML parser knows what it is.)

To create valid XML documents using XSLT, a stylesheet must add a DOCTYPE declaration to the result tree. Because a DOCTYPE declaration isn't an element or a processing instruction, standard methods for adding those to your result tree won't accomplish this. Instead, an XSLT processor knows that it must create a DOCTYPE declaration in your result document when it sees certain specialized attributes in an xsl:output element.

The most important attribute of the xsl:output element is the method attribute, which specifies whether the output document is XML, HTML, or text. Values of "html" or "text" for this attribute specify special treatment which makes it easier to create certain kinds of Web pages and plain text documents; (see section 6.1.2, "HTML as output," page 190, and section 6.5, "Non-XML output," page 202, for more on these). A value of "xml" is the default, so if you see no xsl:output instruction in a stylesheet, its result tree is supposed to represent an XML document.

The xsl:output instruction has other attributes that you can use to control aspects of your XML output, and two of these attributes let you add SYSTEM and PUBLIC declarations to a DOCTYPE declaration in your result. If your xsl:output element has a doctype-system attribute, the XSLT processor adds a DOCTYPE declaration to the result tree with that attribute's value as its SYSTEM identifier. If it also has a doctype-public attribute, it adds this attribute's value to the result's DOCTYPE declaration as a PUBLIC identifier. (An XSLT processor ignores an xsl:doctype-public attribute without an accompanying doctype-system attribute, because an XML document can't have a PUBLIC identifier without a SYSTEM identifier.)

The following example source document conforms to the DocBook DTD:

```
<chapter><title>Chapter 1</title>
  <para>More unexpert, I boast not: them let those</para>
  <para>Contrive who need, or when they need, not now.</para>
```

```
<para>For while they sit contriving, shall the rest,</para>
<para>Millions that stand in Arms, and longing wait</para>
</chapter>
```

The following stylesheet just copies it to the result tree. Because the stylesheet's `xsl:output` instruction includes both `doctype-system` and `doctype-public` attribute specifications, the result will include a DOCTYPE declaration with both of these identifiers:

```
<!-- xq449.xsl: converts xq448.xml into xq450.xml -->
<xsl:stylesheet xmlns:xsl="http://www.w3.org/1999/XSL/Transform"
    version="1.0">

<xsl:output method="xml" doctype-system="../dtds/docbookx.dtd"
    doctype-public="-//OASIS//DTD DocBook XML//EN"/>

<xsl:template match="@*|node()">
  <xsl:copy>
    <xsl:apply-templates select="@*|node()"/>
  </xsl:copy>
</xsl:template>

</xsl:stylesheet>
```

The stylesheet could have had different instructions after that `xsl:output` element to rearrange, rename, or delete the elements, or to perform any of the other XSLT tricks possible on the source tree's nodes as they're copied to the result tree. The DOCTYPE declaration added to the result tree would still look like the one produced by the stylesheet and input document above, as shown here:

```
<?xml version="1.0" encoding="utf-8" ?>
<!DOCTYPE chapter
  PUBLIC "-//OASIS//DTD DocBook XML//EN" "../dtds/docbookx.dtd">
<chapter><title>Chapter 1</title>
  <para>More unexpert, I boast not: them let those</para>
  <para>Contrive who need, or when they need, not now.</para>
  <para>For while they sit contriving, shall the rest,</para>
  <para>Millions that stand in Arms, and longing wait</para>
</chapter>
```

How does the XSLT processor know what to put for the document type (the "chapter" part in "DOCTYPE chapter")? It knows the root element of the document it's creating in the result tree, and that's what an XML document type is: the element that serves as the document's root element.

If the `method` attribute of the stylesheet's `xsl:output` element has a value of "text", then a DOCTYPE declaration for the result tree wouldn't make any sense. If `method` has a value of "html", a DOCTYPE declaration might make sense. Some Web pages, especially XHTML documents, actually do conform to a DTD, so specifying `doctype-system` and `doctype-public` attribute values for such an `xsl:output` element `method` attribute can be useful.

The DOCTYPE declarations added this way can only point to external DTD files. XSLT offers no way to create a result tree DOCTYPE declaration with an internal DTD subset—that is, with DTD declarations between the square brackets, as shown in the first example. The DTD named in your `doctype-system` attribute must have all the declarations that your document needs.

6.10 XML DECLARATIONS

The XML declaration at the beginning of an XML document is not necessary, but it's the best way to say "this is definitely an XML document and here's the release of XML to which it conforms." The following is typical:

```
<?xml version="1.0"?>
```

> **WARNING** Despite its beginning and ending question mark, an XML declaration is *not* a processing instruction; it's a separate kind of markup declaration. In fact, the XML specification explicitly prohibits the processing instruction target (the name right after a processing instruction's opening question mark) from being "xml" or "XML" in order to prevent a processing instruction from being confused with an XML declaration.

An XSLT processor's default behavior is to add an XML declaration to the beginning of an XML document created in the result tree. If your stylesheet includes an `xsl:output` instruction with a `method` value of "text" or "html", the XSLT processor doesn't consider the result tree's document to be XML, so it won't add an XML declaration. If `method` is "xml" or the stylesheet has no `xsl:output` element (in which case the default value of "xml" is assumed), the result is considered an XML document. To show the simplest case, we'll apply the simplest possible stylesheet

```
<!-- xq453.xsl: converts xq454.xml into xq455.xml -->
<xsl:stylesheet xmlns:xsl="http://www.w3.org/1999/XSL/Transform"
  version="1.0"/>
```

to this little document:

```
<test>Dagon his Name, Sea Monster</test>
```

The result, thanks to XSLT's built-in template rules, shows the element's character data with the XML declaration preceding it:

```
<?xml version="1.0" encoding="utf-8" ?>Dagon his Name, Sea Monster
```

Although an XML declaration is optional, when it is included, it must have the version information. As I write this, 1.0 is the only version of the XML specification available. In the example above, after the version information, the XML declaration includes an encoding declaration to tell us how the characters in the document are encoded. While the XML specification considers an encoding declaration to be optional when the document is encoded as UTF-8 or UTF-16, the XSLT specification says that XSLT processors must add one with a value of "utf-8" or "utf-16" if no other encoding value is specified.

You can specify one yourself or change the `version` value by adding encoding and `version` attributes to an `xsl:output` element in your stylesheet. The following stylesheet adds them:

```
<!-- xq456.xsl: converts xq454.xml into xq457.xml -->
<xsl:stylesheet xmlns:xsl="http://www.w3.org/1999/XSL/Transform"
  version="1.0">
  <xsl:output method="xml" version="1.1" encoding="utf-16"/>
</xsl:stylesheet>
```

Using the same input as the previous example this produces the following (although it may not look right in text editors that can't handle UTF-16):

```
<?xml version="1.1" encoding="utf-16" ?>Dagon his Name, Sea Monster
```

What if you don't want an XML declaration in the result of your transformation? For example, I rarely show them in the result of this book's examples because I wanted to make the examples as concise as possible. I suppressed them by adding an `omit-xml-declaration` attribute to most of the sample stylesheets' `xsl:output` elements, like this:

```
<!-- xq458.xsl: converts xq454.xml into xq459.txt -->
<xsl:stylesheet xmlns:xsl="http://www.w3.org/1999/XSL/Transform"
  version="1.0">
  <xsl:output method="xml" omit-xml-declaration="yes"/>
</xsl:stylesheet>
```

The output of this stylesheet applied to the earlier XML document is identical to the output created with the earlier stylesheet, minus the XML declaration:

```
Dagon his Name, Sea Monster
```

6.11   *WHITESPACE: PRESERVING AND CONTROLLING*

XML considers four characters to be whitespace: the carriage return, the linefeed, the tab, and the spacebar space. Microsoft operating systems put both a carriage return and a linefeed at the end of each line of a text file, and people usually refer to the combination as the "carriage return."

XSLT offers several techniques for controlling whitespace in your result document. It's important, however, to remember two things if you get frustrated over a lack of control:

- XSLT is an XML application that was originally designed to convert XML documents into XML documents.

- XML applications often seem to take a cavalier attitude toward whitespace because the rules about the places in an XML document where whitespace doesn't matter sometimes give these applications free rein to add or remove whitespace in certain places.

The moral of the story is that when you're using XSLT to create XML documents, you shouldn't worry too much about whitespace. When using it to create text documents and the whitespace isn't coming out the way you want, remember that XSLT is a transformation language, not a formatting language, and another tool may be necessary to give you the control you need. Extension functions may also provide relief. String manipulation is one of the most popular reasons for writing these functions. (See section 5.5.2, "Using built-in extension functions," page 146, for more. Also see section 3.10, "Empty elements: creating, checking for," page 67, for additional background on some tricks that whitespace can play in XSLT.)

6.11.1 xsl:strip-space and xsl:preserve-space

The `xsl:strip-space` instruction lets you specify source tree elements that should have whitespace text nodes (that is, text nodes composed entirely of whitespace characters) stripped.

Let's look at how this element can affect the following sample source document:

```
<colors>

<color>red</color>

<color>    yellow    </color>

<color>
blue
</color>

<!--
  Next color element has whitespace content.
-->
<color>    </color>

</colors>
```

To establish a baseline, this first stylesheet has no `xsl:strip-space` element. It's just an identity stylesheet—that is, a stylesheet that copies the source tree as is to the result tree.

```
<!-- xq506.xsl: converts xq505.xml into xq507.xml -->
<xsl:stylesheet xmlns:xsl="http://www.w3.org/1999/XSL/Transform"
    version="1.0">

  <xsl:output method="xml" omit-xml-declaration="yes"/>

  <xsl:template match="@*|node()">
   <xsl:copy>
    <xsl:apply-templates select="@*|node()"/>
   </xsl:copy>
  </xsl:template>

</xsl:stylesheet>
```

The result looks just like the source:

```
<colors>

<color>red</color>

<color>    yellow    </color>

<color>
blue
</color>

<!--
  Next color element has whitespace content.
-->
<color>       </color>

</colors>
```

Now we add an `xsl:strip-space` element to have the stylesheet strip whitespace text nodes from the `color` elements:

```
<!-- xq508.xsl: converts xq505.xml into xq509.xml -->
<xsl:stylesheet xmlns:xsl="http://www.w3.org/1999/XSL/Transform"
    version="1.0">

  <xsl:output method="xml" omit-xml-declaration="yes"/>

  <xsl:strip-space elements="color"/>

  <xsl:template match="@*|node()">
   <xsl:copy>
    <xsl:apply-templates select="@*|node()"/>
   </xsl:copy>
  </xsl:template>

</xsl:stylesheet>
```

When applied to the same source tree document, the result looks identical, except that the last `color` element is now an empty element. In the source tree, the element's only content was a text node of whitespace characters, and this node has been stripped:

```
<colors>

<color>red</color>

<color>    yellow    </color>

<color>
blue
</color>

<!--
  Next color element has whitespace content.
-->
<color/>

</colors>
```

Now let's tell the XSLT processor to strip the whitespace nodes from the parent colors element instead of the color elements:

```
<!-- xq510.xsl: converts xq505.xml into xq511.xml -->
<xsl:stylesheet xmlns:xsl="http://www.w3.org/1999/XSL/Transform"
     version="1.0">

  <xsl:output method="xml" omit-xml-declaration="yes"/>

  <xsl:strip-space elements="colors"/>

  <xsl:template match="@*|node()">
   <xsl:copy>
    <xsl:apply-templates select="@*|node()"/>
   </xsl:copy>
  </xsl:template>

</xsl:stylesheet>
```

This has a more drastic effect, because the colors element had many more white-space-only text nodes—all those carriage returns between the color elements. The only carriage returns in the whole document that made it to the result document are the ones that were either inside a color element (before and after "blue") or inside the comment:

```
<colors><color>red</color><color>     yellow     </color><color>
blue
</color><!--
  Next color element has whitespace content.
--><color>     </color></colors>
```

You can list more than one element type name in the xsl:strip-space instruction's elements attribute, as long as their names are separated by whitespace. You can also use an asterisk as this attribute's value to tell the XSLT processor to strip whitespace text nodes from all the elements in the source tree.

The xsl:preserve-space instruction does the opposite of the xsl:strip-space instruction. For all elements listed in its elements attribute, the XSLT processor will leave whitespace text nodes alone. By default, the XSLT processor treats all elements as xsl:preserve-space elements, so you only need it to override an xsl:strip-space instruction. For example, if your source document has twenty different element types and you want to strip whitespace nodes in all of them except the codeListing and sampleOutput elements, you don't have to list the other eighteen in an xsl:strip-space element's elements attribute. Instead, use an asterisk for the xsl:strip-space element's elements attribute value and list the two exceptions as the xsl:preserve-space element's elements attribute value.

```
<!-- xq512.xsl -->
<xsl:stylesheet xmlns:xsl="http://www.w3.org/1999/XSL/Transform"
     version="1.0">

<xsl:output method="xml" omit-xml-declaration="yes"/>
```

```
<xsl:strip-space elements="*"/>
<xsl:preserve-space elements="codeListing sampleOutput"/>

<xsl:template match="@*|node()">
 <xsl:copy>
  <xsl:apply-templates select="@*|node()"/>
 </xsl:copy>
</xsl:template>

</xsl:stylesheet>
```

6.11.2   Indenting

Setting the xsl:output element's indent attribute to a value of "yes" tells the
XSLT processor that it may add additional whitespace to the result tree. The default
value is "no."

WARNING   An indent value of "yes" means that an XSLT processor *may* add whitespace
to the result. The processor is not required to add whitespace, however, so
if setting this value doesn't have the effect you desire, try it with a different
XSLT processor. Or, check the processor's documentation. The Xalan C++
XSLT processor, for example, indents element's zero spaces as default, but
this figure can be reset with the -INDENT command line parameter.

The following stylesheet is the identity stylesheet with the xsl:output element's
indent value set to "yes". In other words, this stylesheet copies all the nodes of the
source tree document to the result tree without making any changes, except that the
XSLT processor may add more whitespace:

```
<!-- xq514.xsl: converts xq516.xml into xq517.xml -->
<xsl:stylesheet xmlns:xsl="http://www.w3.org/1999/XSL/Transform"
    version="1.0">

<xsl:output method="xml" omit-xml-declaration="yes" indent="yes"/>

<xsl:template match="@*|node()">
  <xsl:copy>
    <xsl:apply-templates select="@*|node()"/>
  </xsl:copy>
</xsl:template>

</xsl:stylesheet>
```

With an XSLT processor that does add whitespace, the stylesheet turns this source
document

```
<chapter><title>My Chapter</title>
<para>This paragraph introduces the chapter's sections.</para>
<sect1><title>Section 1 of "My Chapter"</title>
<para>Here is the first section's first paragraph.</para>
<para>Here is the first section's second paragraph.</para>
</sect1>
<sect1><title>Section 2 of "My Chapter"</title>
<para>Here is the first section's first paragraph.</para>
```

```
<sect2><title>Section 2.2</title>
<para>This section has a subsection.</para>
</sect2>
</sect1>
</chapter>
```

into this:

```
<chapter>
   <title>My Chapter</title>

   <para>This paragraph introduces the chapter's sections.</para>

   <sect1>
      <title>Section 1 of "My Chapter"</title>

      <para>Here is the first section's first paragraph.</para>

      <para>Here is the first section's second paragraph.</para>

   </sect1>

   <sect1>
      <title>Section 2 of "My Chapter"</title>

      <para>Here is the first section's first paragraph.</para>

      <sect2>
         <title>Section 2.2</title>

         <para>This section has a subsection.</para>

      </sect2>

   </sect1>

</chapter>
```

The added indenting makes the parent-child and sibling relationships of the elements much clearer, because a child element's tags are indented further than a parent element's tags, and siblings are all indented to the same level. When someone gives you an XML document with no DTD or schema and you need to figure out its structure, a pass through this little stylesheet is a great first step.

The XSLT specification warns us that it's "usually not safe" to set indent to "yes" with documents that contain elements that mix character data with child elements. For example, the first color child of the colors element in the following document has the string "red:" as character data, followed by three shade elements that are children of that color element. The second color element has only character data content (the string "yellow"), and the third one has a structure similar to the first one:

```
<colors>
<color>red:
<shade>fire engine</shade>
<shade>candy apple</shade>
```

```
<shade>brick</shade>
</color>
<color>yellow</color>
<color>blue:
<shade>navy</shade>
<shade>robin's egg</shade>
<shade>cerulean</shade>
</color>
</colors>
```

The same stylesheet indents the elements of this document, but not the first `shade` element in the first and third `color` elements:

```
<colors>

    <color>red:
<shade>fire engine</shade>

        <shade>candy apple</shade>

        <shade>brick</shade>

    </color>

    <color>yellow</color>

    <color>blue:
<shade>navy</shade>

        <shade>robin's egg</shade>

        <shade>cerulean</shade>

    </color>

</colors>
```

The stylesheet doesn't indent those two `shade` elements because that would add character data to the document. Adding whitespace *between* two elements (for example, between a `</color>` end-tag and a `<color>` start-tag in the example) doesn't affect a document's contents, but adding it *within* an element that has character data content adds text that an XML parser considers significant—in other words, it changes the content of the document.

To summarize, an `indent` value of "yes" is useful if every element in your source document has either character data and no elements as content (such as the `shade` elements above) or elements and no character data as content (such as the `colors` element in the example), but can lead to unpredictability if your source document has elements that mix child elements with character data such as the `color` elements above. The spaces that indent the other `shade` elements are also inside the "red" `color` element, but because this whitespace isn't being added to existing character data at those positions, the text nodes that they're in are pure whitespace, so the XML processor will ignore them. (It's a tricky concept. See section 6.11.1, "xsl:strip-space and xsl:preserve-space," page 230, for more on this.)

6.11.3 Adding and removing whitespace with xsl:text

The `xsl:text` instruction adds a text node to the result tree. When result tree whitespace characters—in particular, carriage returns—aren't coming out the way you want them, this element is handy for both adding and preventing whitespace in your result document.

For example, let's say you want to print out the children of this `employee` element with spaces or carriage returns between them:

```
<employee hireDate="09/01/1998">
   <last>Herbert</last>
   <first>Johnny</first>
   <salary>95000</salary>
</employee>
```

In this template rule, the comment shows that a space exists after the `xsl:apply-templates` element that adds the `hireDate` attribute value, and obviously a carriage return exists after that comment and the second and third `xsl:apply-templates` element.

```
<!-- xq529.xsl: converts xq528.xml into xq530.txt -->

  <xsl:template match="employee">
    <xsl:apply-templates select="@hireDate"/> <!-- note space -->
    <xsl:apply-templates select="first"/>
    <xsl:apply-templates select="last"/>
  </xsl:template>
```

Because an XML parser ignores whitespace between elements if that whitespace is the only character data between those elements, the XML parser that reads in the stylesheet and hands it to the XSLT processor won't hand over that space and those carriage returns, so the template creates this result from the source document:

```
09/01/1998JohnnyHerbert
```

The `xsl:text` element is a great way to say "don't throw this whitespace out." As explained in section 6.11.1, "xsl:strip-space and xsl:preserve-space," page 230, element types in your source document can be designated as whitespace-stripping or whitespace-preserving elements. XSLT stylesheets are XML documents too, and `xsl:text` elements are the only whitespace-preserving elements in those documents.

This revision of the previous template illustrates how `xsl:text` elements with a single space as content ensure that those spaces end up in the result:

```
<!-- xq531.xsl: converts xq528.xml into xq532.txt -->
<xsl:template match="employee">
  <xsl:apply-templates select="@hireDate"/><xsl:text> </xsl:text>
  <xsl:apply-templates select="first"/><xsl:text> </xsl:text>
  <xsl:apply-templates select="last"/>
</xsl:template>
```

When applied to the same source document, the revised stylesheet creates a result with spaces separating the values:

```
09/01/1998 Johnny Herbert
```

The `xsl:text` elements in this next version of the template each have a single carriage return as their contents instead of a single space:

```
<!-- xq533.xsl: converts xq528.xml into xq534.txt -->
<xsl:template match="employee">
  <xsl:apply-templates select="@hireDate"/><xsl:text>
</xsl:text>
  <xsl:apply-templates select="first"/><xsl:text>
</xsl:text>
  <xsl:apply-templates select="last"/>
</xsl:template>
```

With the same source document used again, the result of this template has each value separated by a carriage return:

```
09/01/1998
Johnny
Herbert
```

This last template isn't indented very nicely. For those two `xsl:text` elements to each have a single, and only a single, carriage return as their contents, their end-tags must be right at the beginning of the line after the start-tag. If they were indented with the rest of the child elements of the `xsl:apply-templates` element, like this,

```
<!-- xq535.xsl: converts xq528.xml into xq536.txt -->
<xsl:template match="employee">
  <xsl:apply-templates select="@hireDate"/><xsl:text>
  </xsl:text>
  <xsl:apply-templates select="first"/><xsl:text>
  </xsl:text>
  <xsl:apply-templates select="last"/>
</xsl:template>
```

the XSLT processor would add the carriage return and also the two spaces used to indent those end-tags before each value:

```
09/01/1998
  Johnny
  Herbert
```

One handy trick to get around this indenting problem and make stylesheets more readable is to declare a general entity that has an `xsl:text` element with a space or carriage return as its contents and to then reference that entity in the document. This next version of the stylesheet does so for both characters, and references these entities to put a carriage return after the `hireDate` value and a space after the `first` value:

```
<!-- xq537.xsl: converts xq528.xml into xq538.txt -->
<!DOCTYPE stylesheet [
```

```
<!ENTITY space "<xsl:text> </xsl:text>">
<!ENTITY cr "<xsl:text>
</xsl:text>">
]>
<xsl:stylesheet xmlns:xsl="http://www.w3.org/1999/XSL/Transform"
      version="1.0">
<xsl:output method="xml" omit-xml-declaration="yes"/>

<xsl:template match="employee">
  <xsl:apply-templates select="@hireDate"/>&cr;
  <xsl:apply-templates select="first"/>&space;
  <xsl:apply-templates select="last"/>
</xsl:template>

</xsl:stylesheet>
```

The result has the carriage return and space right where the entity references put them:

```
09/01/1998
Johnny Herbert
```

Usually, stylesheets declare entities like this when they need to be used repeatedly in a document. If your stylesheet needs to have many carriage returns or single spaces inserted, declaring entities for them in this manner is often worthwhile because &cr; and &space; are easier to write over and over than the text strings they represent. (See section 4.2, "Entities," page 87, for more on the use of entities in stylesheets.)

An XML processor will not delete a carriage return in an element with other character data, but sometimes you don't want that carriage return. The xsl:text element can help here, too, as easily as it can help to add carriage returns. For example, if we want to add the contents of the preceding source document to the result tree with the labels "Hire Date:" and "Name:" preceding each line, we might try

```
<!-- xq539.xsl: converts xq528.xml into xq540.txt -->
<!DOCTYPE stylesheet [
<!ENTITY space "<xsl:text> </xsl:text>">
<!ENTITY cr "<xsl:text>
</xsl:text>">
]>
<xsl:stylesheet xmlns:xsl="http://www.w3.org/1999/XSL/Transform"
      version="1.0">
<xsl:output method="xml" omit-xml-declaration="yes"/>

<xsl:template match="employee">
  Hire Date:
  <xsl:apply-templates select="@hireDate"/>&cr;
  Name:
  <xsl:apply-templates select="first"/>&space;
  <xsl:apply-templates select="last"/>
</xsl:template>

</xsl:stylesheet>
```

The result shows a carriage return after each label:

```
Hire Date:
09/01/1998

Name:
Johnny Herbert
```

If we don't want those carriage returns, we can wrap those labels in `xsl:text` elements. Doing so splits the carriage returns after those labels so that they are no longer next to non-whitespace characters and will therefore be ignored by the XML processor that hands this stylesheet to the XSLT processor:

```
<!-- xq541.xsl: converts xq528.xml into xq542.txt -->
<xsl:template match="employee">
  <xsl:text>Hire Date: </xsl:text>
  <xsl:apply-templates select="@hireDate"/>&cr;
  <xsl:text>Name: </xsl:text>
  <xsl:apply-templates select="first"/>&space;
  <xsl:apply-templates select="last"/>
</xsl:template>
```

The result has the labels on the same line as the relevant data:

```
Hire Date: 09/01/1998
Name: Johnny Herbert
```

Whether you're trying to add carriage returns or delete them, the `xsl:text` instruction is great for controlling how carriage returns are added to your result tree.

6.11.4 Adding tabs to your output

A stylesheet can add tabs to output using the character reference "	". For example, let's say we want to convert this source document into a text file that uses tabs to line up columns of information:

```
<employees>

  <employee hireDate="04/23/1999">
    <last>Hill</last>
    <first>Phil</first>
    <salary>100000</salary>
  </employee>

  <employee hireDate="09/01/1998">
    <last>Herbert</last>
    <first>Johnny</first>
    <salary>95000</salary>
  </employee>

  <employee hireDate="08/20/2000">
    <last>Hill</last>
    <first>Graham</first>
    <salary>89000</salary>
  </employee>

</employees>
```

Ample use of this character reference in this stylesheet

```
<xsl:stylesheet xmlns:xsl="http://www.w3.org/1999/XSL/Transform"
    version="1.0">
<xsl:output method="text"/>
<!-- xq524.xsl: converts xq525.xml into xq526.txt -->

<xsl:strip-space elements="*"/>

<xsl:template match="employees">
Last&#9;First&#9;Salary&#9;Hire Date
----&#9;-----&#9;------&#9;----------
<xsl:apply-templates/>
</xsl:template>

<xsl:template match="employee">
  <xsl:apply-templates select="last"/>
  <xsl:text>&#9;</xsl:text>
  <xsl:apply-templates select="first"/>
  <xsl:text>&#9;</xsl:text>
  <xsl:apply-templates select="salary"/>
  <xsl:text>&#9;</xsl:text>
  <xsl:apply-templates select="@hireDate"/><xsl:text>
</xsl:text>
</xsl:template>

</xsl:stylesheet>
```

produces this result from that source document:

```
Last      First    Salary   Hire Date
----      -----    ------   ----------
Hill      Phil     100000   04/23/1999
Herbert   Johnny   95000    09/01/1998
Hill      Graham   89000    08/20/2000
```

When the stylesheet's first template sees an `employees` element, it adds a two-line header to the result tree before applying the appropriate templates to the children of the `employees` element: one line consists of the field names separated by "	" character references, and another line contains several groups of hyphens, each group separated by the same character reference.

The only possible child of the `employees` element is the `employee` element, and its template rule individually applies templates (in this case, the default XSLT template that outputs an element's text content) to its children with the "	" character reference between each one. This character reference doesn't always have to be inside an `xsl:text` instruction (note that it's not in the stylesheet's first template), but if it had been added without this element in the second template, the XSLT processor would have ignored it. Remember, like carriage returns and the spacebar space, tab characters are considered whitespace, and an XSLT processor ignores whitespace characters between elements if they're the only characters there and not enclosed by an `xsl:text` instruction.

TIP	Although stylesheets are easier to read when elements are indented to show their levels of nesting, if you're concerned about controlling whitespace, extraneous whitespace in your stylesheet can cause alignment problems with your output. This is why this section's examples are not always indented.

Defining a general entity for this "<xsl:text>	</xsl:text>" string can make the stylesheet easier to read, especially if you call the entity "tab":

```
<!DOCTYPE stylesheet [
  <!ENTITY tab "<xsl:text>&#9;</xsl:text>">
  <!ENTITY cr "<xsl:text>
</xsl:text>">
]>
<xsl:stylesheet xmlns:xsl="http://www.w3.org/1999/XSL/Transform"
    version="1.0">
<xsl:output method="text"/>
<!-- xq527.xsl: converts xq525.xml into xq526.txt -->

<xsl:template match="employees">
Last&tab;First&tab;Salary&tab;Hire Date
----&tab;-----&tab;------&tab;----------
<xsl:apply-templates/>
</xsl:template>

<xsl:template match="employee">
  <xsl:apply-templates select="last"/>&tab;
  <xsl:apply-templates select="first"/>&tab;
  <xsl:apply-templates select="salary"/>&tab;
  <xsl:apply-templates select="@hireDate"/>&cr;
</xsl:template>

</xsl:stylesheet>
```

This stylesheet has the same effect as the previous one, but is easier to read. As long as I was defining a "tab" entity, I defined a "cr" one as well for "carriage return," which also makes the stylesheet easier to read. (See section 4.2, "Entities," page 87, for more on defining and referencing entities in XSLT and XML.)

6.11.5   Normalizing space

Imagine that your source document has extra whitespace in places, but not consistently, and you want to get rid of this whitespace to make the document consistent. For example, the first employee element in the following example has no extra spaces or carriage returns within its child elements, but the second one has plenty:

```
<employees>

  <employee hireDate="09/01/1998">
    <last>Herbert</last>
    <first>Johnny</first>
    <salary>95000</salary>
  </employee>
```

```
<employee hireDate="    04/23/1999">
    <last>
Hill
</last>
    <first>

    Phil

</first>
    <salary>100000
</salary>
  </employee>

</employees>
```

A simple stylesheet to create comma-delimited versions of each employee's data, like this,

```
<!-- xq546.xsl: converts xq543.xml into xq548.txt -->
<xsl:stylesheet xmlns:xsl="http://www.w3.org/1999/XSL/Transform"
    version="1.0">
<xsl:output method="xml" omit-xml-declaration="yes"/>

<xsl:template match="employee">

  <xsl:apply-templates select="@hireDate"/>
  <xsl:text>,</xsl:text>
  <xsl:apply-templates select="first"/>
  <xsl:text>,</xsl:text>
  <xsl:apply-templates select="last"/>

</xsl:template>

</xsl:stylesheet>
```

creates output that includes all that extra whitespace:

```
09/01/1998,Johnny,Herbert

    04/23/1999,

    Phil

'
Hill
```

The `normalize-space()` function, in addition to converting strings of multiple space characters into a single space, deletes any leading and trailing spaces from the string passed to it as an argument. (See section 5.7.1, "Extracting and comparing strings," page 153, for more on this function.) Using this function can solve the problem with the preceding stylesheet:

```
<!-- xq544.xsl: converts xq543.xml into xq547.txt -->
<xsl:stylesheet xmlns:xsl="http://www.w3.org/1999/XSL/Transform"
    version="1.0">
<xsl:output method="xml" omit-xml-declaration="yes"/>

<xsl:template match="employee">
```

```
  <xsl:value-of select="normalize-space(@hireDate)"/>
  <xsl:text>,</xsl:text>
  <xsl:value-of select="normalize-space(first)"/>
  <xsl:text>,</xsl:text>
  <xsl:value-of select="normalize-space(last)"/>
<!-- Following alternative won't work:
  <xsl:apply-templates select="normalize-space(@hireDate)"/>
  <xsl:text>,</xsl:text>
  <xsl:apply-templates select="normalize-space(first)"/>
  <xsl:text>,</xsl:text>
  <xsl:apply-templates select="normalize-space(last)"/>
-->
</xsl:template>

</xsl:stylesheet>
```

Note the comment in the second half of the "employee" template rule. We can't just insert the `normalize-space()` function inside the `select` attributes of the previous stylesheet's `xsl:apply-templates` instructions, because this function returns a string, and `xsl:apply-templates` expects to see a node set expression as the value of its `select` attribute. So, the template uses `xsl:value-of` instructions instead. The `normalize-space()` function works, and the result is formatted consistently:

```
09/01/1998,Johnny,Herbert

04/23/1999,Phil,Hill
```

6.12   GENERATING IDS AND LINKS

XSLT's `generate-id()` function generates a unique ID for a node passed to it as an argument. This ID starts with a letter so that you can use it as the value of an XML ID attribute. For example, the following stylesheet copies an XML document and adds a `uid` ("unique ID") attribute to each `chapter`, `sect1`, and `sect2` element. The `xsl:value-of` instruction uses the `generate-id()` function in the stylesheet's single template to create a value for these attributes:

```
<xsl:stylesheet xmlns:xsl="http://www.w3.org/1999/XSL/Transform"
    version="1.0">
<xsl:output method="xml" omit-xml-declaration="yes"/>
<!-- xq462.xsl: converts xq463.xml into xq464.xml -->

  <xsl:template match="chapter | sect1 | sect2">
    <xsl:copy>
      <xsl:attribute name="uid">
        <xsl:value-of select="generate-id(.)"/>
      </xsl:attribute>
      <xsl:apply-templates select="@*|node()"/>
    </xsl:copy>
  </xsl:template>
```

```
  <xsl:template match="@*|node()">
    <xsl:copy>
      <xsl:apply-templates select="@*|node()"/>
    </xsl:copy>
  </xsl:template>

</xsl:stylesheet>
```

The stylesheet turns this XML document

```
<chapter>
<para>Then with expanded wings he steers his flight</para>
<figure><title>"Incumbent on the Dusky Air"</title>
<graphic fileref="pic1.jpg"/></figure>
<para>Aloft, incumbent on the dusky Air</para>
<sect1>
<para>That felt unusual weight, till on dry Land</para>
<figure><title>"He Lights"</title>
<graphic fileref="pic2.jpg"/></figure>
<para>He lights, if it were Land that ever burned</para>
<sect2>
<para>With solid, as the Lake with liquid fire</para>
<figure><title>"The Lake with Liquid Fire"</title>
<graphic fileref="pic1.jpg"/></figure>
</sect2>
</sect1>
</chapter>
```

into this:

```
<chapter uid="N134711680">
<para>Then with expanded wings he steers his flight</para>
<figure><title>"Incumbent on the Dusky Air"</title>
<graphic fileref="pic1.jpg"/></figure>
<para>Aloft, incumbent on the dusky Air</para>
<sect1 uid="N134683456">
<para>That felt unusual weight, till on dry Land</para>
<figure><title>"He Lights"</title>
<graphic fileref="pic2.jpg"/></figure>
<para>He lights, if it were Land that ever burned</para>
<sect2 uid="N134684064">
<para>With solid, as the Lake with liquid fire</para>
<figure><title>"The Lake with Liquid Fire"</title>
<graphic fileref="pic1.jpg"/></figure>
</sect2>
</sect1>
</chapter>
```

Your XSLT processor may generate different values with the generate-id() function. In fact, if you run the same stylesheet with the same input document a second
time, your XSLT processor may not generate the same ID values that it generated the
first time. However, if you call generate-id() more than once in one run with
the same node as an argument, the processor generates the same ID value each time

for that node. Because unique IDs are popular ways to identify link destinations, this consistency of the generate-id() function makes it a great way to generate links.

For example, section 5.1.3, "'For' loops, iteration," page 118, demonstrates how to copy a document, such as the previous one, adding a list of all its illustrations at the beginning of the result document. If we make the result tree version an HTML file, we can use the generate-id function to turn each entry of this opening illustration list into an HTML link to the img element in the body of the document containing the illustration:

```
<!-- xq465.xsl: converts xq463.xml into xq466.html -->
<xsl:stylesheet xmlns:xsl="http://www.w3.org/1999/XSL/Transform"
      version="1.0">

  <xsl:output method="html"/>

  <xsl:template match="chapter">
    <html><body>

      <!-- Generate a list of picture titles, with each
           title linking to the picture in the poem below. -->
      <b>Pictures:</b><br/>
      <xsl:for-each select="descendant::figure">
        <a href="#{generate-id(graphic)}">
        <xsl:value-of select="title"/></a><br/>
      </xsl:for-each>

    <xsl:apply-templates/>
    </body></html>
  </xsl:template>

  <xsl:template match="para">
    <p><xsl:apply-templates/></p>
  </xsl:template>

  <xsl:template match="graphic">
    <!-- Image and title as caption, centered. -->
    <center><a name="{generate-id(.)}"><img src="{@fileref}"/></a>
    <b><xsl:value-of select="../title"/></b></center>
  </xsl:template>

  <!-- Suppress figure title because "graphic" template
       rule already added it to result tree. -->
  <xsl:template match="figure/title"/>

</xsl:stylesheet>
```

With the source document above, this stylesheet creates the following HTML document:

```
<html>
    <body>
        <b>Pictures:</b>
        <br>
        <a href="#N134691840">"Incumbent on the Dusky Air"</a>
        <br>
```

```
            <a href="#N134692416">"He Lights"</a>
            <br>
            <a href="#N134757920">"The Lake with Liquid Fire"</a>
            <br>
<p>Then with expanded wings he steers his flight</p>

<center>
            <a name="N134691840"><img src="pic1.jpg"></a>
            <b>"Incumbent on the Dusky Air"</b>
        </center>
<p>Aloft, incumbent on the dusky Air</p>

<p>That felt unusual weight, till on dry Land</p>

<center>
            <a name="N134692416"><img src="pic2.jpg"></a>
            <b>"He Lights"</b>
        </center>
<p>He lights, if it were Land that ever burned</p>

<p>With solid, as the Lake with liquid fire</p>

<center>
            <a name="N134757920"><img src="pic1.jpg"></a>
            <b>"The Lake with Liquid Fire"</b>
        </center>

</body>
</html>
```

The stylesheet uses the `generate-id()` ID twice:

- As the `xsl:for-each` instruction in the "chapter" template rule adds each `figure` element's `title` to the result tree for the "Pictures:" list at the beginning of the result document, it puts each of these `title` elements inside of an HTML a element to link to the appropriate picture in the main part of the document. Each of these a elements has an `href` attribute to indicate the link destination. An `href` attribute that begins with a pound sign ("#") looks for the link destination in the same document. Specifically, it looks for another a element with a name attribute value equal to the part after the pound sign in the link origin. For example, an a start-tag of `<a href="#a123">` links to an a element with an `<a name="a123">` start-tag elsewhere in the same document.

  Instead of the string "a123" identifying each link destination, this stylesheet uses the `generate-id()` function to make up an identifying string. Because the `graphic` element node is passed to it as an argument, the function creates an ID string for each of the three graphic elements: "N134691840", "N134692416", and "N134757920".

- To create the link destinations, the "graphic" template rule puts each HTML img element in the result tree inside of an a element. These img elements use the value of the source tree graphic elements' `fileref` attributes as their src value, and the a elements use the `generate-id()` function to create the values for their name attributes. Passing this function an argument of "." is the same as passing it `self::node()`, which, in this case, means passing it the `graphic` element node, so the XSLT processor generates an ID value for each `graphic` node. These are the same three nodes for which the earlier use of the `generate-id()` created IDs, and the XSLT processor creates the same three values: "N134691840", "N134692416", and "N134757920". When this HTML file is displayed with a Web browser, each link in the opening "Pictures:" list will now go to the corresponding picture in the document.

This consistency in the `generate-id()` function's treatment of a particular node, even if it generates an ID for it more than once, is the key to the function's power. These graphic elements didn't even have IDs in the source document. With the help of this function, their equivalent in the result document has them, and other elements in that document can use those IDs to link to them.

6.13   *XSL* AND *XSLT*: CREATING ACROBAT FILES AND OTHER FORMATTED OUTPUT

XSL is the Extensible Stylesheet Language, a W3C standard for specifying the visual or audio presentation of an XML document. "Visual presentation" refers to details such as fonts, margins, bolding, italicizing, and other page layout issues. Audio presentation refers to the pitch, speed, volume, and other parameters of a spoken voice communicating a document. As I write this, with the XSL spec in Candidate Recommendation status, I know of no program that can do anything with a stylesheet that has audio properties specified, but several do exist that can turn XML documents into attractive pages suitable for publishing.

XSLT's relationship with XSL can be confusing. They have similar names, and they both offer specialized elements that you assemble into stylesheets that convert XML documents into something else. Technically, XSLT is a part of XSL; XSL was designed to be a language for transforming and formatting documents, and the "Transformations" part of this plan (the "T" in "XSLT") proved so valuable that the W3C's XSL Working Group split XSLT into its own specification. Now, when people refer to "XSL," they usually mean the formatting part.

Before XSLT became its own spec describing the conversion of XML documents into other XML documents (or even into non-XML documents), the original plan for this transformation language was to use it to convert XML documents into trees of formatting objects. Formatting objects are specific elements from the XSL namespace that describe the presentation of the document's information. Although XSLT was split out to be separate, it's still very good for this.

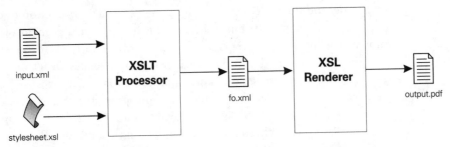

Figure 6.3 An XSLT processor can convert an XML file into a formatting object XML file suitable for rendering by an XSL processor.

Before we look at an example using XSLT to create an XSL formatting object document, let's consider a short XSL document created by hand so that we can get a feel for the structure of formatting object documents:

```
<!-- xq501.xml -->
<fo:root xmlns:fo="http://www.w3.org/1999/XSL/Format">

  <fo:layout-master-set>

    <fo:simple-page-master>
      <fo:region-body/>
    </fo:simple-page-master>

  </fo:layout-master-set>

  <!-- Optional fo:declaration elements can go here. -->

  <fo:page-sequence>

    <!-- A sequence of pages. -->

    <fo:flow>
      <fo:block>Him thus intent Ithuriel with his spear</fo:block>
    </fo:flow>

  </fo:page-sequence>

</fo:root>
```

A formatting object stylesheet document uses elements from the http://www.w3.org/1999/XSL/Format namespace. The namespace prefix declared for this namespace is usually "fo" (for "formatting object"). The document element is `fo:root`, an element with two required child elements:

1 `fo:layout-master-set` has the "masters" that set constraints for pages, regions, and other general aspects of the document's layout.

2 `fo:page-sequence` describes how to create a specific sequence of pages in the document. There's no limit to how many of these a document can have.

In the preceding sample document, the `fo:layout-master-set` uses the simplest master, `fo:simple-page-master`, to set the relevant values to their defaults.

An `fo:page-sequence` typically has a series of `fo:flow` flow object elements that make up the actual content of the document. Our example has one `fo:flow` element to add the phrase "Him thus intent Ithuriel with his spear" to the formatting object tree.

An XSL processor turns these elements into whatever is appropriate for the output formats it supports. FOP ("Formatting Object Processor"), the XSL renderer originally written by James Tauber and available through the XML Apache project (xml.apache.org), can turn the preceding document into a PDF file that looks like that in figure 6.4 when displayed in Adobe Acrobat.

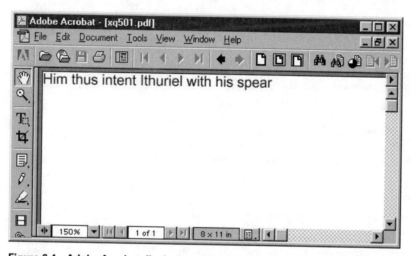

Figure 6.4   Adobe Acrobat displaying a PDF file created by FOP from a simple XSL formatting object file

The text is right up against the left and top edges of the "paper," because no margins were specified, so most laser printers wouldn't be able to print this little document. It's still an impressive achievement, though. With a little XML markup and an open-source program unaffiliated with any major software company, we've created a working Acrobat document.

Let's look at how we can use XSLT to create a more complex XSL document suitable for FOP rendering. For input, the following poem document has a `title` element and an in-line `prop` element for proper names. Elements of both types will be formatted differently from the rest of the poem's text. We want line breaks after each `verse` of the poem, and we want a little extra space after the `title` in the final Acrobat version:

```
<poem>
  <title>"Paradise Lost" excerpt</title>
  <verse>Him thus intent <prop>Ithuriel</prop> with his spear</verse>
```

```
<verse>Touched lightly; for no falsehood can endure</verse>
<verse>Touch of Celestial temper, but returns</verse>
<verse>Of force to its own likeness: up he starts</verse>
<verse>Discovered and surprised.</verse>
</poem>
```

Our XSLT stylesheet will read this poem document and convert it to an XSL stylesheet, or "formatting object file," suitable for conversion into an Acrobat file by FOP. The XSLT stylesheet, which converts this document to an XSL formatting object file, declares two namespaces in its `xsl:stylesheet` start-tag: one to identify the XSLT instructions to the XSLT processor and one to identify the XSL elements to the rendering program. (See section 4.3, "Namespaces," page 92, for more on the use of namespaces in XSLT.)

```
<!-- xq503.xsl: converts xq502.xml into xq504.xml -->
<xsl:stylesheet version="1.0"
    xmlns:xsl="http://www.w3.org/1999/XSL/Transform"
    xmlns:fo="http://www.w3.org/1999/XSL/Format">

  <xsl:template match="/">

    <fo:root>

      <fo:layout-master-set>
        <fo:simple-page-master>
          <fo:region-body margin-top="36pt"
              margin-bottom="36pt" margin-left="36pt"
              margin-right="36pt"/>
        </fo:simple-page-master>
      </fo:layout-master-set>

      <fo:page-sequence>
        <fo:flow flow-name="xsl-region-body">
          <xsl:apply-templates/>
        </fo:flow>
      </fo:page-sequence>

    </fo:root>

  </xsl:template>

  <xsl:template match="verse">
    <fo:block font-size="10pt" font-family="Times">
      <xsl:apply-templates/>
    </fo:block>
  </xsl:template>

  <xsl:template match="title">
    <fo:block font-size="14pt" font-weight="bold"
        space-before.optimum="12pt"
        space-after.optimum="12pt">
      <xsl:apply-templates/>
    </fo:block>
  </xsl:template>
```

```
<xsl:template match="prop"><!-- proper names -->
  <fo:inline font-style="italic">
    <xsl:apply-templates/>
  </fo:inline>
</xsl:template>

</xsl:stylesheet>
```

When the XSLT processor finds the root ("/") of the source tree, the stylesheet's first template rule adds the result XSL stylesheet's fo:root document element to the result tree. It also adds that fo:root element's fo:layout-master-set and fo:page-sequence child elements to the result tree. The fo:layout-master-set element resembles the one in the earlier example except that the fo:region-body element in its fo:simple-page-master doesn't leave all its parameters at their default values. Instead, it sets the top, bottom, left, and right margins to 36 points, or half an inch.

The fo:page-sequence element has one fo:flow object, and this element's contents in the result tree will be determined by the xsl:apply-templates instruction between the fo:flow tags in the XSLT stylesheet. Regardless of what this stylesheet's template rules do with the nodes that the XSLT processor finds hanging off the source tree's root node, the nodes that they add to the result tree will be between these fo:flow tags in the result document.

The stylesheet's three remaining template rules turn parts of the poem document into formatting objects to go inside this fo:flow element. The first of the three sets the verse elements to 10 point text in the Times font family. The second sets the title element to 14 point bold text. The font-family is left at the default value, which happens to be Helvetica for the FOP XSL formatter.

The "title" template rule also sets space-before.optimum and space-after.optimum attribute values. Related attribute values include space-before.minimum, space-before.maximum, and the corresponding space-after attribute values. The opportunity to set three different parameters to control the amount of allowable space before or after a given text block lets you specify exactly how much leeway you want to give to a page layout engine's automated decisions about these settings.

The poem's title and verse elements are both added to the formatting object result tree as fo:block elements. They're each their own block of text. You can set block-oriented parameters for them such as the amount of space to put before and after each block.

The final template rule adds a fo:inline element to the result tree for prop elements. This tells the XSL processor to treat elements of this type as part of their surrounding block instead of treating each one as its own block. Emphasized words, technical terms set in a different font, and, in this case, a single proper name to be italicized are typical elements that make good candidates for inline rendering instead of block rendering.

When this stylesheet is run with the poem source document shown previously, it creates the following result (I added carriage returns and indenting to make the result easier to read, but these won't affect the FOP program's treatment of them):

```
<?xml version="1.0" encoding="UTF-8"?>
<fo:root xmlns:fo="http://www.w3.org/1999/XSL/Format">
<fo:layout-master-set><fo:simple-page-master>
<fo:region-body margin-top="36pt" margin-bottom="36pt"
     margin-left="36pt" margin-right="36pt"/>
</fo:simple-page-master>
</fo:layout-master-set><fo:page-sequence><fo:flow>
<fo:block font-size="14pt" font-weight="bold"
    space-before.optimum="12pt"
    space-after.optimum="12pt">"Paradise Lost" excerpt</fo:block>
<fo:block font-size="10pt"
    font-family="Times">Him thus intent
<fo:inline font-style="italic">Ithuriel</fo:inline>
 with his spear</fo:block>
<fo:block font-size="10pt" font-family="Times">
Touched lightly; for no falsehood can endure</fo:block>
<fo:block font-size="10pt" font-family="Times">
Touch of Celestial temper, but returns</fo:block>
<fo:block font-size="10pt" font-family="Times">
Of force to its own likeness: up he starts</fo:block>
<fo:block font-size="10pt" font-family="Times">
Discovered and surprised.</fo:block>
</fo:flow></fo:page-sequence></fo:root>
```

FOP turns this document into the PDF file displayed by Acrobat in figure 6.5.

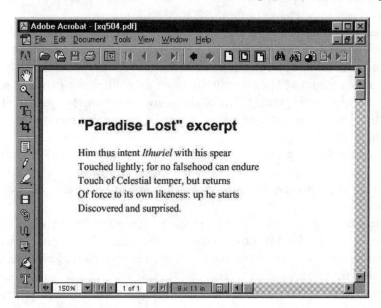

Figure 6.5 Adobe Acrobat displaying a PDF file created by FOP from a more complex XSL formatting object file

CHAPTER 6 SPECIALIZED INPUT & OUTPUT

A glance through the W3C XSL specification (see http://www.w3.org/TR/xsl) reveals many other settings that you can assign to your formatting objects along with those shown in the examples above. These include `fo:page-number`, `fo:list-item`, `fo:table-and-caption`, and many others.

For now, FOP only converts formatting object files to Acrobat PDF files, but that's pretty useful. Other XSL engines will certainly appear to convert these files to other formats, whether RTF or other vendors' own rendering formats. Any given rendering engine may not support the entire XSL spec. For example, it will be awhile before all audio properties are supported by one package, and some visual ones may be difficult to support as well. Still, it's a great way to create nice-looking documents on multiple platforms using nothing but free software and open standards.

6.14 SPLITTING UP OUTPUT INTO MULTIPLE FILES

A classic XML transformation task is the splitting of a large source document into multiple result documents. For example, when preparing a large book for web delivery, you probably want to split it up so that each chapter gets converted to a separate HTML file, because the entire book would be too large to send to a web browser.

The XSLT 1.0 specification has no provisions for splitting up output into multiple documents. This ability is so useful, however, that nearly every XSLT processor offers an `extension` element that lets you do this.

Instead of picking one XSLT processor's syntax for splitting up output documents, or trying to cover all of them, this section shows the syntax for doing so with the `xsl:document` element described in the W3C's XSLT 1.1 Working Draft. Although the W3C XSL Working Group eventually decided to discontinue work on XSLT 1.1 in order to fully devote their energy to XSLT 2.0, XSLT 1.1's `xsl:document` element is based on several existing implementations of this potential XSLT feature and will provide a model for future implementations until a XSLT 2.0 Recommendation eventually makes the `xsl:document` syntax official.

> **WARNING**   Double-check your own processor's syntax for splitting up a result tree into multiple documents. It may be a variation on the syntax shown in this section.

Imagine that the following document is much bigger than it appears here. We want to convert the document to HTML, and we want each chapter stored in its own separate HTML file, for a total of three result documents.

```
<story>

  <chapter><title>Chapter 1</title>
    <para>A Dungeon horrible, on all sides round</para>
    <para>More unexpert, I boast not: them let those</para>
  </chapter>

  <chapter><title>Chapter 2</title>
```

```
    <para>Contrive who need, or when they need, not now.</para>
    <para>For while they sit contriving, shall the rest</para>
  </chapter>

  <chapter><title>Chapter 3</title>
    <para>Millions that stand in Arms, and longing wait</para>
    <para>So thick a drop serene hath quenched their Orbs</para>
  </chapter>

</story>
```

The following stylesheet converts our document into a set of HTML files:

```
<!-- xq560.xsl: converts xq552.xml into xq561.html (chap1.html),
     xq562.html (chap2.html), and xq563.html (chap3.html) -->
<xsl:stylesheet xmlns:xsl="http://www.w3.org/1999/XSL/Transform"
    version="1.0">
  <xsl:output method="xml" omit-xml-declaration="yes"/>

  <xsl:template match="chapter">
    <xsl:variable name="chapNum"><xsl:number/></xsl:variable>

      <xsl:document href="chap{$chapNum}.html">
        <html><body>
            <xsl:apply-templates/>
        </body></html>
      </xsl:document>

  </xsl:template>

  <xsl:template match="chapter/title">
      <h1><xsl:apply-templates/></h1>
  </xsl:template>

  <xsl:template match="para">
      <p><xsl:apply-templates/></p>
  </xsl:template>

</xsl:stylesheet>
```

The first template rule's xsl:document element splits the source tree document, putting each html element into its own result tree (and file). Its href attribute specifies a location for each output file, using a variable named chapNum in the href value to create a different filename for each HTML file: chap1.html:

```
<html><body><h1>Chapter 1</h1>
  <p>A Dungeon horrible, on all sides round</p>
  <p>More unexpert, I boast not: them let those</p>
</body></html>
```

chap2.html:

```
<html><body><h1>Chapter 2</h1>
  <p>Contrive who need, or when they need, not now.</p>
  <p>For while they sit contriving, shall the rest</p>
</body></html>
```

and chap3.html:

```
<html><body><h1>Chapter 3</h1>
  <p>Millions that stand in Arms, and longing wait</p>
  <p>So thick a drop serene hath quenched their Orbs</p>
</body></html>
```

In addition to href, the xsl:document element has other attributes that give you much of the same control over the output that the attributes of the xsl:output element give. For example, doctype-system and doctype-public give the result document DOCTYPE declarations; and method eases the creation of plain text and older format HTML files. There is also omit-xml-declaration, as well as other attributes. (See section 6.9, "Valid XML output: including DOCTYPE declarations," page 225, section 6.1.2, "HTML as output," page 190, section 6.5, "Non-XML output," page 202, and section 6.11.2, "Indenting," page 233, for more on how these attributes can control the format of your output.)

PART **3**

Appendices

Appendix A is a quick reference to XSLT syntax, showing you the various elements that you can use in your XSLT stylesheets and their attributes, with pointers back to the page in this book where the element is introduced.

Appendix B describes the use of several free and commercial XSLT processors, showing how to process a sample document and stylesheet with them.

XSLT quick reference

This quick reference to XSLT syntax divides up the elements from the XSLT namespace into three categories:

- *Top-level elements*, which are children of the `xsl:stylesheet` element that give general instructions about creating the result tree.

- *Instruction elements*, which tell the XSLT processor to add something to the result tree.

- Miscellaneous other elements: the `xsl:stylesheet` element, its synonym `xsl:transform`, the `xsl:import` element, which is not considered a top-level element because it has to come in the spreadsheet before any other top-level elements, and elements with specific roles inside various instruction elements: `xsl:when` and `xsl:otherwise` from the `xsl:choose` instruction, `xsl:with-param` from the `xsl:call-template` instruction, and `xsl:sort` from the `xsl:apply-templates` or `xsl:for-each` instructions

Terms such as "top-level," "instruction," and all the other terms you see used in this quick reference are defined in the Glossary. Also see section 5.11, "Using the W3C XSLT specification," page 182 for background on these terms.

The quick reference table uses DTD content model syntax, which is very similar to the regular expression syntax used by Perl and many other tools with their roots in Unix, to describe the allowable content of each XSLT element as well as legal attribute values:

- A plus sign (+) means "one or more."

- An asterisk (*) means "zero or more."

- A question mark (?) means "zero or one"—in other words, that something is optional and can appear only once.

- A comma separates two items in a series that must appear in that order. For example, the content model of "when+,otherwise?" for `xsl:choose` means that this element consists of one or more `xsl:when` elements followed by an optional `xsl:otherwise` element.

- A pipe symbol (|) separates two options in a choice. For example, "'yes' | 'no'" as the potential values for the `xsl:value-of` element's `disable-output-escaping` attribute show that it can be either the literal string "yes" or the string "no".

Quoted values show literal values as they must appear, and italics name a type of expression that may be inserted. For example, the `xsl:sort` element's `data-type` attribute's legal values of "'text' | 'number' | *qname-but-not-ncname*" show that it can either be the literal strings "text" or "number" or a QName that isn't an NCName. (See the glossary for descriptions of both of these terms.)

For each element's attributes, the tables below have a column to show whether the attribute is required and another to show whether it's an attribute value template (AVT). The title of each column also points to the page number where that XSLT element is introduced if it is covered in this book.

A.1 TOP-LEVEL ELEMENTS

▶ **xsl:attribute-set** (see page 80)

content `xsl:attribute*`		
attributes	**required**	**AVT**
name= *qname*	yes	
use-attribute-sets= *qnames*		

▶ **xsl:decimal-format**

content Empty		
attributes	**required**	**AVT**
name= *qname*		
decimal-separator= *char*		
grouping-separator= *char*		
infinity= *string*		
minus-sign= *char*		
NaN= *string*		

► **xsl:decimal-format** *(continued)*

attributes	required	AVT
percent= *char*		
per-mille= *char*		
zero-digit= *char*		
digit= *char*		
pattern-separator= *char*		

► **xsl:include** (see page 128)

content Empty

attributes	required	AVT
href= *uri-reference*	yes	

► **xsl:key** (see page 172)

content Empty

attributes	required	AVT
name= *qname*	yes	
match= *pattern*	yes	
use= *expression*	yes	

► **xsl:namespace-alias** (see page 98)

content Empty

attributes	required	AVT
stylesheet-prefix= "#default"	*prefix*	yes	
result-prefix= "#default"	*prefix*	yes	

► **xsl:output** (see page 192 and page 216)

content Empty

attributes	required	AVT
method= "xml"	"html"	"text"	*qname-but-not-ncname*		
version= *nmtoken*		
encoding= *string*		
omit-xml-declaration= "yes"	"no"		
standalone= "yes"	"no"		

▶ **xsl:output** (see page 192 and page 216) *(continued)*

attributes	required	AVT
doctype-public= *string*		
doctype-system= *string*		
cdata-section-elements= *qnames*		
indent= "yes" | "no"		
media-type= *string*		

▶ **xsl:param** (see page 169)

content *template*

attributes	required	AVT
name= *qname*	yes	
select= *expression*		

▶ **xsl:preserve-space** (see page 231)

content Empty

attributes	required	AVT
elements= *tokens*	yes	

▶ **xsl:strip-space** (see page 231)

content Empty

attributes	required	AVT
elements= *tokens*	yes	

▶ **xsl:template** (see page 7)

content (param*, *template*)

attributes	required	AVT
match= *pattern*		
name= *qname*		
priority= *number*		
mode= *qname*		

▶ xsl:variable (see page 164)

content *template*		
attributes	**required**	**AVT**
name= *qname*	yes	
select= *expression*		

A.2 INSTRUCTIONS

▶ xsl:apply-imports

content xsl:with-param*

▶ xsl:apply-templates (see page 13)

content (xsl:sort | xsl:with-param)*		
attributes	**required**	**AVT**
select= *node-set-expression*		
mode= *qname*		

▶ xsl:attribute (see page 78)

content *template*		
attributes	**required**	**AVT**
name= *qname*	yes	yes
namespace= *uri-reference*		yes

▶ xsl:call-template (see page 132)

content xsl:with-param*		
attributes	**required**	**AVT**
name= *qname*	yes	

▶ xsl:choose (see page 114)

content (when+, otherwise?)

▶ xsl:comment (see page 85)

content *template*

▶ **xsl:copy** (see page 58)

content *template*

attributes	required	AVT
use-attribute-sets= *qnames*		

▶ **xsl:copy-of** (see page 59)

content Empty

attributes	required	AVT
select= *expression*	yes	

▶ **xsl:document** (see page 248)

content *template*

attributes	required	AVT
href= *uri-reference*	yes	yes
method= "xml" | "html" | "text" | *qname-but-not-ncname*		yes
version= *nmtoken*		yes
encoding= *string*		yes
omit-xml-declaration= "yes" | "no"		yes
standalone= "yes" | "no"		yes
doctype-public= *string*		yes
doctype-system= *string*		yes
cdata-section-elements= *qnames*		yes
indent= "yes" | "no"		yes
media-type= *string*		yes

▶ **xsl:element** (see page 48)

content *template*

attributes	required	AVT
name= *qname*	yes	yes
namespace= *uri-reference*		yes
use-attribute-sets= *qnames*		

▶ **xsl:fallback** (see page 145)

content *template*

▶ **xsl:for-each** (see page 143)

content (sort*, *template*)		
attributes	**required**	**AVT**
select= *node-set-expression*	yes	

▶ **xsl:if** (see page 111)

content *template*		
attributes	**required**	**AVT**
test= *boolean-expression*	yes	

▶ **xsl:message** (see page 114)

content *template*		
attributes	**required**	**AVT**
terminate= "yes" l "no"		

▶ **xsl:number** (see page 208)

content Empty		
attributes	**required**	**AVT**
level= "single" l "multiple" l "any"		
count= *pattern*		
from= *pattern*		
value= *number-expression*		
format= *string*		yes
lang= *nmtoken*		yes
letter-value= "alphabetic" l "traditional"		yes
grouping-separator= *char*		yes
grouping-size= *number*		yes

▶ **xsl:processing-instruction** (see page 105)

content *template*		
attributes	**required**	**AVT**
name= *ncname*	yes	yes

▶ **xsl:text** (see page 89 and page 241)

content text (PCDATA)

attributes	required	AVT
disable-output-escaping= "yes" | "no"		

▶ **xsl:value-of** (see page 71)

content Empty

attributes	required	AVT
select= *string-expression*	yes	
disable-output-escaping= "yes" | "no"		

▶ **xsl:variable** (see page 164)

content *template*

attributes	required	AVT
name= *qname*	yes	
select= *expression*		

A.3   NO CATEGORY

▶ **xsl:import** (see page 130)

content Empty

attributes	required	AVT
href= *uri-reference*	yes	

▶ **xsl:otherwise** (see page 114)

content *template*

▶ **xsl:sort** (see page 221)

content Empty

attributes	required	AVT
select= *string-expression*		
lang= *nmtoken*		yes
data-type= "text" | "number" | *qname-but-not-ncname*		yes
order= "ascending" | "descending"		yes
case-order= "upper-first" | "lower-first"		yes

► **xsl:stylesheet** (see page 8)

content (import*, *top-level-elements*)		
attributes	**required**	**AVT**
id= *id*		
extension-element-prefixes= *tokens*		
exclude-result-prefixes= *tokens*		
version= *number*	yes	

► **xsl:transform** (see page 8)

content (import*, *top-level-elements*)		
attributes	**required**	**AVT**
id= *id*		
extension-element-prefixes= *tokens*		
exclude-result-prefixes= *tokens*		
version= *number*	yes	

► **xsl:when** (see page 114)

content *template*		
attributes	**required**	**AVT**
test= *boolean-expression*	yes	

► **xsl:with-param** (see page 133)

content *template*		
attributes	**required**	**AVT**
name= *qname*	yes	
select= *expression*		

A P P E N D I X   B

Running XSLT processors

B.1   RUNNING XSLT PROCESSORS

Because the XSLT specification is about taking an XML document stored in a source tree in memory and converting it into a result tree in memory, the specification deliberately avoids any talk of how to get a document into that source tree and out of that result tree. (See section 1.1.2, "Documents, trees, and transformations," page 6, for more on this.) By doing this, the specification leaves XSLT processors more flexibility in how they read the documents:

- An XSLT processor can be built into (or plugged into) a web browser. When the browser reads in a document that has a stylesheet specified for it, the browser applies the stylesheet to that document and displays, the result of the transformation.

- An XSLT processor can be made available as a programming library in a particular programming language. The documentation with that XSLT processor tells the user the syntax of that language to use in order to pass a document and stylesheet to the XSLT processor and to get the result back.

- An XSLT processor can be run from a command prompt: the DOS command prompt in a Windows operating system, a shell in a Unix-based operating system such as Linux, or whatever command line is available in your operating system.

269

(See section 6.2, "Browsers and XSLT," page 192, for information on the current and future roles of XSLT processors in web browsers. For information on using an XSLT processor from a programming library, see the documentation for that programming library.)

XSLT processors run from a command line also have their own documentation. Most have several things in common. This appendix describes a few popular and interesting XSLT command line processors to give you a taste of what you can expect from them as well as an awareness of the features that can make one stand out from the pack. A printed book could never have an exhaustive, up-to-date list of XSLT processors. Use this appendix as a starting point and then go to http://www.xmlsoftware.com/xslt to explore what is currently available. Devotees of the Perl and Python programming languages in particular should go to http://www.xmlsoftware.com/xslt and check out this web page's offerings.

TIP   Command line XSLT processors and programming libraries are often packaged together, because once you've created one, the other is easily included. A programming library, then, may include a command line processor as an example of how to call the library's XSLT processor. Or a command line processor may include its source code so that you can use it in your own projects without calling the processor from the command line.

All XSLT processors need to know two basic pieces of information: the source document to read into the source tree, and the stylesheet to apply to the source tree document. Although you'll usually want to tell the XSLT processor what to do with the result tree document, sometimes this isn't a required parameter, because a command line processor may scroll the result up your screen if you don't specify a destination for that output. At a Windows or UNIX command prompt, the greater-than character (">") tells the operating system to send the output to a text file instead of the screen, so this is a popular way to store an XSLT result tree document on these operating systems. For example, the following command line uses the Sablotron processor to apply the xq553.xsl stylesheet to the xq338.xml input file and to store the output in xq339.html:

```
sabcmd xq553.xsl xq338.xml  > xq339.html
```

Another important piece of information to pass to an XSLT command line processor is the value of any parameters that you want to set. The use of parameters in XSLT stylesheets is described in section 5.8.2, "Parameters," page 169. This appendix uses an example from that section to demonstrate how to invoke each command line processor. This way, you can see how an important aspect of running XSLT processors varies from one processor to another.

Each section of this appendix shows how to apply this stylesheet

```
<!-- xq553.xsl: converts xq338.xml into xq339.html. -->

<xsl:stylesheet xmlns:xsl="http://www.w3.org/1999/XSL/Transform"
```

```
        version="1.0">

<xsl:output method="html"/>

  <xsl:param name="bodyTextSize">10pt</xsl:param>

  <xsl:template match="winery">
   <b><font size="{$bodyTextSize}"><xsl:apply-templates/>
   <xsl:text> </xsl:text>
   <xsl:value-of select="../@grape"/></font></b><br/>
  </xsl:template>

  <xsl:template match="product">
   <i><font size="{$bodyTextSize}">
    <xsl:apply-templates/></font></i><br/>
  </xsl:template>

  <xsl:template match="year | price">
   <font size="{$bodyTextSize}"><xsl:apply-templates/></font><br/>
  </xsl:template>

</xsl:stylesheet>
```

to this document:

```
<wine grape="Cabernet">
  <winery>Duckpond</winery>
  <product>Merit Selection</product>
  <year>1996</year>
  <price>11.99</price>
</wine>
```

Each application of the stylesheet will pass a bodyTextSize value of "8pt" to the stylesheet to override the default value of "10pt" shown in the stylesheet, producing this result:

```
<?xml version="1.0" encoding="utf-8"?>
  <b><font size="8pt">Duckpond Cabernet</font></b><br/>
  <i><font size="8pt">Merit Selection</font></i><br/>
  <font size="8pt">1996</font><br/>
  <font size="8pt">11.99</font><br/>
```

With no bodyTextSize value passed to the XSLT processor, the size attributes would have the default value of "8pt".

```
  <b><font size="10pt">Duckpond Cabernet</font></b><br>
  <i><font size="10pt">Merit Selection</font></i><br>
  <font size="10pt">1996</font><br>
  <font size="10pt">11.99</font><br>
```

For each XSLT processor covered, this appendix lists the following information:

Homepage	The URI of the processor's homepage for more information.
Platforms	Operating systems under which you can run it. If Java is listed as the platform, you should be able to run the processor on any operating system that has a Java virtual machine installed.
XML parser used	A key reason that XSLT stylesheets are XML documents is that XSLT processors can leave mundane parsing details to another XML parser. This section lists the parser used and also tells you whether you can plug in another parser.
Version tested	The release of the XSLT processor tested for this appendix. By the time you read this, it will probably have been updated, and much of the information here will be superseded.
Cost	The cost of the processor, if any.
API or source included	The Application Programming Interface (if available) is included so that you can use the XSLT processor from within your programs. If the full source code of the parser is included, that, too, is noted here.
Command line help	What you enter at the command line to display a list of all command line options.
Other documentation included	The documentation included, such as HTML or text files.
Installation instructions	Where to find installation instructions, usually as a relative pathname. For example, if this entry says install\readme.html and you installed the program in a directory named c:\prog\whatever, look for the installation instructions in c:\prog\whatever\install\readme.html. If you don't see it there, compare the release number of the version you're installing with the one described here. The location of the instructions may have changed.

With a Java-based XSLT processor, the program being executed from the command line will most likely be the Java Virtual Machine (JVM). For Java processors, I used the Blackdown (http://www.blackdown.org) JVM for Linux under Linux, and Sun's JVM under Microsoft Windows operating systems.

Under Windows, some Java processors such as Saxon and XT make an executable "stub" (a small EXE File that automates the process of running the Java program) available to run the XSLT processor with Microsoft's JVM (which comes with Internet Explorer), so you don't have to specify the class path and other information normally necessary to run a Java program.

When you do run an XSLT processor by calling the JVM directly, check to see which releases of JVMs that processor was tested with. The installation will tell you which jar files you'll need and where to put them.

B.2   SAXON

Developed by	**Michael Kay**
Homepage	**http://users.iclway.co.uk/mhkay/saxon/**
Platforms	**Java; Windows executable stub included**
XML parser used	**Microstar's Ælfred included; others can be plugged in**
Version tested	**6.0.1**
Cost	**Free**
API or source included	**Both**
Command line help	`java com.icl.saxon.StyleSheet -?`
Other documentation included	**a directory full of HTML files**
Installation instructions	**See** `doc/index.html#Installation` **after unzipping the distribution file.**

Running it with the samples shown:

```
java com.icl.saxon.StyleSheet xq338.xml xq553.xsl bodyTextSize=8pt
```

Michael Kay of the German database company Software AG (SAG) (and formerly of the British software and services company ICL, which accounts for the "icl" in many Saxon-related URIs) wrote Saxon as a collection of tools for processing XML documents. The main tool is its XSLT processor. Kay is on the W3C XSL Working Group, and as one of the leading experts on XSLT, his XSLT processor is one of the most popular.

B.3   XT

Developed by	James Clark
Homepage	http://www.jclark.com/xml/xt.html
Platforms	Java; Windows executable stub available.
XML parser used	Clark's XP used as the default, but must be downloaded from http://www.jclark.com/xml/xp. Others can be plugged in.
Version tested	19991105
Cost	Free
API or source included	Both
Command line help	`java com.jclark.xsl.sax.Driver`
Other documentation included	One HTML file.
Installation instructions	xt.htm

Running it with the samples shown:

```
java com.jclark.xsl.sax.Driver xq338.xml xq553.xsl bodyTextSize=8pt
```

Along with many other tremendous contributions to the XML and SGML worlds (for example, he came up with the name "XML"), James Clark is the editor of the XSLT specification. XT was one of the first XSLT processors to become available, but by now its only interest is historical. James wrote it as a proof of concept in the early days of the XSLT 1.0 Working Draft and never updated it to implement the full XSLT 1.0 Recommendation. After he announced in November of 1999 that he would not continue work on XT, a group was formed at http://4xt.org to continue XT development without him, because he made the source freely available.

B.4 iXSLT

Developed by	Infoteria
Homepage	http://www.infoteria.com/en/contents/product/ixslt/
Platforms	Windows
XML parser used	(not given)
Version tested	2.0c
Cost	$150 for Developer's Edition; bulk discounts available.
API or source included	A DLL accessible from C++ programs and a COM version are included.
Command line help	`ixslt -h`
Other documentation included	Several HTML files.
Installation instructions	Readme.html

Running it with the samples shown:

```
ixslt -i:xq338.xml xq553.xsl -p:bodyTextSize=8pt
```

Infoteria's iXSLT is the XSLT processor entry in their suite of XML processing products. It's written in C++, and it's very, very fast. Their inclusion of COM and DLL versions of iXSLT make it a good XSLT processor to incorporate into larger Windows applications.

Unlike many other XSLT processors, it costs money, but in a workplace where support from a software vendor is an issue to consider when purchasing software (being a commercial software vendor, they make support available), the cost of iXSLT should be a minor issue.

B.5 XALAN-JAVA

Developed by	Apache Software Foundation
Homepage	http://xml.apache.org/xalan-j/
Platforms	Java
XML parser used	Comes with the Apache Xerces parser; others can be plugged in.
Version tested	2.0.D05 beta
Cost	free
API or source included	Open source
Command line help	`java org.apache.xalan.xslt.Process`
Other documentation included	Extensive HTML documentation
Installation instructions	docs/getstarted.html

Running it with the samples shown:

```
java org.apache.xalan.xslt.Process -IN xq338.xml -XSL xq553.xsl -
PARAM bodyTextSize 8pt
```

According to their homepage at http://xml.apache.org, the goals of the Apache XML project are "to provide commercial-quality standards-based XML solutions that are developed in an open and cooperative fashion, to provide feedback to standards bodies (such as IETF and W3C) from an implementation perspective, and to be a focus for XML-related activities within Apache projects." Much of the Xalan Java and C++ XSLT processors were originally developed at IBM before being donated to the Apache project. (See the following page for Xalan-C++.)

B.6   XALAN-C++

Developed by	Apache Software Foundation
Homepage	http://xml.apache.org/xalan-c/
Platforms	Windows, Linux, AIX
XML parser used	Apache's Xerces C++
Version tested	1.0.0
Cost	free
API or source included	Open source
Command line help	`testXSLT`
Other documentation included	Extensive HTML documentation
Installation instructions	xml-xalan/c/docs/getstarted.html

Running it with the samples shown:

```
testXSLT -IN xq338.xml -XSL xq553.xsl -PARAM bodyTextSize 8pt
```

The Apache Xalan C++ XSLT processor is very fast, and binaries are available for Windows, Linux, and AIX. I didn't find the tested release quite as robust as its home page claims. For example, when running the command line shown above under Linux, it assumed that the passed parameter was a number, and because "8pt" isn't, it converted the parameter to the string "NaN" for "Not a Number." Also, its error messages can be quite cryptic. I'm sure they'll straighten this out. With a name like `testXSLT` for the binary, I imagine that they plan to do more work on it.

I tend to use this processor first for most XSLT work because of its speed, because they have Windows and Linux binaries available, and because I feel that the Apache XML project is worth supporting. (See section B.5, "Xalan-Java," page 276, for more on the Apache XML project.) If a given stylesheet causes me problems, I'll try it with another processor to see if that processor's error messages can shed more light on the problem than Xalan C++ does. As with the Xalan Java parser, the original work on this processor was done at IBM before they donated it to the Apache project.

Developed by	Ginger Alliance
Homepage	http://www.gingerall.com/charlie-bin/get/webGA/act/sablotron.act
Platforms	Linux, Windows NT, Solaris, FreeBSD, OpenBSD, OpenServer, and UnixWare.
XML parser used	James Clark's Expat. Download this from: http://sourceforge.net/projects/expat. If the DLL filename includes its version number, rename it to `explat.dll` before moving it in a directory on your path.
Version tested	0.50
Cost	free
API or source included	Open source (Mozilla Public License or Gnu Public License)
Command line help	`sabcmd --help`
Other documentation included	Not with installation; see web page.
Installation instructions	INSTALL_WIN text file

Running it with the samples shown:

```
sabcmd xq553.xsl xq338.xml $bodyTextSize=8pt
```

Czechoslovakia's Ginger Alliance developed Sablotron as part of a larger application framework product they market named Charlie. It's written in C++, so it's very fast. Along with the source code, they make binaries available for Windows, Linux, and Solaris, and report that it's been compiled on other Unix boxes as well.

Their download page also has a Perl package that encapsulates the C API, making it possible to do XSLT processing from within Perl programs.

B.8   MSXSL

Developed by	Microsoft
Homepage	http://msdn.microsoft.com/code/sample.asp?url=/msdn-files/027/001/485/msdncompositedoc.xml
Platforms	Windows
XML parser used	msxml3.dll which as of this writing must be down-loaded separately. Eventually, I'm sure the default msxml.dll included with Internet Explorer will be good enough.
Version tested	3.0
Cost	free
API or source included	source included
Command line help	`msxsl -?`
Other documentation included	a Word file: msxsl.doc
Installation instructions	The downloadable file is a self-extracting executable that creates msxml.exe and msxsl.doc.

Running it with the samples shown:

```
msxsl xq553.xsl xq338.xml bodyTextSize=8pt
```

Microsoft's free MSXSL parser is small and fast. As far as I can tell, the version I tested only creates files with an encoding of UTF-16, and it ignored an encoding attribute of the xsl:output method setting it to "UTF-8". (The strings "UTF" and "encoding" didn't show up anywhere in the source code when I searched for them.)

glossary

Italicized terms in each definition have their own entries in the glossary.

attribute value template   When an XSLT processor sees an attribute value that is interpreted as an attribute value template, it replaces any *expression* surrounded by curly braces with the result of evaluating that *expression*. For example, it replaces "{2+2}" with "4" or "{substring('abcde',4)}" with "de".

axis   A *location step's* axis describes the relationship of a set of *nodes* to the *context node* in terms of where they are on the *source tree*. For example, in the location step `child::wine`, the `child` axis part tells an XSLT processor to look at the child nodes of the context node. (The `wine` node test part tells us the name of the nodes that we want in that axis.) See section 2.2, "Axes," on page 24 for more.

comma-separated value (CSV) files   A CSV file is a text file with a record on each line and a comma separating each field of those records. A line of a CSV file that holds a last name, first name, hire date, and salary field might look like this:

```
'Hill','Phil','20001122',80000
```

The pipe ("|") and tab character are also popular for delimiting fields in such files. Most spreadsheet programs and database managers can read CSV files very easily.

context node   An *XPath* term, in XSLT, context node generally refers to the *source tree node* that the XSLT processor is currently handling. Inside of an `xsl:for-each` loop, the context node is the one currently being processed by the loop; in a *template rule* (and outside an `xsl:for-each` loop), it's usually the *node* that matched the pattern in the `xsl:template` element's match attribute to trigger the template rule.

expanded-name An expanded-name is an attribute or element's name and its name-space URI (if this namespace isn't null) taken together. For the `xsl:stylesheet` element, the expanded-name would be "http://www.w3.org/1999/XSL/Transform" and "stylesheet."

expression An expression is a term or combination of terms that gets evaluated by the processor to determine what the term describes—a number, a set of *nodes*, a string value, or a Boolean value. The term itself can include numbers, strings, Boolean values, function calls, or *XPath node* set descriptions.

extension An extension is an addition to the set of elements or functions that make up the XSLT language in order to let a *stylesheet* do more than the XSLT specification requires. For example, if you wrote a function that could be called from a stylesheet to return a string value of the current date, that would be an extension function. See section 5.5, "Extensions to XSLT," on page 143 for more information.

formatting objects In XSL, the specific elements from the XSL *namespace* that describe how to visually or aurally present the document's information are called formatting objects. See section 6.13, "XSL and XSLT: creating Acrobat files and other formatted output," on page 247 for more information.

instantiate In the world of object-oriented development, a class declaration describes the structure and behavior of a certain class of objects. When one of these objects (also known as an "instance" of that class) is created in memory, we say that it's instantiated. In XSLT, a *template* describes the structure of something to add to the *result tree*, and when an instance of that template is added to the result tree, we say that the template is being instantiated.

instruction An instruction is an element from the XSLT *namespace* that tells the XSLT processor to add something to the *result tree*.

literal result element An element in an XSLT *stylesheet* that is not in the XSLT *namespace* (that is, not a special XSLT element) nor an *extension* element is a literal result element, and an XSLT processor will pass it along to the *result tree* unchanged.

location step An *XPath expression* consists of one or more location steps separated by slashes. Each location step can have up to three parts: an *axis* specifier, a required *node test*, and an optional *predicate*. The XPath expression "child::wine[@grape='Merlot']" has one step, and "wines/wine/attribute:year" has three. See section 2.1, "Location paths, axes, node tests, and predicates," on page 24 for more information.

markup The markup is the text in a document that describes that document's structure and properties. In an XML document, the tags, entity references, and declarations are the markup.

namespace A collection of element type names and attribute names is called a namespace. A namespace declaration at the beginning of an XML document usually gives a *URI* identifying a namespace (for example, http://www.w3.org/ 1999/XSL/Transform for the XSLT namespace) and a namespace prefix (used in the document), to show which elements and attributes belong to that namespace (for XSLT, usually "xsl"). See section 4.3, "Namespaces," on page 92 for more information.

NCName The XSLT specification defines many of the components of XSLT syntax as *NCNames*, a term that comes from the *W3C Namespace* specification. To simplify a little, an *NCName* is any name that begins with a letter or underscore and doesn't have a colon in it ("NC" = No Colon"). The name can't have a colon because it may have a *namespace* prefix added to its beginning, or it may serve as a namespace prefix itself. Either way, a colon would act as a separator between the prefix and the remainder of the name, which is why these names on either side of the colon aren't allowed to have colons in them. (See also QName, on page 284).

node When a document (either a source or result document) is represented as a tree, each component of the tree is called a node. Six kinds of nodes can be on a tree: element nodes, attribute nodes, text nodes, processing instruction nodes, comment nodes, and *namespace* nodes. The root element of one of these documents is not the root node of a *source tree* or *result tree* that holds that document; it is the child of a root node created specifically for that tree. This way, a comment or processing *instruction* outside of that root element can be represented as a *sibling* node on that tree.

node test The part of an *XPath expression location step* that names which of the *nodes* in the specified *axis* are being addressed is called a node test. In the *XPath expression* "child::title" the "title" node test shows that the expression refers to the `title` elements in the `child` axis. In the XPath expression "preceding-sibling::*" the asterisk shows that the *expression* refers to elements of any name in the `preceding-sibling` axis. See section 2.3, "Node tests," on page 41 for more information.

open source Open source describes software in which the source code is freely available to anyone who wants to examine it and make their own modifications and contributions. Modified versions must be redistributed under the same terms as the original version.

pattern Patterns are used to specify a set of conditions that a node must meet for some action to take place on it. Pattern syntax uses a subset of *XPath expressions* that limit you to using the `child` and `attribute` axes. In XSLT, they are most often used in the `match` value of `xsl:template` *template rules*. They are also used in the `xsl:key` element's `match` attribute and the `xsl:number` element's `count` and `from` attributes.

predicate A predicate is an optional part of an *XPath expression's location step* that specifies a condition for filtering out some of the *nodes* selected by the *axis* and *node test* parts of the location step. For example, in the one-step XPath expression "child::wine[@grape='Merlot']", the predicate in square brackets shows that, of all the *context node's* children that are `wine` elements, we want only the ones with a `grape` attribute value of "Merlot". See section 2.4, "Predicates," on page 43 for more information.

principal node type A principle node type is the type of *node* in a *source tree* or *result tree* to which a particular *axis* refers. The `attribute` axis refers to a set of attribute nodes: the `namespace` *axis* refers to *namespace* nodes, and the other axes all refer to element nodes. Knowing an axis's principal node type is how you can tell that while the *XPath expression* `ancestor::price` selects all the `price` elements that are ancestors of the *context node,* the *XPath expression* `attribute::price`, on the other hand, refers to a `price` attribute of the context node.

QName A QName is a "Qualified Name" that includes an optional *namespace* prefix and colon before a required "local part," which is an *NCName*. For example, the value of an `xsl:template` element's name attribute is a QName. A QName can be a simple name like "glossaryEntry" or it can include a *namespace* prefix and colon, as with "snee:glossaryEntry".

result tree A result tree is a tree structure in memory where an XSLT processor assembles the result of its transformation. Most XSLT processors can also write out this tree as a file that would be considered the output document, although they are not required to do so. See also *source tree*.

sibling In a tree structure, one *node's* sibling node is any other node that has the same parent node.

source tree A tree structure of *nodes* in memory that stores the input document is called a source tree. An XSLT processor goes through this tree, applying any relevant *template rules* in the *stylesheet* to each node, and stores the result in the *result tree*. Most XSLT processors can read a document from a disk file or communications connection into this source tree, although they are not required to do so. See also *result tree*.

stylesheet   In XSLT, a stylesheet is a set of instructions describing the transformation of XML documents of a particular document type. This set of *instructions* is stored in a specialized XML document with the `stylesheet` element from the http://w3.org/1999/XSL/Transform *namespace* as the `document` element.

template   The part of a template rule that gets evaluated for addition to the *result tree* is called the template. A template may contain XSLT *instructions*, *extension* elements, and *literal result elements*.

template rule   A template rule is the basic building block of an XSLT *stylesheet*, represented by an `xsl:template` element in the stylesheet. A template rule has two parts: a match *pattern* (the value of the `xsl:template` element's `match` attribute), which describes the *source tree nodes* to which the rule applies and a *template* (the contents of the `xsl:template` element) to add to the *source tree* when such a node is found.

top-level element   A top-level element is a special XSLT stylesheet element (that is, an element from the http://w3.org/1999/XSL/Transform *namespace*) that is a child of the stylesheet's `xsl:stylesheet` document element. Except for `xsl:template`, which specifies a *template rule* for the stylesheet, the other top-level elements specify general instructions about the stylesheet such as global variables, other stylesheets to import, and instructions about storing the output. Nearly all XSLT elements that are not top-level elements are used in the *templates* within the template rules.

URI   Uniform Resource Identifiers (URI) are the system for naming resources on the web. Web address URLs such as http://www.snee.com are the most common form of URIs.

W3C   The World Wide Web consortium (W3C) is a group of companies and universities around the world working to develop and promote common protocols for use on the web.

well-formed XML document   A well-formed XML document is an XML document that conforms to the basic structural rules of an XML document as described by the W3C XML specification. For a well-formed document to also be a valid XML document, it must specify a DTD or schema of rules about the structure of documents of that particular document type (that is, it must specify a list of rules about subelements that can make up each element and the attributes that go with each element) and it must conform to that structure.

XPath   Sometimes, when processing one part of a source document tree, you want the XSLT processor to get some information from another part of the document. The mini-language developed as part of XSLT for specifying the path through the document to the required information is called "XPath." XPath lets you say things like "get the `revisionDate` attribute value of the element before the context node element's `chapter` ancestor element." XPath proved useful enough that the *W3C* split it into a specification separate from XSLT so that other specifications can more easily take advantage of it. See chapter 1, "A brief tutorial," on page 3, for more information.

XSL   The Extensible *Stylesheet* Language (XSL) is a *W3C* standard for specifying the visual or audio presentation of an XML document. "Visual presentation" refers to details such as fonts, margins, bolding, italicizing, and other page layout issues. Audio presentation refers to the pitch, speed, volume, and other parameters of a spoken voice communicating a document. XSLT, which specifies transformations to an XML document, began as part of the XSL specification before being split out into its own spec. See chapter 1, "A brief tutorial," on page 3, and section 6.13, "XSL and XSLT: creating Acrobat files and other formatted output," on page 247, for more information.

XSLT   Extensible Stylesheet Language Transformation (XSLT) is a W3C specification specifying an XML-based language for describing the transformation of XML documents into other XML documents, HTML documents, or any desired text format. See chapter 1, "A brief tutorial," on page 3, for more information.

XSLT processor   An XSLT processor is a program that can apply an XSLT *stylesheet* to an XML document stored in a *source tree* and then create a *result tree* based on the transformation *instructions* stored in that *stylesheet*. Typical XSLT processors can also read an XML document into the source tree and write out the result of the source tree as an output file.

index

axis *(continued)*

child 25

defined 24, 281

descendant 35

descendant-or-self 35, 37

following 32

following-sibling 29

namespace 40–41

parent 25

preceding 32

preceding-sibling 29

self 39

axis specifiers 26, 118, 185

B

Balise 5

biggest value, finding 181

Blackdown JVM 272

Boolean expressions

in predicate 43

`xsl:if` and 113

`boolean-expression` 117

Brown, Mike J. 161

browsers

HTML and 190

XSLT and 192

built-in template rules 12, 52, 56, 58, 137

not relying on 137

shown 225

C

C 186

C++ 5, 118, 133

XSLT processor 275

Candidate Recommendation 183

carriage returns 107, 207, 230, 233, 239

adding 93

preventing 205

skipped numbers and 216

See also `xsl:text`

case conversion 159

case statements 110

(`xsl:choose`) 114

ceiling() function 151

characters

mapping with `translate()` function 156

child axis 25

abbreviation 26

child subelement

testing for 113

Clark, James 274, 278

colons 185

COM XSLT processor 275

combining elements 69

command line XSLT processor 192

command prompt

running XSLT processor from 269

commas

adding to a list 139

as separator in large numbers 208

comma-separated value (CSV) files

defined 281

comment 42

adding to your result tree 84

converting to elements 86

nodes 60, 184

reading from source tree 86

comment() node test 86

concat() function 155, 162

constants and variables 164, 166

contains() function 75, 136, 155, 162

content, reusing 202

context node 39, 113, 185

defined 24, 281

control statements 110

copying tags, attributes, and contents 70

count attribute of `xsl:xsl-number` 209, 211

count() function 61, 113, 151

counting

comments and other nonelement nodes 63

elements 61

elements and subelements 113

elements with a particular attribute set 62

nodes 61

CSV files 204

curly braces 14, 26, 56, 115, 166

variables and parameters 166

when selecting attribute values 77

XSLT specification and 117

D

E

3D User Iterfaces with Java 3D

Jon Barrilleaux
Softbound, 528 pages, $49.95, August 2000
ISBN 1-884777-90-2

Ebook Edition
PDF files 14 MB, $13.50
Ebook edition only available from publisher's site:
www.manning.com/barrilleaux

A practical guide on how to design and implement the next generation of sophisticated 3D user interfaces on present-day PCs without exotic devices like head-mounted displays and data gloves.

Written for user-interface designers and programmers, the book systematically discusses the problems and techniques of letting users view and manipulate rich, multidimensional information. It teaches how to tackle the design challenges of 3D user interfaces which support such tasks as e-commerce, product configuration, system monitoring, and data visualization.

"Jon Barrilleaux should be given a standing ovation for producing such an excellent piece of work for a topic (Java 3D) that desperately needs more documentation."

—j3d.org

Web Development with JavaServer Pages

Duane K. Fields and Mark A. Kolb
Softbound, 584 pages, $44.95, April, 2000
ISBN 1-884777-99-6

Ebook edition
PDF files, 14 MB, $13.50
Ebook edition only available from publisher's site:
www.manning.com/fields

This best-selling book will teach you how to create dynamic content—personalized, customized, and up-to-the minute—a key ingredient of site development on the World Wide Web today. It covers all aspects of JSP development, as well as comparisons to similar dynamic content systems such as CGI, Active Server Pages, Cold Fusion, and PHP. It clearly demonstrates the advantages offered by JSP as a full-featured, cross-platform, vendor-neutral technology for dynamic content generation.

Full coverage of JSP 1.1 syntax teaches beginners the basics. More advanced readers can jump straight into techniques for mixing databases and web pages, how to make an elegant and scalable architecture, and even subtleties such as how JSP helps to better divide the labor between page designer and programmer. Detailed code and good design techniques are included, as well as complete reference materials on JSP tags and the JSP API.

"...the best offering, head and shoulders above the rest for both the Web designer and the Java developer interested in picking up JSP skills. None of the other JSP books offer the same depth of coverage on the different JSP topics."

—JavaWorld

For ordering information visit www.manning.com

Server-Based Java Programming

Ted Neward
Softbound, 592 pages, $49.95, July 2000
ISBN 1-884777-71-6

Ebook edition
PDF files, 7 MB, $13.50
Ebook edition only available from publisher's site:
www.manning.com/Neward3

Java programming seen from the enterprise-wide view. Shows how to turn nuts-and-bolts J2EE techniques toward enterprise-wide goals such as fault tolerance, scalability, and less new development on each project. Techniques demonstrate how business development in Java can approach the fabled Three Zeroes: Zero Development, Zero Deployment, and Zero Administration.

"This book covers everything: threads, control, extensions, classloaders, sockets, servlets, persistence, objects, architecture, design—everything. Written for experienced programmers to take them to new heights in programming practices and design..."

—Swynk.com